Praise for Michael J. Gelb's *Discover Your Genius*

"*Discover Your Genius* offers a cornucopia of pithy insights, pr͟ ideas, and cerebral gossip. . . . Range freely, choose anyplac͟ you are guaranteed rich rewards and authentic wisdom."
                              —Tony Schwartz, author of *What ͟*

"Imagine what you could accomplish with Gandhi, Shakespeare, D͟ ͟, or Queen Elizabeth I as your personal mentor! In *Discover Your Genius,* Michael Gelb brings to life a 'dream team' of history's most extraordinary, inspiring minds. Captivating, playful, and profound, this book will guide you to the fulfillment of your own dreams for a richer, more beautiful life."
                         —Debbie Ford, bestselling author of *The Secret of the Shadow*

"Michael Gelb is a genius at helping you 'discover your genius': Each chapter by itself is worth far more than the price of the entire book!"
                              —Tony Buzan, author of *The Mind Map Book*

"*Discover Your Genius* is a rich repast, and one certain to expand the reader's mind and mettle. It offers the inner story of some of the great minds of history, giving us powerful clues to genius—theirs as well as our own."   —Jean Houston, author of *A Mythic Life*

"I truly admire the insightful way in which [Gelb] has probed and exposed the essence of the 'genius.' . . . Just as each of these great thinkers 'took a leap' from the ordinary and the known, [Gelb] too has 'leaped' beyond the dry scholarship of the academic world to open up a new view of these illustrious geniuses. . . . Engaging, inspiring, and informative."
                              —Jennings Wagoner, Ph.D., University of Virginia,
                              Curry School of Education

"[Gelb has] the graceful ability to synthesize masses of material into accessible prose without sacrificing historical context."
                              —Carole Fungaroli Sargent, Ph.D.,
                              Georgetown University Department of English

© Mark Finkenstaedt

About the Author

MICHAEL J. GELB, a renowned innovator in the field of creative thinking and leadership development, is the bestselling author of *How to Think Like Leonardo da Vinci, Body Learning, Samurai Chess,* and *Present Yourself!* Since 1978, Gelb has conducted seminars around the world for such companies as British Petroleum, IBM, DuPont, Microsoft, Merck, and Nike. He lives in Edgewater, New Jersey.

Discover Your Genius

DISCOVER YOUR GENIUS

*How to Think Like History's
Ten Most Revolutionary Minds*

Michael J. Gelb

ILLUSTRATIONS BY
NORMA MILLER

Quill

An Imprint of HarperCollinsPublishers

This book presents nutrition and exercise information that may or may not be right for you. In view of the complex, individual, and specific nature of health and fitness problems, this book is not intended to replace professional medical advice. Every individual is different. Before starting any diet or exercise program, get your doctor's approval. The publisher and the author expressly disclaim any responsibility for any loss or risk incurred as a consequence of the application of the contents of this book.

Grateful acknowledgment is made to Norma Miller for her portraits of the ten geniuses found in this book.

HarperCollins books may be purchased for educational, business, or sales promotional use. For information please write: Special Markets Department, HarperCollins Publishers Inc., 10 East 53rd Street, New York, NY 10022.

First Quill edition published 2003.

Designed by Lindgren/Fuller Design

The Library of Congress has catalogued the hardcover edition as follows:
Gelb, Michael.
    Discover your genius: how to think like history's ten most revolutionary
minds/Michael J. Gelb.—1st ed.
        p.   cm.
    ISBN 0-06-621376-2
    1. Creative thinking. 2. Creative thinking—Problems, exercises, etc. 3. Gifted persons—Case studies. I. Title.
    BF408 .G365 2002
    153.3'5—dc21   2001039503

ISBN 0-06-093790-4 (pbk.)

03 04 05 06 07 ❖/RRD 10 9 8 7 6 5 4 3 2 1

To my parents, Joan and Sandy Gelb,
whose example brings to life these sacred words:

Happy are those who find wisdom
She is more precious than jewels,
And nothing you desire can compare with her
Her ways are ways of pleasantness, and all her paths are peace.

~ゥ

The Talmud says, "In the world to come each of us
will be called to account for all the good things
God put on earth that we refused to enjoy." My
wish for you is that you will use the wisdom of
these great characters to keep that session as brief
as possible.

—MICHAEL J. GELB

CONTENTS

Michael Gelb invites us to explore and apply the essential qualities of ten geniuses in a uniquely engaging personal manner. These extraordinary individuals all changed the world, and Gelb guides us to use their inspiration and example to change the way we look at our lives. <u>Each of the geniuses he introduces was driven by an unquenchable passion for their particular kinds of truth and beauty.</u> Copernicus's act of remodeling the heavens, for example, was one of aesthetic cleansing, creating, as he claimed, a harmonious celestial body or perfect temple where the efforts to save the old theory had resulted in a monstrous structure.

We all have experienced the surprise at how different a street looks when we turn around and see it from another point of view. Most of history walks in one direction. Some geniuses have enabled us to turn around and look the other way, backwards or sideways. Leonardo, for example, noted how the so-called vanishing point toward which furrows in a ploughed field appear to converge seems to move with us as we walk beside the field. The genius not only alters our viewpoint, but also pulls our perspective into line with his or hers.

Through some magnificent act of insight, intuition, inspiration, brain wave, conviction, whatever we might call it, the genius sees or senses something from a different perspective. Their new perspective provides a view that ultimately proves so compelling that we can never see things in quite the same way again. What they see is often a bigger picture than we can readily grasp. And they can do this because they sense how the parts fit into the whole, the deeper harmonic resonance of things that may seem on the surface to be unrelated.

Originally conceived as an external guardian spirit, the notion of genius (from the root *genare,* "to generate, or beget") evolved by the Renaissance to represent an innate talent, or special kind of in-built virtue in a specific area of accomplishment. Some argue, however, that the notion of individual genius is fundamentally flawed, nothing more than a construct of the Romantic era of the late eighteenth and early nineteenth centuries. The Romantics themselves captured the notion that there is something beyond reason in the supreme achievements of those who transcended the limitations that beset even their ablest contemporaries. Through the history of genius there runs a persistent strain, picked up by Shakespeare, that to be transformingly great you might, perhaps, need to be a bit mad.

There is a sense in which resorting to metaphors of the transcendent is inevitable in talking about genius. This might just be a matter of cliché. But I don't think so. Understanding genius requires awareness of context, cultural milieu, history, and more, yet the individual component remains. We still can't define it directly, pin it down by verbal formula. But, we can recognize it when we see or sense it (even though it may take centuries to do so), and can gain a grip on its elusive quality through creative imagination.

Is it daft to attempt to model our selves on the transcendent genius of a Copernicus, Brunelleschi, or Einstein? No, not if we consider that all these great minds applied essential principles of focus and purposefulness to the clarification of their core insights. Moreover, in the face of the monstrous structure of mass-media culture, the emphasis in these pages on a personal access to genius, beauty, and truth can enrich our lives aesthetically, intellectually, and morally.

Of course we will all be able to quibble with Michael Gelb's choices while recognizing the exemplary nature of those he has included, not as exemplary human beings in all cases, but as exemplary of what humans can potentially achieve, if only we believe in what we can do.

—*Martin Kemp, Professor of the History of Art at the University of Oxford*

ACKNOWLEDGMENTS

The challenge of combining accessibility with accuracy in bringing these great figures to life for you could not have been met without the help of an extraordinary "genius board" of advisers. I am very grateful to these exceptional scholars for their critiques and contributions:

Professor Roger Paden
Professor Jacqueline Eales
Piero Sartogo
Professor Roy Ellzey
Professor Jill Shepherd
Professor Carole Fungaroli
Dr. Win Wenger
Grandmaster Raymond Keene, O.B.E.
Professor Martin Kemp
Professor Jennings Wagoner

In addition to serving on the "genius board," Grandmaster Raymond Keene, O.B.E., and Professor Jacqueline Eales of Canterbury University provided in-depth, comprehensive academic research support for this project.

Special thanks to Audrey Ellzey, who organized and integrated the work of the "genius exercise" teams.

I'm grateful to all who participated in and offered feedback on the exercises, including Bobbi Sims, Dr. Roy Ellzey, Dr. Sheri Philabaum, Laura Sitges, Paul Davis, Michele Dudro, Karen Denson, David Owen, D'jengo Saunders, Lin Kroeger, Annette Morgan, Bridget Belgrave, Roben Torosyan,

Jeannie Becker, Gwen Ellison, Karen Lee, Katie Carey, Ron Gross, Stacy Forsythe, Virginia Kendall, Forrest Hainline, Jr., and Dr. Dale Schusterman.

This project also benefited from the critical reading and feedback generously offered by Jean Houston, Barbara Horowitz, Mark Levy, Merle Braun, Lyndsey Posner, Ken Adelman, Lisa Lesavoy, Stella Lin, Jaya Koilpiilai, Dr. Marvin Hyett, Alex Knox, Beret Arcaya, Lori Dechar, and Sir Brian Tovey.

Audrey Ellzey, Professor Roy Ellzey, Grandmaster Raymond Keene, and Professor Robert Greenberg served as brilliant sounding boards for the selection of the musical masterpieces designed to enhance your appreciation of the genius qualities.

"Danke" to Eileen Meier for helping me create the space to write. *"Grazie"* to Nina Lesavoy for making the right connections and nurturing the vision. And *"merci"* to my super office staff: Denise Lopez, Ellen Morin, and Mary Hogan.

My external editor, Tom Spain, who also edited *How to Think Like Leonardo da Vinci,* provided superb constructive feedback in the development and manifestation of these ideas. Thanks to former HarperCollins editor Joe Veltre for shepherding this book through its intermediate phases with a quiet confidence and to my current editor, Kelli Martin for her enthusiasm, thoroughness, and dedication in ushering this project into the world. I'm also very grateful to Trena Keating for championing this project in its early stages. I feel incredibly fortunate to have discovered Norma Miller, and am honored by her willingness to embrace this book and help bring the geniuses to life through her remarkable portraits.

And, as always, I'm grateful to Muriel Nellis and Jane Roberts of Literary and Creative Artists for pulling the right levers in the engine room of success.

Since 1978 I've had the privilege of working with many of the most creative leaders in business internationally, leaders who strive to apply the genius principles in their personal and professional lives. Some who were especially helpful in this project include Ed Bassett, Tim Podesta, David Chu, Dennis Ratner, Jim D'Agostino, Marcia Weider, Debbie Dunnam, Nina Lesavoy, Eddie Oliver, Ketan Patel, Marv Damsma, Tony Hayward, Gerry Kirk, Mark Hannum, Susan Greenburg, and Harold Montgomery.

Discover Your Genius

On the Shoulders of Giants

You were born with the potential for genius. We all were; just ask any mother.

In 1451, in the Italian seaport of Genoa, a new mother saw it in the eyes of her firstborn child, unaware that the scintillating power of the 100 billion neurons in his brain would one day redefine the shape of the planet on which she lived. Decades later, the wife of a prosperous Polish merchant saw it in the eyes of her baby, though she would never have dared to predict that the connections his adult mind would eventually make would effectively reorder the universe. Three centuries and an ocean away, a woman of land and privilege didn't know that what she saw in the eyes of her child was the dawn of the capacity to grasp and synthesize the essence of Classical, Renaissance, and Enlightenment thinking—and reinvent the notion of personal liberty for centuries to come.

Few of us may claim to be geniuses, but almost every parent will tell you of the spark of genius they saw the first moment they looked into their new baby's eyes. Your mother saw it too. And although she may not have realized it, the newborn brain she saw at work shared the same miraculous potential as the infant minds that would one day achieve the greatness described above.

Even if you have yet to revolutionize anyone's ideas about the planet or its inhabitants, you came into the world with the same spark of genius beheld so long ago by the mothers of Christopher Columbus, Nicolaus Copernicus, and Thomas Jefferson. By its very design, the human brain harbors vast potential for memory, learning, and creativity. Yours does too—far more than you may think. The 100-billion-neuron tally is a simple fact of human physiology, according to the great neurologist Sir Charles Sherrington, who described the human brain as "an enchanted loom" ready to weave a unique tapestry of creative self-expression.

But its power can be as elusive as it is awesome, and can be unlocked only with the knowledge of how to develop that potential, and put those hundreds of billions of fact-learning, connection-building neurons to work in the most effective, creative ways possible. It's far from automatic. We must learn to make the most of what we have—even if that requires us to accept on faith the premise that we have more than we're already using.

Fortunately, we don't have to do it alone. History has produced enough intellectual giants to convince anyone of the potential power of the human brain. Familiar to all of us, their discoveries and innovations have shaped the world in which we live. But as indebted as we are to them for the fruits of their mental labor, we can also turn to the most revolutionary minds in history for guidance and inspiration on how to use our brains to realize our own unique gifts. For just as they have shown us the way in geography, astronomy, and government, these great minds can also show us the way to our own full potential. We needn't aspire to the same incomparable heights to learn from their accomplishments; after all, they've already done their work. But who among us doesn't have to restructure our universe, redefine our world, or renegotiate our relationships with others on an almost daily basis? Indeed, such are the dynamics by which our individuality is developed and expressed.

The full expression of our unique genius does not come without our concerted effort; it requires our embarking upon a deliberate plan for

We were all infant prodigies.

—Thomas Mann

personal development. In a world that drives us down toward a lowest common denominator of taste, thought, and feeling, we all need all the help we can get in manifesting the best in ourselves. Think about it: your brain is the most powerful learning and creative problem-solving system in the world. But most of us know less about how our brains work than we do about our cars. Of course, cars come with instruction manuals and brains don't; even in school, most of us spend more time studying history, mathematics, literature, and other subjects than trying to understand and apply the most important subject of all, learning how to learn.

The individuals whom history recognizes as revolutionary geniuses have done a better job than most of harnessing the mind power with which they were born. Part of their success can be attributed to an intuitive understanding of how to learn. You can learn anything you want to, and you'll surprise yourself with what you can achieve when you know how to learn. In *Discover Your Genius* you'll develop that understanding for yourself. And as you apply the wisdom of history's great minds, you'll improve your mental abilities as you get older.

Study and in general the pursuit of truth and beauty is a sphere of activity in which we are permitted to remain children all our lives.
—ALBERT EINSTEIN

Imagine unleashing your creativity by enjoying the benefits of the mental play that helped inspire the theory of relativity. Or evaluating your business climate with the combination of keen observation and an open mind that yielded the theory of evolution. Or navigating your life path with the same love of knowledge and truth that spawned all of Western philosophy.

The individuals behind these revolutions of thought live on in our collective memory as models for tackling the challenges that lie ahead. The difference between your mind and theirs is smaller than you think, and is less determined by inborn capacity than by passion, focus, and strategy—all of which are yours to develop. Harvard biologist Edward O. Wilson writes that the great minds of history "were obsessed; they burned within. But they also had an intuitive grasp of inborn human nature accurate enough to select commanding images from the mostly inferior thoughts that stream

For the first time in human history the genius of the human race is available for all to harvest.

—JEAN HOUSTON, PH.D., AUTHOR OF *THE POSSIBLE HUMAN* AND *JUMP TIME*

through the minds of all of us. The talent they wielded may have been only incrementally greater, but their creations appeared to others to be qualitatively new. They acquired enough influence and longevity to translate into lasting fame, not by magic, not by divine benefaction, but by a quantitative edge in powers shared in smaller degree with those less gifted. They gathered enough lifting speed to soar above the rest."

In *Discover Your Genius* you'll learn how ten of history's greatest geniuses gained the "lifting speed" they needed to change the world. You'll see how they identified and embraced the "commanding images" that led them to the revolutionary ideas we now know so well. Through practical exercises, you'll discover how their breakthrough thinking principles can help you sharpen your edge for real-world results. And by getting to know these ten extraordinary individuals, you'll glimpse the boundless range of human potential in ways that will ignite your own passion for growth and inspire you to soar to new heights of professional success and personal fulfillment. Most important, by studying the lives and minds of others, you will learn to be more fully and truly yourself.

You have been modeling yourself on others all your life. That potential genius into whose eyes your mother gazed was soon returning her look, mirroring her smile, discovering how to be a person by doing what other people did. Learning through imitation is central to the mental development of many species, humans included. But as we become adults, we gain a unique advantage: we can choose whom and what to imitate. We can also consciously select new models to replace the ones we outgrow. It makes sense, therefore, to choose the best role models to inspire and guide us to the realization of our potential.

Ever since I was a child I've been fascinated by the nature of genius, an interest that has evolved into my profession and life passion: guiding others to discover and realize their own potential for genius. As an exploration of that passion, I spent years immersed in studying the life and work of

Leonardo da Vinci, perhaps the greatest genius who ever lived. In addition to painting the eternally magnificent *Mona Lisa* and *Last Supper*, Leonardo designed ball bearings, gearshifts, underwater diving equipment, and, most incredibly, a parachute—long before anyone was able to fly (now that's thinking ahead!). Leonardo's amazing leaps of imagination and his ability to think far ahead of his time fired my passion for incorporating the lessons of genius into my own life and the lives of my students.

The expression of that passion, *How to Think Like Leonardo da Vinci*, has helped readers around the world claim this towering figure of history, a true giant of mind and spirit, as a personal guide to meeting the challenges of contemporary life. By approaching Leonardo's unique genius as the sum of seven distinct principles that they can study and emulate, readers have been able to make this supreme genius a role model all their own.

Whom have you chosen to inspire and guide you in your life thus far? Who are your greatest heroes and heroines, your most inspirational role models? If you have already begun the process of mastering and implementing the seven da Vincian principles, you know firsthand the profound impact that your chosen role models can have on your life—and, in true da Vincian fashion, you are ready to discover what you can learn from other role models. There's no need to limit yourself to Leonardo; after all, one hallmark of genius is the ability to internalize and integrate the thoughts and examples of previous great thinkers. Albert Einstein, for example, kept above his bed a portrait of Sir Isaac Newton, who himself advised that we can see farther if we "stand on the shoulders of giants."

But on whose shoulders should we stand? This book arose from contemplation of the following three questions:

- In addition to Leonardo, who are the most revolutionary, breakthrough-thinking geniuses in human history?
- What is the essential lesson we can learn from each of these great minds?
- How can we apply the wisdom and experience of these great minds to bring more happiness, beauty, truth, and goodness to our lives, and the

lives of our children, in the midst of accelerating change, rampant materialism, and cultural chaos?

Discover Your Genius will bring you the incomparable power of ten of the most revolutionary, influential minds the world has known. If this pragmatic approach to history is new to you, you are in for a treat; immersing yourself in the life and work of history's greatest breakthrough thinkers provides rich nourishment for your mind and spirit. As you learn to "stand on their shoulders," you'll discover the truth of Mark Twain's statement: "Really great people make you feel that you, too, can become great."

YOUR GENIUS DREAM TEAM

In the pages that follow you will have the opportunity to get to know ten of the most amazing people who have ever lived. Each of these extraordinary individuals embodies a special "genius" characteristic that you are invited to emulate and integrate into your daily life.

Each genius is presented in a brief biography illustrating the role of the key principle in his or her life and work. We then explore how that principle can and does relate to you, including a self-assessment to measure its current impact, and a special highlight on the principle's potential application in the twenty-first-century world of work. Most important, you are offered an opportunity to enjoy a series of practical exercises to develop your mastery of each principle, and to implement its time-tested power in your own life today.

A reporter with whom I recently shared the principles of *Discover Your Genius* raised a concern that you may recognize. "I like basketball, but whatever I do I'll never be like Michael Jordan," he said. "So how can anyone even think of being like Leonardo, Einstein, or Elizabeth I?" I know how he feels; it's normal to feel humble when contemplating genius in any area of life. If

I simply compare myself to Michael Jordan, my sense of prowess on the courts is obliterated instantly. However, if instead of comparing I think about applying some of the individual components of Jordan's mastery—his focus, his awareness of his fellow players, the way he learned to move his feet on defense, and his commitment to developing his game at all levels throughout his career—then I'm inspired and better prepared to play my best.

Michael Jordan is to basketball what Leonardo da Vinci is to creativity. Leonardo had Leon Battista Alberti and Filippo Brunelleschi as his role models, Michael had Julius Erving and Elgin Baylor. A manual for aspiring hoopsters should start with Michael, but then it might move on to elucidate the special qualities of other legendary players. The fluid movement of Dr. J. and Elgin Baylor, the ball handling of Bob Cousy, the defense of Bill Russell, the passing of Magic Johnson, the body positioning of Karl Malone, the poise of Larry Bird, and the perfect shooting form of Cheryl Miller.

This book is your guide to learning from humanity's all-time/all-star breakthrough-thinking, revolutionary-genius dream team. To assemble this team I searched for the most world-shaking ideas, discoveries, and innovations in history. I looked for breakthroughs of thought, action, or creation that are stunningly original as well as being universally and eternally relevant and useful, that can be largely attributed to a particular individual. Of course, every great breakthrough is the result of a complex weaving of influences, effort, and serendipity. The most advanced, creative, and original thinking is always a product of historical context and the influences of previous geniuses, mentors, and collaborators on the mind of the originator. Nevertheless, although there is an undeniable aspect of subjectivity to the process, one can identify the most important threads in the tapestry of revolutionary genius.

Of course, your list of the ten most revolutionary minds might include different names. My aim is not to provide an "ultimate" list, but to inspire you to discover your own genius through the study of these archetypal figures. In discussing this project with people from all walks of life in the course of its development, I have invariably encountered enthusiastic, often heated, debate about who should be included. I'm delighted when people make a strong case for someone I've left out; in fact, there is a great deal to be gained from making your own list of exceptional people and aiming to embody their best qualities.

But first allow me to introduce the dream team of geniuses from whom you'll be learning how to think. You've already met three as newborn babies; here's the full team, along with the principles we will explore for each.

Plato (CIRCA 428–348 B.C.): *Deepening Your Love of Wisdom*

The love of wisdom—philosophy—and its manifestation in the quest for truth, beauty, and goodness, is the thread that weaves through the lives of all the great minds you'll get to know in the pages that follow. Plato, our first genius, is the seminal figure in this grand tapestry. Whenever you ask for a definition of something, or wonder about the essence of things, you are expressing the influence of Plato. If you consider yourself an idealist, you are deeply indebted to him. If you are more of a skeptic, then you question idealism in terms that he pioneered. Plato's influence on our view of the world is difficult to overstate. The wisdom of Socrates, teacher of Plato, is known to us primarily through Plato's writings. And Aristotle, tutor of Alexander the Great and one of history's most powerful and influential thinkers, was Plato's student.

Plato raised fundamental questions that will inspire you to strengthen your ability to think for yourself, to learn, and to grow. The knowledge of learning how to learn is perhaps the most important knowledge we can possess, and Plato's timeless wisdom is an ideal starting point for its development.

Plato also beckons us to care about more than just personal growth, challenging us to think about making a better world. If you feel disturbed by the moral relativism of our culture and its leaders, if you care deeply about goodness and justice, if you feel that education should be a primary force in building a better society, then you are already thinking in the tradition of Plato.

Filippo Brunelleschi (1377–1446): *Expanding Your Perspective*

Architect of the dome of Florence's cathedral, Brunelleschi engineered the structural embodiment of the shift of consciousness that we now call the Renaissance: the rebirth of the classical ideal of power and potentiality vested in the individual. Brunelleschi's Duomo stands as an antidote to the worldview conveyed by Gothic cathedrals before it, which awed their visitors into accepting the premise that all power was invested above. As the effective inventor of visual perspective, Brunelleschi influenced the accomplishments of Alberti, Donatello, Masaccio, Michelangelo, and Leonardo. Brunelleschi had to expand and maintain his personal goal-oriented perspective as well; only by overcoming tremendous political and personal adversity and finding ingenious solutions to everyday problems was he able to complete his dome and change our understanding of space forever.

Brunelleschi's genius can help you broaden your perspective to see a big picture no one else has visualized, and inspire you to keep your eyes on the prize to make that vision real. If you ever feel challenged to keep your perspective, if you find yourself getting caught up in the small stuff, then Filippo Brunelleschi is someone you must get to know.

Christopher Columbus (1451–1506): *Going Perpendicular: Strengthening Your Optimism, Vision, and Courage*

Where Plato and Brunelleschi ventured into metaphorical oceans of uncertainty, Columbus literally followed his genius across an unknown sea. In a time when most explorers sailed parallel to the coastline in their expeditions, hugging the land as closely as possible, Columbus set out at a direct right angle to the shore, straight out into the unknown, with results we all know well.

Columbus's genius can inspire you to pursue your unfulfilled dream—be it a new career, a new way of being in relationship, a chance to develop a hidden talent or to live in a different part of the world. If you ever feel restless, frustrated, or bored with the safe coastline of habit, then Columbus's uncanny optimism, compelling vision, and profound courage can help you navigate through life's unknown waters.

Nicolaus Copernicus (1473–1543): *Revolutionizing Your Worldview*

The Polish astronomer Copernicus's publication of *The Revolution of the Heavenly Spheres* in 1530 led to the classic example of a paradigm shift—a major change in or reversal of a fundamental frame of reference for understanding the world. By offering a carefully presented theory that the earth orbits a stationary sun, Copernicus eclipsed the classical astronomy view of the universe centered around a still, flat earth that had dominated human consciousness for 1,400 years.

Copernicus's genius for conceptualizing a radically different universe could not be more timely than it is today. Paradigm shifts are happening faster and more dramatically than ever before, as radical developments in computer technology, communication, genetics, geopolitics, and the new economy promise to revolutionize our world, many times over, in the next few decades. If you are concerned about adapting gracefully to this time of change and transformation, then Copernicus and his genius will speak to you.

Queen Elizabeth I (1533–1603): *Wielding Your Power with Balance and Effectiveness*

The most intimate paradigm shift of the last few decades has been driven by the expansion of women's rights and power—a process that can be traced to the remarkable rise and reign of England's Queen Elizabeth I. Combining skills that have been generally regarded as "masculine"—influencing her environment, getting things done, and acting aggressively when necessary—and "feminine"—receptivity to counsel, empathy for her rivals, and sensitivity to her people—Elizabeth stands as an archetype of the balance and integration of traditional notions of masculine and feminine power.

Elizabeth is a reminder to us all of how to use our power wisely, at home or at work. If you are seeking somehow to increase your individual power, or are struggling with questions of the balance of masculine and feminine power in professional and personal relationships, then Elizabeth and her reign offer unique and inspiring lessons that resonate today.

William Shakespeare (1564–1616): *Cultivating Your Emotional Intelligence*

Just as most of Western philosophy flows from Plato, so can much of our drama, literature, and conception of ourselves be seen as a stream fed by Shakespeare, Queen Elizabeth's most illustrious subject. In his works he captures, as no one has done before or since, the broad spectrum of human experience and self-awareness, articulating elements of the psyche in a manner that is both universal and eternal. Central to his genius is his unique ability to appreciate the essence of human experience, a mission so many of his characters also embark upon (often with tragically less success). He does so (and his characters try to do so) by cultivating both intrapersonal ("To thine own self be true") and interpersonal ("I know you all!") intelligence.

Knowing oneself and knowing how to work effectively with others is even more important in "these most brisk and giddy-paced times." If you strive to be true to yourself, if you wish to deepen your insight and understanding of others, if you're fascinated by the drama of everyday life, and if you know that "all the world's a stage" and you wish to play your roles with wit and grace, then the Bard is your indispensable ally.

Thomas Jefferson (1743–1826): *Celebrating Your Freedom in the Pursuit of Happiness*

Almost three centuries passed before the rebirth of the ancient Greek ideal of individual power begun in the Italian Renaissance could be enshrined and protected by democratic, republican systems of government. Articulated by a succession of geniuses, many of them revolutionary in the most literal sense, the ideals of individual liberty, equality, and justice find their supreme expression in the birth of the United States of America. Of all the Founding Fathers, Thomas Jefferson, the author of the Declaration of Independence, left liberty's greatest testament.

As the founder of the University of Virginia, Jefferson was a leader in helping others gain access to the inner freedom that comes from the power of education. He also pioneered the adoption of the first law establishing religious freedom. A multitalented model of the Renaissance man, the "sage of Monticello" inspires us to fulfill our potential and celebrate our freedom. If you strive to make the most of your "life, liberty and pursuit of happiness," then you owe it to yourself to deepen your understanding of Thomas Jefferson.

Charles Darwin (1809–1882): *Developing Your Power of Observation and Opening Your Mind*

The recipient, like Jefferson, of a large inheritance that furthered his career, Darwin followed his university studies in medicine and theology with a five-year mission to study Pacific flora and fauna, most notably in the Galapagos Islands. Rather than reaffirming the prevailing worldview—that life on earth was an instantaneous and unchanging creation of an omnipotent Creator—Darwin reached a different conclusion, which he articulated in one of the most influential books ever written: *The Origin of Species by Means of Natural Selection.*

The comprehensive, painstaking, and detailed observations from which Darwin formulated the theory of evolution are testimony to the power of seeing the world clearly, without prejudice or preconception. His is a marvelous example of the open mind, the consciousness that embraces change and creates the future. As we explore the process by which he made his discoveries, you'll learn to use his example to expand your consciousness, manage change, and create your future.

Mahatma Gandhi (1869–1948): *Applying the Principles of Spiritual Genius to Harmonize Spirit, Mind, and Body*

The prime mover of Indian independence, Mahatma Gandhi and his example of moral persuasion through nonviolent protest influenced the human rights movements led by Martin Luther King, Nelson Mandela, His Holiness the Dalai Lama, and many others. For Gandhi political action and spiritual practice went hand-in-hand. Although he came from a Hindu background, Gandhi was a student of all the world's major spiritual traditions; his integration and practical application of the ideals of Christ, Buddha, and the Baghavad Gita is an expression of a profound gift of spiritual genius.

Gandhi once described his lifelong goal as simply "self-realization," which to him meant "to see God face to face." By all accounts, his tremendous charisma, or "soul force," indicated that his relationship with God was a close one; in large part because he said what he believed and put into practice what he said, his spirit, mind, and body were in supreme harmony. Whatever your goals, his example of mental, physical, and spiritual harmony can help you be more true to your highest self.

Albert Einstein (1875–1955): *Unleashing Your Imagination and Combinatory Play*

Although Einstein began to achieve global renown after the publication of the special theory of relativity in 1905, his superstar status wasn't conferred fully until a solar eclipse in 1919, when a British scientific expedition measuring the curve of light deflection found it was exactly consistent with Einstein's predictions. The president of Britain's Royal Society commented that Einstein's theory was "one of the greatest—perhaps the greatest—of achievements in the history of human thought." So profound were the implications that the *Times* of London called for nothing less than "a new philosophy of the universe . . . that will sweep away nearly all that has hitherto been accepted as the axiomatic basis of physical thought."

Einstein maintained that the secret of his genius was his ability to look at problems in a childlike, imaginative way. He called it "combinatory play." If you like to doodle and daydream, then you are already following in Einstein's footsteps. Perhaps you'd like to learn new ways to use your imagination to solve complex problems? Maybe you dream of bringing a more lighthearted and playful approach to managing the serious issues of daily life. If you want to bring more creativity to your life, at work and at home, then welcome Einstein to your arsenal of genius.

I encourage you to immerse yourself in the lives and teachings of the geniuses who inspire you most. My study of Leonardo has been one of the richest experiences of my life, as has been the research for *Discover Your Genius*. You'll find that all the people included become more fascinating the more you learn about them.

> *. . . what counts most in the long haul of history is seminality, not sentiment.*
>
> —EDWARD O. WILSON

You'll also find that none of them is perfect, as has been widely reported in our culture's drive to expose our leaders' every flaw. The revolutionary geniuses we will get to know aren't offered for wholesale consumption. Rather, we'll aim to extract the very best of their example, and their creations, to enrich our lives. My aim is to make the essence and archetype of each of these extremely complex individuals accessible to you. Einstein set the benchmark for this endeavor when he said that "things should be made as simple as possible, not simpler."

My hope is that you'll be inspired to read the full biographies and study the original works of the extraordinary individuals we'll explore. And, most importantly, that you will embody this timeless wisdom to bring more happiness, beauty, truth, and goodness to your life. Cicero wrote of Socrates: "[He] called down philosophy from the skies and implanted it in the cities and homes of men." Let's call down the wisdom of our revolutionary geniuses and implant it in our lives, today.

<hr />

CRITERIA FOR
SELECTION TO THE DREAM TEAM

UNIVERSALITY OF IMPACT. Although nine of ten of the geniuses selected are Western, they are nonetheless universal in their impact. Western culture* has proven thus far to be the dominant influence in the world, partly through the influence of the revolutionary minds profiled in the following pages. The need to logically define the criteria for selection in order for you to consider accepting this perspective, for example, can be traced back to Plato and his student Aristotle, and the fact that you're reading in English owes much to Elizabeth I.

ORIGINAL, REVOLUTIONARY BREAKTHROUGHS THAT ARE REASONABLY ATTRIBUTABLE TO AN INDIVIDUAL. Put yourself into the mind of an "Einstein" living about 6,000 years ago. One day you happen to see some boulders rolling down the side of an embankment. The next day you chance to observe

<hr />

*Francis Bacon, a genius of the Enlightenment, a close runner-up to our top ten, observed that printing, gunpowder, and the magnetic compass, "changed the appearance of the whole world." These three revolutionary innovations (not to mention pasta!) all originated in China. If the Ming emperor hadn't called back his fleet in 1433 and instituted a policy of isolationism, this book might be written in Chinese with a very different cast of characters.

as a rotten tree trunk falls and rolls down the same slope. That night you dream of the boulder and the tree trunk, rolling, rolling, and rolling. You wake up with the ancient-language equivalent of "aha," because you've had a vision: you can build a sacred shrine to your gods by using fallen tree trunks to roll giant slabs of stone along the surface of the earth. From ancient times through to the present, the creative individual makes connections that others don't see, some of which are so original and powerful that they change the world forever.

Of course, we can't know who first harnessed fire, rigged up a plow, or invented the wheel. And modern insights into cultural evolution and systems theory give us pause before trumpeting the glories of an individual outside the fabric of his Zeitgeist. Nevertheless, the ten figures in this book were clearly individuals of extraordinary originality, whose towering achievements and revolutionary breakthroughs changed the world. They stand as amazing individuals and enduring archetypes from whom we can draw inspiration and guidance.

UTILITY FOR YOU. Shakespeare noted that "there was never yet the philosopher that could endure the toothache patiently." In other words, philosophy and inspiring ideas are fine, but how do they apply in actual practice? My most important criterion for selecting this genius roster is its practical value for you.

Thomas Jefferson, one of the incredible geniuses you'll get to know better, presided over the American Philosophical Society for Promoting Useful Knowledge. In this society's charter we read: "Knowledge is of little use, when confined to mere speculation: But when speculative truths are reduced to practice, when theories, grounded upon experiments, are applied to the common purposes of life; and when, by these . . . the arts of living made more easy and comfortable, and, of course, the increase and happiness of mankind promoted; knowledge then becomes really useful."

The approach of *Discover Your Genius* is based on practice, grounded in experience, in application to "the common purposes of life." The primary focus of the book is to offer you a treasure trove of guidance in "the arts of living" and to increase your happiness.

All the valuable things, material, spiritual, and moral,

which we receive from society can be traced back through

countless generations to certain creative individuals.

—ALBERT EINSTEIN

~◡

A FEW QUESTIONS
FROM THE LAST DINNER PARTY

Why only one woman and only one person of color?
Men and women and humans of every race are all equally gifted with
the potential for genius. All groups haven't, of course, had equal access
to the opportunity of developing that gift. And many women and
minorities who managed to develop their gifts against the odds have
been unfairly denied appropriate recognition. My wish is that the
ideas and inspiration of the great minds profiled here will touch and
empower all. In selecting the geniuses for inclusion in the book, gender and race were not used as criteria. Elizabeth I and Gandhi are
included not as an expression of affirmative action, but purely on
merit.

How could you leave out Sir Isaac Newton?
I consider Newton a revolutionary genius of equal stature to Einstein, and,
Newton also manifested the same fundamental genius quality of imagination and combinatory play. Yet I chose Einstein based on the ultimate criterion of "utility for you" because he's more current and therefore easier
to get to know.

It was, however, very hard to choose between them, just as it was difficult to choose Copernicus over Galileo and Thomas Jefferson over Benjamin Franklin. In the case of these close calls I've included a piece or sidebar about the runners-up, so Newton is profiled in the Einstein chapter, Galileo and Kepler are sidebars in the Copernicus chapter, and Benjamin Franklin is featured prominently in the chapter on Thomas Jefferson.

What about Christ and Buddha?
I decided to eliminate from consideration figures who are broadly viewed as divine inspirations for the formation of religions. Why? Well, I've got a lot of chutzpah, but not enough to write *How to Think Like the Son of God*.

Why no musicians? How could you leave out Beethoven and Mozart?
I love music, and consider Mozart, Beethoven, George Gershwin, and Ella Fitzgerald, among many others, to be geniuses. But in the vast scope of history, music serves more as a reflection, rather than a driver, of the changes in consciousness wrought by the likes of Copernicus, Jefferson, and Einstein. Beethoven captured the sound of freedom in his Ninth Symphony, but Jefferson did much more to make people actually free.

Nevertheless, music is so important that, with the help of a wonderful team of musical cognoscenti, I've chosen a piece of music that is evocative of the spirit and accomplishments of each of our breakthrough thinkers. I hope that you'll enjoy listening to the recommended selections in concert with your enjoyment of each great mind. (*Discover Your Genius* classical music CD available from 1-800-427-7680 and www.springhillmedia.com).

What about Leonardo da Vinci?
He got the last book all to himself!

HOW TO GET
THE MOST FROM THIS BOOK

The title *Discover Your Genius* has an intentional double meaning. The aim of the book is to help you discover and apply your own potential for genius, and at the same time to help you discover the "genius" or "geniuses" who inspire you the most.

Overview the Whole Book First

To get the most from this adventure in genius, begin by scanning the entire book. Spend some time musing on the genius portraits (see below) and develop a feel for the whole pantheon. Then, if you are more comfortable with a linear progression, read the chapters in order, which will give you a chronological presentation. Feel free, however, to skip around and approach the revolutionary geniuses in any order that appeals to you. You may wish to go straight to the genius who beckons you most strongly and immerse yourself in his or her life and wisdom as your point of departure.

CONTEMPLATE THE ILLUSTRATIONS

As you approach each genius chapter, spend a few minutes contemplating the portrait that goes with it. The images of the ten geniuses that appear in these pages were commissioned by the author from artist Norma Miller especially for this book. Miller's portraits, which have graced the cover of *Time* magazine, are known for their numinous, soulful aliveness. The artist was challenged to capture the genius quality in each of these original watercolors and to bring it to life for you.

Norma's comments on the process of creating the images are offered here in the hope that they will enhance your enjoyment and inspiration:

"Even though each portrait had its own particular set of challenges, there were similarities to the creative process for all of them. The first challenge was to lose self-consciousness—not to worry if the image I was painting was looking like the person; that is the sure route to a lifeless portrait. You might say that I worked from the inside of the person until eventually an image evolved. One of the fascinating aspects about portraiture is that it is the aura and 'feel' of a person that brings them to life, not the accuracy of the features.

"As a life-drawing teacher, I have often observed the student's need to seek the security of wanting every mark that is put on paper to look like something recognizable. To have the drawing look like something as soon as possible, often the inclination is to do an outline and fill it in—to work from the outside in. In fact, just the reverse should happen—to draw from the inside; the outside always has a magical way of taking care of itself. I soon realized that there are no obvious facial characteristics that can depict particular traits of genius. In fact, it soon became apparent that genius had much to do with combining many traits, some which even seemed at odds with one another, such as playfulness and seriousness, optimism and fear, or freedom and responsibility. Through these seeming paradoxes a subtle sense of these unique, complex characters began to emerge. The emphasis became the 'soul' of the person, and doesn't the soul emanate from the eyes? Indeed, the more I got to 'know' each genius, the more fascinated I became with not how we look at them, but rather, how they look at us and the world."

Reflect on the Self-Assessments

However you arrive at a given chapter, take a few minutes to reflect on its self-assessment questions before proceeding to the exercise section. You needn't formulate or write exact answers to the self-assessments; you may want to simply muse on the questions and allow them to percolate in your mind. After you complete the exercises from a chapter, return to your self-assessment and note any changes in attitudes that the exercises may have brought to light.

Enjoy the Exercises

Some of the genius exercises are lighthearted and fun while others require profound self-reflection and inner work. Start with the ones that seem most appealing, and don't feel compelled to do them in the order in which they are presented. Find your own pace and rhythm for enjoying and exploring the exercises. One early reader compared the exercises to a big box of Belgian chocolates, commenting, "I can't eat them all at once but I look forward to unwrapping and enjoying one each day!"

Keep a Genius Notebook / Journal

In a classic study of mental traits of genius, Catherine Cox examined 300 of history's greatest minds. She found that geniuses in every field—from painting, literature, and music, to science, the military, and politics —tended to have certain common characteristics. Most notably, she discovered that geniuses enjoy recording their insights, observations, feelings, poems, and questions in personal notebooks or through letters to friends and family.

So, in the manner of all the geniuses whom we will explore, keep a notebook to express your insights, musings, and observations as you journey through these great minds. You can use the same notebook to record your reflections on the self-assessments and your responses to the exercises in the book.

If you are required to write for your job, or at school, you are probably asked to do so in a linear, orderly fashion; most bosses don't tell us to let our minds go free and be creative when writing a business plan or filling out an expense report. But in your genius notebook you are encouraged to do just that. Scholars criticized Leonardo da Vinci for the seemingly random nature of his notebooks, to which he never provided either an index or a table of contents. Leonardo's notes feature sketches of birds in flight and water flowing, observations on the anatomy of a cat, jokes, dreams, and shopping lists, all appearing on the same page. Like most of the great minds you'll be exploring, Leonardo intuitively trusted the natural flow of his associative process—the combinatory play that Einstein advocates. Practice this free play in response to the inspiration of each revolutionary genius. As you record and reflect on the ideas and insights that inspire you, they will become imprinted in your psyche at a deeper level.

Form a Group to Explore the Genius Exercises

Many of the workshop attendees and others who have been introduced to the *Discover Your Genius* program have reported that they enjoy forming discussion and combinatory play groups to explore the geniuses further, and to compare notes on the exercises for embodying each principle. You'll find some suggestions for hosting your own "genius salons" and a few simple, delicious recipes to inspire your creativity and delight your friends. Feel free to use modern methods to access ancient truths; forming e-mail groups to explore the geniuses and mine their qualities can prevent geographical restrictions from limiting your creative potential, and the Internet can yield a wealth of important and interesting facts.

Practice Imaginary Dialogues with the Geniuses

You can deepen the impact of genius thinking in your life by creating an imaginary dialogue with great minds. "Conversing" with geniuses of the past—or present—is great fun and usually quite enlightening. To get the most from your genius dialogues, record the "responses" in your notebook.

Niccolo Machiavelli (1469–1527), a strong candidate for inclusion in the list of history's most revolutionary thinkers, developed many of his ideas through imaginary dialogues with great minds of the past. Adorned in his courtly robes, Machiavelli regularly retired to his private office where he engaged in questioning the great minds of history and recording their responses. As he noted:

"Study the actions of illustrious men, to see how they have borne themselves, examine the causes of their victories and defeats, so as to imitate the former and avoid the latter.

"Above all, do as illustrious men do, who take as their example, those who have been praised and famous before them, and whose achievements and deeds still live in the memory, as it is said Alexander the Great imitated Achilles and Caesar imitated Alexander."

Machiavelli explains this practice further:

"I take off my work-day clothes, filled with dust and mud, and don royal and curial garments. Worthily dressed, I enter into the ancient courts of the men of antiquity, where warmly received, I feed on that which is my only food and which was meant for me. I am not ashamed to speak with them and ask them the reasons of their actions, and they, because of their humanity, answer me. Four hours can pass and I feel no weariness; my troubles forgotten, I neither fear poverty nor dread death. I give myself over entirely to them. And since Dante says that there can be no science [understanding] without retaining what has been understood, I have noted down the chief things in their conversation."

Let's begin our genius dialogue with Plato, the father of Western philosophy.

Plato

(CIRCA 428–348 B.C.)

Deepening Your Love of Wisdom

Beauty is truth, truth beauty . . .

—JOHN KEATS

Think for a moment of the teachers who have had the most lasting and profound impact on you. Chances are, they helped you see the essence of something dear to you for the first time, or inspired you to cultivate a lasting love for that subject, or perhaps instilled in you ideals that are still with you today. If you were lucky enough to have had such influential teachers in your life, you know the feelings of warmth and gratitude their memories evoke, for they set you on the path toward becoming the person you want to be.

My visual inspiration was drawn from Raphael's depiction in his magnificent School of Athens *of what he thought Plato must have looked like—legend has it that Raphael used Leonardo da Vinci as the model for Plato. I used this archetype of what a great philosopher looks like as my launching point. I wanted Plato to look as though he was observing and thinking at the same time, a process that embodies wisdom.*—Norma Miller

Those teachers, and the fires they kindled in you, were also your first introduction to the tradition of teaching and learning that can be traced back to our first revolutionary genius. The personification of the ancient Greeks' cultural love of wisdom, Plato is one of a line of teachers and students of legendary intellectual prowess that begins with Socrates, teacher of Plato, who then passed on his wisdom to Aristotle, who became the tutor of Alexander the Great. But Plato stands tallest among these giants, exerting more influence on us today than you may realize: for example, so much of what the favorite teachers noted above are remembered for—the pursuit of the essence of something, the celebration of ideals, even the

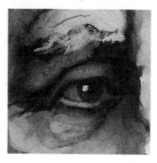

love of learning—came to us from Plato. If, as Charles Freeman writes in *The Greek Achievement*, "the Greeks provided the chromosomes of Western Civilization," then Plato sequenced the DNA.

Plato set the table for the feast of the Western intellectual dialogue; one twentieth-century philosopher went so far as to characterize the subsequent Western philosophical tradition as consisting "by and large of footnotes to Plato." The underlying premise that informed the writing of this book—that each of us, yourself included, possesses a divine spark that can be awakened and nurtured into a full expression of our spiritual and creative gifts—is itself a neo-Platonic assumption. Even Leonardo da Vinci was expressing an essentially Platonic notion when he wrote in his notebook, "The desire to know is natural to good men," and "For in truth great love is born of great knowledge of the thing loved." In fact, Plato was the central influence of the classical wisdom whose rebirth marked the Renaissance that Leonardo personified.

There is an eye of the soul which is

more precious than ten-thousand bodily eyes,

for by it alone is truth seen.

—PLATO

TEACHER AND STUDENT

Plato's birth into a distinguished and politically well-connected Athenian family came near the onset of the Peloponnesian War. The war exacerbated an atmosphere of political turmoil in his homeland that lasted until he was in his early twenties. Originally oriented to a career in politics, Plato became disenchanted by the cutthroat struggle for power between the oligarchic and democratic factions in Athens. As he wrote, "I was disgusted and drew back from the wickedness of the times."

Plato's uncles and older brothers had studied with Socrates before his birth, so we can be reasonably sure that he was exposed as a child to the teachings of the master. And it is with Socrates that an appreciation of Plato must begin. Born in Athens in 469 B.C., Socrates dedicated his life primarily to the pursuit of moral goodness and the search for truth.

When one of his friends asked the Oracle at Delphi whether anyone was wiser than Socrates, the Oracle replied: "NO." Socrates overcame his embarrassment at being considered the wisest man of his time by interpreting the distinction as recognition of his most important knowledge: the knowledge of his own ignorance. He believed that the Oracle's intention was to bring him and others closer to goodness and truth by helping them realize their fundamental ignorance of these essentials. Rejecting the mantle of "expert" or even "teacher," Socrates practiced profound intellectual humility, describing himself as a "midwife of ideas."

The process of the questing mind, critical and open, is the core of the Socratic approach. Socrates embodied the Delphic command to "know thyself." His admonition, "The unexamined life is not worth living" is the point of departure for anyone who seeks wholeness and enlightenment. Socrates believed that happiness was to be achieved not through external achievement, material wealth, or status, but rather through living a life that nurtures one's soul.

Socrates found his finest student in Plato, but their relationship was cut short when the Athenian democratic government sentenced Socrates to death in 399 B.C., on what Plato called "a monstrous charge, the last that could be made against him, the charge of impiety." His disillusionment with Athens at its worst, Plato left for years of study abroad, seeking recourse through philosophy—literally, "the love of wisdom," from the Greek roots *philein* meaning "loving" and *sophia* meaning "wise." As "law and morality were deteriorating at an alarming rate," he wrote, he was ultimately "forced . . . to the belief that the only hope of finding justice for society or for the individual lay in true philosophy."

PLATO'S RENAISSANCE

In 1486, at the age of twenty-three, Pico della Mirandola asserted his stature as one of the high priests of Plato's renaissance when he presented his remarkable "Oration on the Dignity of Man," a neo-Platonic perspective on creation that is as inspiring to students of human potential today as it was when first presented more than 500 years ago. In it Pico proclaims that we humans, unlike other creatures, have unlimited potential to create our own stature in life. He writes:

"Neither an established place, nor a form belong to you alone, nor any special function we have given you, O Adam, and for this reason, that you have and possess, according to your desire and judgment, whatever place, whatever form, and whatever functions you shall desire. The nature of other creatures, which has been determined, is confined within the bounds prescribed by us. You, who are confined by no limits, shall determine for yourself your own nature, in accordance with your own free will, in whose hand I have placed you.

"I have set you at the center of the world, so that from there you may more easily survey whatever is in the world. We have made you neither heavenly nor earthly, neither mortal nor immortal, so that, you may fashion yourself in whatever form you shall prefer. You should be able to descend among the lower forms of being, which are brute beasts; you shall be able to be reborn out of the judgment of your own soul into the higher beings, which are divine."

A PHILOSOPHY OF KNOWLEDGE

Plato's love of wisdom is best appreciated by considering his fundamental philosophy of knowledge on which his political, educational, and moral philosophy are all based. Of course, a full understanding of the ideas that Plato developed and expressed through his celebrated dialogues would require a lifetime of scholarly inquiry. Nevertheless, his most important idea, and the famous metaphor with which he chose to express it, reveal more than a glimpse of his genius.

In Plato's view, the world we experience is a pale reflection of an ideal world, a permanent and unchanging realm he calls the world of Forms. Our everyday world is changing constantly, with everything in it a mere

According to the Neo-Platonists, since the self shares the same structure as the world, by knowing the self, one can know the world.

—PROFESSOR ROGER PADEN ON THE NEO-PLATONIC LOVE OF WISDOM

impermanent expression of its true essence, which resides in the world of Forms. For example, in your hand you hold a book, but it is only because you know the eternal essence, or form, of "bookness" that you are able to recognize this particular book. Similarly, you recognize an apple or a cat as a manifestation of the ideal form of "appleness" or "catness."

The world of Forms is hierarchically organized, with Beauty, Truth, and Goodness at the top of the hierarchy. Plato reasoned that before birth all human souls have access to the world of pure beauty, truth, and goodness but that when we are born, we forget. The philosopher's mission is to lead the way back to the beauty, truth, and goodness we have forgotten.

Imagine a perfect circle.

We can conceive the form of a perfect circle and the circle can be formally defined as pi r squared (πr^2).

Now draw a circle. As you draw you will introduce imperfections. Even Leonardo and Michelangelo drew imperfect circles. And a computer can't draw a perfect circle either, because its pixels aren't perfect.

Nevertheless, the ideal form of the perfect circle is known to us, Plato would say, from before birth.

In book seven of *The Republic* Plato introduces his most famous metaphor for the world of forms and its relation to our everyday experience: "I want you to go on to picture the enlightenment or ignorance of our human condition somewhat as follows. Imagine an underground chamber, like a cave with an entrance open to the daylight and running a long way underground. In this chamber are men who have been prisoners there since they were children, their legs and necks being so fastened that they can only look straight ahead of them and cannot turn their heads."

Plato goes on to describe the prisoners' restricted view. Their "reality" is limited to the shadows reflected on the wall of the cave by a fire burning behind them. Plato then asks, "think what would naturally happen to them if they were released from their bonds and cured of their delusions."

He describes the prisoners' difficulty in adjusting to the brightness and overcoming the illusions of his former "shadow-reality"—a realm that the prisoners had not known was a mere shadow of the world of light, just as ours is a limited reflection of the world of Forms.

For Plato, it is the philosopher who overcomes his fear, breaks his chains, and ventures out of the cave to seek the light. And it is love, of wisdom, goodness, truth, and beauty, that is the philosopher's driving force. Plato's true philosopher, who escapes the cave and knows the light of the form of the Good, also returns to guide others to enlightenment.

THE POWER OF LOVE

[Beauty] is eternal, unproduced, indestructible;
neither subject to increase or decay . . . All other things
are beautiful through a participation of it . . .
This is the divine and pure . . . the beautiful itself.

—PLATO

~‿

The concept of love that Plato saw as so central to enlightenment is different from the love of which we speak so casually today. When Plato speaks of the "love of wisdom," he really means it. For Plato, passionate love of beauty, truth, and goodness was the way out of the cave. This loving force, known to the Greeks as Eros, may begin with physical desire and personal affection but evolves to a more universal, spiritual plane. (Thus the contemporary phrase "Platonic relationship," though typically used to suggest that a relationship is not carnal, actually refers to a friendship based on the pursuit and shared recognition of pure truth, beauty, and goodness.)

Love is expressed through rigorous work in Plato's world; disciplined study and intensive training in reasoning are prerequisites for understanding true knowledge. Still, the process by which Plato suggests we experience a full realization of the form of the Good bears some resemblance to a romantic consummation. Describing oneness with the form of the Good, he writes: "If the lover is attuned to the object with which he would be united, the result is delight, pleasure and satisfaction. When the lover is united with the one he loves, he finds peace; relieved of his burden, he finds rest." And speaking through Socrates' voice in the Symposium, Plato emphasizes that "human nature will not easily find a better helper than love."

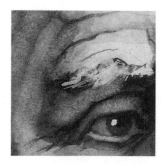

THE GENIUS WITHIN

Plato returned to Athens for his crowning achievement: the creation in 379 B.C. of the Academy, the first university in the Western world. If Platonism were a religion, then learning and teaching would be its forms of worship, and the Academy would be its temple. Entrance to it was predicated on successful completion of what we now call elementary and secondary education. Although information about specialized subjects was included in the curriculum, the primary focus of a Platonic education was "reminding" the student of the knowledge inherent in the human soul.

Plato reasoned that the most important knowledge was already inside the student. Therefore, the role of the teacher was to facilitate the student's realization of this inner knowing through Socratic questioning leading to independent thought. In the Dialogue entitled "Meno," for example, Plato's Socrates quizzes a young slave boy about the Pythagorean theorem. The boy, who has no training of any kind in geometry, initially leaps to false answers. But Socrates' stream of questioning soon brings the boy to realize that his conclusions are faulty. Eventually Socrates' questions stimulate the boy to solve the problem correctly. Socrates then argues that the boy's geometrical knowledge was innate, and that he was serving not as a teacher, but merely as a midwife of recollection. Just as the student's discovery of the proofs of geometry can be drawn out by skilled questioning, so, Plato argues, can realization of virtue, justice, and beauty.

Plato emphasizes that "we must reject the conception of education professed by those who say that they can put into the mind knowledge that was not there before . . ." For Plato, anything worth knowing is already known, and must be remembered and reclaimed by the soul.

Plato's conception of the soul involves three parts, organized hierarchically, from lowest to highest, as the physical ("the appetites"), the imaginative ("the passions") and the intellectual ("reason"), and his ideal society is structured with three corresponding classes: manual laborers (physical), artisans and soldiers (imaginative), and the philosophers and guardians of society (intellectual). Here we see the basis for the modern world's criticism of Plato, from the understandable objection to his rigid class system and his misguided suggestion that artists and poets be censored because of their potentially disruptive influence, to the charge that his notion of the ideal state, led by a benevolent king and elite "guardians," has been misused to justify the absolutist and authoritarian tendencies of numerous corrupt governments through the ages.

Yet careful readers of Plato's *Republic* cannot fail to recognize the emphasis he places on the thorough training, moral integrity, and self-denial required of his ideal society's leaders. And, in contrast to the conventions of his time, Plato believed that women could qualify as "guardians" of society and as philosopher queens! Overall, the fairest criticism of *The*

Republic may be that, in advocating an ideal society, Plato is guilty of attempting the impossible. As Aristotle put it: "In framing an ideal we may assume what we wish, but we should avoid impossibilities."

As the father of philosophy, Plato stands as an enduring archetype of the love of wisdom. Although Aristotle questioned the framing of an ideal society in *The Republic*, he nevertheless saw Plato as an ideal teacher. Aristotle wrote:

> *Of that unique man whose name is not to come*
> *   from the lips of the wicked*
> *Theirs is not the right to praise him—*
> *Him who first revealed clearly*
> *By word and by deed*
> *That he who is virtuous is happy*
> *Alas, not one of us can equal him.*

Summary of Achievements

▲ Plato is the seminal figure of Western philosophy.

▲ He introduced the logical concept of "definition."

▲ He formulated the basis of the modern university, and the idea of primary and secondary education in preparation for the university.

▲ He championed the process of reasoning and independent thought and formulated the concept of education as drawing out the knowledge of the student, rather than stuffing it in.

▲ Despite his tough stance on artists in *The Republic,* Plato's Dialogues qualify him as a great literary genius. As *The Encyclopedia of Philosophy* points out, "Greek prose reached its peak in the writings of Plato. His flexibility, his rich vocabulary, his easy colloquialism and high rhetoric, his humor, irony, pathos, gravity, bluntness, delicacy and occasional ferocity, his mastery of metaphor, simile and myth, his swift delineation of character—his combination of these and other qualities puts him beyond rivalry."

▲ He brought the teachings of Socrates to the world and taught Aristotle.

PLATO AND YOU

Chances are that you picked up this book as an expression of your own love of wisdom. It is the spirit that drives you to increase your knowledge and improve yourself, and your cultivation of it will reward you in the subsequent chapters and beyond. In the self-assessment and exercises that follow, you'll have the opportunity to examine your own life in the tradition of Socrates and Plato, but we'll proceed in the spirit of the Renaissance neo-Platonists, with a bit more emphasis on the ecstatic elements!

Before you begin, you may wish to consider Plato's delightfully ironic relevance to our world today. Plato reasoned that reality was unchanging and that it possessed a definitive structure. He argued that the "good life" was to be discovered in conforming to that structure. The crux of the change from ancient to modern thought is the shift of focus from a hierarchical, uniform, static world of absolutes to a "matrixed" world of diverse, dynamic, uncertain relativity. Quantum physics, most notably Nobel Prize–winner Werner Heisenberg's famous "uncertainty principle," is a symbol of a world that now easily dismisses "absolutes." But although the modern world has rejected many of Plato's answers, the fundamental questions he raised—"What is virtue and how can we cultivate it?" "How can we live in a way that nurtures the soul?"—are perhaps more important now than ever. And Werner Heisenberg himself was moved to write that one of his life goals was "To meditate in peace on the great questions Plato raised."

Please begin your own meditations by musing on the following self-assessment. Reflect on these Platonic themes and then, after you complete the exercises, return to the self-assessment and reflect again and note any shift in your responses:

PLATO:
DEEPENING YOUR LOVE OF WISDOM
SELF-ASSESSMENT

- ☐ My happiness is based on my success at work.

- ☐ My happiness is based on how others see me.

- ☐ My happiness is based on my financial success and material possessions.

- ☐ My happiness is based on nurturing my soul.

- ☐ I have a well-reasoned perspective on goodness and a strong code of ethics and moral behavior.

- ☐ I'm committed to moral, law-abiding behavior, even if I don't feel like it.

- ☐ I believe that virtue is its own reward

- ☐ I seek the essence of beauty every day.

- ☐ I ask probing, challenging questions of myself and others

- ☐ I have a rational, well-considered philosophy of life.

- ☐ I examine my life—my philosophy, values, and contribution to society—with a searching, critical eye.

- ☐ For which principles would I be willing to sacrifice my life?

EXERCISES

THINKING LIKE PLATO/
DEEPENING YOUR LOVE OF WISDOM

Life must be lived as play.

—PLATO

~⁀

PRACTICE WONDER

In a world of "been there, done that" and "whatever . . ." wonder is often considered naïve and "unhip." But "wonder" is the root of "wonderful" and the beginning of the philosophical quest. Webster offers the following synonyms: admiration, appreciation, astonishment, reverence, surprise, amazement, and awe.

In your notebook, make a list of ten wonderful things, memories, imaginings, observations, dreams, or experiences that fill you with amazement, reverence, and awe.

Appreciation of wonder, every day, is a marvelous way to invite your mind to stay open and increase your enjoyment of life. Poet Samuel Taylor Coleridge called wonder the "living power and prime agent of all human perception." In the words of twentieth-century genius Buckminster Fuller, "Dare to be naïve!"

CONTEMPLATE BEAUTY

. . . at last the vision . . . of a single science,

which is the science of beauty everywhere.

—PLATO

~

The goal of the philosophical quest is direct apprehension of the universal creative intelligence through questioning, contemplation, and profound reflection. For Plato, truth, goodness, and beauty are woven together in a supreme tapestry of perfect form. Of these, beauty is the one most accessible to the senses.

As Plato wrote:

"For he who would proceed aright . . . should begin in youth to visit beautiful forms . . . out of that he should create fair thoughts; and soon he will of himself perceive that the beauty of one form is akin to the beauty of another, and that beauty in every form is one and the same."

▲ Explore the meaning of "the Beautiful" in your life by making a list of ten of the most beautiful things you've ever seen, touched, felt, tasted, thought, smelled, heard, or experienced in any way. Your list can include anything you perceive as beautiful: it might include, for example, a painting, a face, a piece of music, a sunset, a flower, a touch, a concept, or a cake!

▲ After you've made your list, jot down, in a phrase or two, your reflections on what makes each of those things beautiful.

▲ Then look for the common elements in your examples.

▲ Now experiment with expressing your own definition of the essence of beauty in a sentence or two, or perhaps in a few lines of poetry or haiku.

This is Emily Dickinson's expression of the Platonic quest for beauty:

> Beauty crowds me till I die,
> Beauty, mercy have on me!
> But if I expire today,
> Let it be in sight of thee

PLATONIC LOVE: BEAUTY AND ROMANCE

A wonderful way to deepen your appreciation of beauty while enhancing your love life is to reflect on and express your perceptions of the deep beauty you experience, or remember, in your partner. When most people fall in love they see straight through to the essence of beauty in their beloved. But then, as the pressures of making a life with someone grow, that original inspiration is obscured. True romance is remembering and celebrating that beauty, with a sense of wonder, in the midst of the mundane. Hold the image of someone you love in mind and then write down your experience of the way in which that person manifests the form of Beauty. Then, consolidate your reflections in a simple card and give it to your partner. As you refresh your ability to see the beauty in others you'll be rewarded by discovering that they can't help but see it in you.

MEDITATE ON LIGHT

For Plato the supreme form of the Good was represented by the sun. Both Socrates and Plato equated wisdom and goodness with light. Socrates tells us:

"In order that the mind should see light instead of darkness, so the entire soul must be turned away from this changing world, until its eye can learn to contemplate reality and that supreme splendor which we have called the good.

Hence there may well be an art whose aim it would be to effect this very thing."

Poet Ted Hughes practiced and taught a form of this art. He prepared his students to write poetry with this simple meditation on light that you may enjoy. Sit comfortably in a dark, quiet room. Place a single candle on a table, light it, and watch the flame. Keep your eyes soft but focused. When your mind wanders, return to the light of the flame. This is a wonderful practice to prepare yourself for any creative endeavor; try it before sketching, painting, drawing, or writing poetry.

Another inspiring meditation on light is to watch the sunrise and sunset on the same day. Of course, the Light that Plato urges us to seek is ultimately within. As the Chandogya Upanishad expresses it: "There is a light that shines beyond all things on earth, beyond the highest, the very highest heavens. This is the light that shines in your heart."

APPRECIATE AND NURTURE POTENTIAL

Aristotle, Plato's greatest student, formulated the philosophical concept of potentiality. For Aristotle the motive force in the cosmos is the tendency of everything to become what it is meant to be. Aristotle remained true to his teacher (although he disagreed on many other points) by positing that all things develop true to their Form. Thus, human sperm and ovum are a potential baby and an acorn is a potential oak tree.

In early spring the great sunflower fields near Plato's birthplace in Athens seem empty. The first-time visitor sees nothing. But the farmers have already planted millions of seeds. And the farmers foresee, with the right conditions of rain, soil, and sunshine, flowing fields of giant yellow sunflowers. For the farmer, the sunflowers "exist," even before they can be seen, because he knows their potential and the necessary conditions for their full flowering.

What are the seeds within your own soul that have yet to flower fully? Shed some light on your unrealized potential by doing a ten-minute stream-of-consciousness writing exercise on one of the following topics.

- What are the "right conditions" necessary for the full flowering of my soul?
- What am I meant to be?
- My true potential is . . .
- My strongest undeveloped talent is . . .

HOW TO DO A
STREAM-OF-CONSCIOUSNESS EXERCISE

Stream-of-consciousness writing is a marvelous tool for appreciating and nurturing your potential. You can use it to express your love of wisdom as you plumb the depths of any question you wish to explore. Stream of consciousness simply involves writing your thoughts and associations as they occur, without editing.

The secret of effective stream-of-consciousness writing is to *keep your pen moving*; don't lift it away from the paper or stop to correct your spelling and grammar, just write continuously.

Stream-of-consciousness writing yields lots of nonsense and redundancy, but can lead to profound insight and understanding. Don't worry if you seem to be writing pure gibberish; this is actually a sign that you are overriding the habitual, superficial aspects of your thought process. As you persevere, keeping your pen on the paper and moving it continuously, you'll eventually open a window through which your intuitive intelligence will shine. Bear in mind the poet's motto: "Write drunk, revise sober."

You may wish to dedicate a special notebook just for stream-of-consciousness writing.

Dedicate a minimum time for each stream-of-consciousness session. You'll probably need at least five minutes to get your intuitive mind flowing.

Take a ten-minute break after each stream-of-consciousness session. Then go back to your notebook and read what you have written aloud. Highlight the words or phrases that speak to you most strongly.
Look for themes, insights, the beginnings of poems, and more questions to explore.

In addition to appreciating and cultivating your own potential, strive to see and nurture the gifts of those around you. Do you appreciate and encourage the full potential of your spouse or significant other? Your children? Your colleagues at work? Your students? Hold the image of each significant person in your life, one at a time, and contemplate the emergence of their full potential and self-expression. Note your reflections on anything you could do, or perhaps something you could stop doing, that might facilitate their growth.

Our modern Olympic games are another aspect of the legacy of the ancient Greek achievement. When Olympic gold medals are awarded, winners are invariably asked the secret of their success. Almost without exception they answer, "I owe it to my [mom, dad, coach, teacher, brother, friend, priest, etc.] who always believed in me." The best coaches, parents, and friends see the potential in the people around them and help them discover something inside that they might never have known without that external encouragement. Be the person whose belief in the potential of those around you inspires their best.

THE 100 QUESTIONS

For Plato and his teacher, Socrates, the process of questioning is the key to deepening wisdom. When Leonardo da Vinci emphasized that "The desire to know is natural to good men," he was expressing the "rebirth" or "renaissance" of a fundamentally Platonic ideal. One of the most popular and powerful exercises from *How to Think Like Leonardo da Vinci* involves writing out, in stream-of-consciousness style, 100 questions. This exercise goes right to the heart of deepening your love of wisdom and so it is "reborn" here. But now you'll be guided through it by an excerpt from the "genius journal" of Roben Torosyan, Ph.D.

"I had the most interesting and strange experience last night. I thought I was hallucinating. It all started when I was reading *How to Think Like Leonardo da Vinci* and decided I wanted to try the Hundred Questions exercise. The instructions, which turned out to be very important, read as follows:

" 'In your notebook, make a list of a hundred questions that are important to you. Your list can include *any kind of question* as long as it's something you deem significant: anything from "How can I save money?" or "How can I have more fun?" to "What is the meaning and purpose of my existence?" and "How can I best serve the Creator?"

" '*Do the entire list in one sitting.* Write quickly; don't worry about spelling, grammar, or repeating the same question in different words (recurring questions will alert you to emerging themes). Why a hundred questions? The first twenty or so will be off the top of your head. In the next thirty or forty, themes often begin to emerge. And in the latter part of the second half of the list you are likely to discover unexpected but profound material.'

"I was especially intrigued to see if I'd arrive at anything unexpected or profound at the end, as I felt sure I already knew my questions. Initially, I had questions like 'How can I find what's right for me?' and 'How can I not be distracted as easily?' Many questions revolved around wanting to achieve more balance and harmony. Another theme was how to get beyond my own narcissism.

"After filling a page with twenty questions, I was already a little tired. It was late (about 11:20 P.M. when I began), and I had to get up at 7:10 A.M. for yoga. I felt, 'I don't HAVE to do it one sitting. Why should I?' But I liked the idea of following the directions as best I could, even if only to see what would happen if I did exactly what was intended—like a mini-experiment. So I made a leap of faith, assumed the author may have really intended *100* questions for some reason, and kept going, hoping maybe I'd find out something in the end.

"By question 47, I had a deeper than usual flash: 'How can I probe deep within me, to live like a genius, utterly unconcerned with others' judgments, only interested in the problem at hand?' Some nagging themes also repeated regularly, such as, 'How can I respect myself enough to protect my time.' It got hard again after question 60, after I had filled four pages. I was exhausted and felt like I couldn't possibly go on. Again I reread the instructions, and looked for the part about what happens with the latter half of the 100. I decided that I knew I could stop if I wanted to, but that instead I WOULD stick it through—because, as I told myself, I really didn't know WHAT would happen if I did it *all*. Part of me didn't believe anything really profound or unexpected would come out of it.

"Sure enough, from question 88 to 89 there was a sudden and very marked shift. I went from, 'What else matters besides the practical in life?' to 'Where is the light, the source of power and divinity—the source and inspiration for all?' At the time I was writing this, I was also aware of a change in my bodily condition, as if I was tripping on a psychedelic drug or getting into some other state of mind. As I felt the pen press into the paper in my journal, it actually felt for a moment as if something or someone or some energy was driving the writing for me, moving my pen.

"I said to myself then in a blur, 'This isn't me, right now—something's passing through me.' I believe I may have had some form of an altered state of consciousness experience.

"On reflection, it is interesting how the quality and kind of questions changed; from egocentric preoccupations, and other concerns about what I or we can do, to eventually a mystical transcendental state of mind entirely. Interestingly, I was aware of and could have written some so-called profound questions earlier, but they felt contrived at that point, without my having gone through the process.

"For me, this all shows how incredibly important it is to let ourselves really get into any project, almost lose our self-consciousness and abashedness to get immersed in whatever we're doing, whatever we're exploring, to LET ourselves have each experience—beyond clichés, and breaking through detached coolness or mindlessness—as fully as possible. THAT seems to be 'living,' no?"

Experiment with "deepening your love of wisdom" by doing the 100 questions exercise. Then, as Roben did, make notes in your journal about what you learn from the process.

Here are the instructions again:

In your notebook, make a list of a hundred questions that are important to you. Your list can include *any kind of question* as long as it's something you deem significant: anything from "How can I save money?" or "How can I have more fun?" to "What is the meaning and purpose of my existence?" and "How can I best serve the Creator?"

Do the entire list in one sitting. Write quickly; don't worry about spelling, grammar, or repeating the same question in different words (recurring questions will alert you to emerging themes). Why a hundred questions? The first twenty or so will be off the top of your head. In the next thirty or forty, themes often begin to emerge. And in the latter part of the second half of the list you are likely to discover unexpected but profound material.

LIVE THE EXAMINED LIFE

The Enlightenment philosopher John Stuart Mill made a pointed defense of the Platonic notion of the importance of living an examined life when he wrote: "It is better to be a human being dissatisfied than a pig satisfied; better to be Socrates dissatisfied than a fool satisfied. And if the fool, or the pig are of a different opinion, it is because they only know their own side of the question. The other party to the comparison knows both sides."

In other words, from a Socratic/Platonic perspective ignorance isn't bliss, and the quest for morality in our lives is the highest priority for our examination, even if it makes us uncomfortable.

Explore the state of your moral universe in the ways that follow.

EXAMINE THE MORAL PHILOSOPHY IMPLICIT IN THE MEDIA

I don't know who discovered water, but it definitely wasn't a fish. Just as fish are immersed in water, we are so surrounded by advertising, marketing, and media that we can become dulled to the effects they have on our moral awareness.

Ask Yourself

What role did advertising and marketing play in the formation and maintenance of my moral compass? How does it affect me now? How does it aim to shape my values and behaviors? How do advertising and marketing influence the moral development of my children? Experiment by flipping through a few of the channels on your television and getting a quick read on the moral content or message of each channel.

Professor Paden emphasizes: "No random acts of kindness and senseless acts of beauty for Plato. For Plato, acts of kindness help make one kind, and exposure to beauty draws us toward the real. Both make us better people and should be systematically pursued."

Then write in your journal, or discuss with a friend, the underlying moral messages of any of the advertisements in the magazines you read, the billboards you pass on the road, or on the radio and television shows you enjoy.

How do these types of influences affect your soul?

EXAMINE YOUR RELATIONSHIP TO VIRTUE

The word "ethics" comes from the Greek word *ethos,* which means "character" or "habitual way of life." Plato and Aristotle reasoned that character must be cultivated through practice and exposure to positive role models. Both Plato and Aristotle thought that virtue was learned in a social setting. They argued that we must maintain a social context that encourages the development of a good character.

Consider the following questions to guide you in your quest for virtue:

What is your most significant virtue and how did you acquire it?
What is your most significant vice and how did you acquire it?

What should you read, listen to, and watch on TV to cultivate virtue?

Is it possible to be happy without being virtuous?

How can you help to cultivate virtue in your children?

Who are your role models for virtue?

What virtues of theirs do you most admire? Why?

Could you think of better role models?

Who are your anti−role models? What vices do they exemplify?

How could you change your milieu to lead you in the direction of greater virtue?

PUT ON A TOGA PARTY

Living the "examined life" is hard work, but both Socrates and Plato also knew how to have a good time. Try a Greek toga party in their honor, not the *Animal House* version, but rather, a modern expression of the original Platonic *The Symposium*. Invite your guests to come dressed as ancient Greeks and to bring their favorite poems or essays about love. Serve a variety of simple Greek delicacies (available in any Greek deli and now in most supermarkets), such as Kalamata olives, hummus, artichoke hearts, feta cheese, hot pita bread, dates, figs, honey, and yogurt.

For a toga party recipe, try this:

Symposium *Lamb Delight*
(Serves 4)

8 lamb sausages (d'Artagnan is an excellent and
   widely available brand)
2 shallots
8 cloves of garlic
One pound of boneless lamb loin
Sprinkles of dried oregano, salt, pepper and hot red
   pepper flakes
Half a pound of Greek feta cheese
8−12 artichoke hearts
16−20 pitted Kalamata olives

Cook the sausage in a frying pan and set it aside. Then sauté the shallots and garlic in some Greek olive oil. Cut the lamb loin into bite-size pieces and add it to the shallot-garlic mixture, on a low flame, stirring gently with the spirit of Platonic Love. Sprinkle in the salt, pepper, oregano, and hot red pepper flakes.

When the meat is cooked to your taste, add the sausage and stir in the crumbled feta cheese and then the olives and artichoke hearts.

Let it simmer for a few minutes and then serve over rice, orzo, or couscous.

Most important, keep the wine flowing. Plato invokes the timeless phrase "in vino veritas," and in the original *Symposium* everyone invoked Bacchus—god of wine—by imbibing continuously. Socrates was renowned for his ability to drink more than anyone else without showing the effects. As the evening progresses, and the wine flows, ask each guest to recite his or her ode to love and give a prize for the most evocative, moving expression (a laurel wreath and a bottle of wine make great prizes).

Ron Gross, author of *Socrates' Way* and leader of the Seminar on Creativity at Columbia University, comments on the value of this kind of informal philosophical exchange: "I encourage my students to elevate their conversations with friends by inviting a discussion of what people mean when they use some key term or phrase such as 'love,' 'justice,' 'friendship,' or 'doing the right thing.' It's astonishing how differently people define such terms. Sharing different perspectives in a respectful and creative way enhances many social occasions that might otherwise glide along much closer to the ground."

Gross adds, "Plato's Dialogues are conversations among friends. *The Crito, The Timaeus, The Euthyphro* are all written in the style of a conversation that might take place at a dinner party. So if Plato could sit in on a great dialogue between your friends Dave and Ellen, he might turn it into 'The Dave' or 'The Ellen'!"

THEME EXPLORATION: ESCAPE FROM THE CAVE

The twentieth-century philosopher Georges Gurdjieff noted that many people are living in a "shadow realm," like the one described in Plato's metaphor of the cave. He wrote, "Man is asleep," and he advocated a practice called "self-remembering."

One of Gurdjieff's tools for encouraging self-remembering was working with a theme to encourage greater awareness. Theme work is a powerful tool for awakening your inner genius. Choose a theme for the day and record observations in your notebook. You can jot down your thoughts throughout the day, or just make mental notes to be recorded in your notebook at a quiet time before sleep. Aim to make accurate, nonevaluative observations. Speculation, opinion, and theory are fine, but actual observation offers the richest resource.

Begin your theme work by exploring the metaphor of the cave in everyday life. Ask yourself: What are the habits and influences that dull my awareness on a daily basis? And how is that "dulling" manifest in my body?

APPEARANCE AND REALITY

What is real? What is mere appearance? How can we know the difference? These three questions gave birth to philosophy. Before Plato and Socrates, the "pre-Socratic" philosophers argued that reality was fundamentally different from appearances. Parmenides posited that reality was "one" and unchanging, while Heraclitus proposed that it was "flux." For Pythagoras reality was "music," for Thales it was "water," and for Democritus it was composed of "atoms."

Plato's laurels as the father of philosophy rest partly on his organization and integration of the multiplicity of pre-Socratic ideas with the teachings of his teacher. As Roger Paden, professor of the philosophy of ethics at the George Mason University, explains:

"For the Greeks, one who knows only appearances is fundamentally ignorant . . . The first step in philosophy, as in life, is to realize that appearances are somehow illusory—not completely, but generally. The second step is to realize that there is a reality behind them. The third is to know that reality. The last is to understand appearances in terms of that underlying reality. Connect that to the cave story and you will see that, for Plato, the stable reality behind appearances are the forms, united by the single form of the Good. Appearances are a shadow of the forms and need to be understood in terms of the forms."

Learning to distinguish between appearance and reality is the basis of wisdom in everyday life as well as the essence of the philosophical quest. Take "appearance and reality" as a theme for a day and record your observations of the most notable discrepancies between them. The appearance/reality distinction is a powerful lens through which to view everything, from a suit of clothes to a smile.

For Plato, anything worth knowing is already known, and must be remembered and reclaimed by the soul. This Platonic notion is expressed poetically in these lines from T. S. Eliot's "The Four Quartets."

> *We shall not cease from exploration*
> *And the end of all our exploring*
> *Will be to arrive where we started*
> *And know the place for the first time.*

PLATO AT WORK

In his classic study of leadership entitled *On Becoming a Leader*, Warren Bennis reports that outstanding leaders share a fundamental commitment to personal growth. In other words, they are committed to deepening their love of wisdom, to living the examined life that Socrates urges. The finest leaders build "learning organizations" by modeling an openness to learning in their own behavior.

Although Plato's ideal of a philosopher king or queen doesn't align with our modern democratic philosophy of government, it is a marvelous metaphor for business leadership. Leaders in rapidly changing organizations must be guardians of the essence of core competencies and champions of the ideals, or forms, of corporate vision and moral integrity. And they must empower people through Socratic questioning to make those ideals real. The most effective leaders make wise decisions by encouraging a democracy of ideas, mining the intellectual capital at every level of the organization.

The way to invest in the intellectual capital around you is, of course, to ask questions. The Socratic method is an extremely effective technique for leaders and an essential practice in the art of empowerment. Effective leaders are skilled at asking carefully worded questions, guiding people to greater understanding of issues and problems until appropriate solutions became obvious. They praise helpful ideas and correct faulty ones by continuing to ask carefully chosen questions. They rarely appear to be directing the discussion or to have all the answers, yet that is often the case. By guiding people to think things through for themselves, the Platonic leader encourages shared pride and ownership of the solutions generated.

Ed Bassett, senior vice president at Du Pont, comments on Plato's relevance to his work: "The secret of leading in a rapidly changing environment is to be committed to living the examined life oneself. Our organization has evolved dramatically in the course of the last twenty years, but our core values have remained constant. Our workplace had become far more diverse, our technologies have changed almost beyond recognition, but the essence of what we do—solving our customers' most important business problems—remains the same. Leaders must learn to be flexible and creative in tactics, and adaptable to shifts in culture and style, while holding to guiding principles of vision and ethics as though they were Platonic ideals."

PLATO'S MUSIC: THE SOUNDS OF TRUTH AND BEAUTY

Plato set the tone of the Western philosophical tradition with his dialogues on questions of truth, beauty and goodness. Through their development of four-part counterpoint, four voices that share the melody back and forth almost like a verbal dialogue, composers of the Baroque period—most notably Johann Sebastian Bach—provide a supreme expression of this tradition. Listen, for example, to Bach's Brandenburg Concertos, his "Six Suites for Unaccompanied Cello" or the Toccata and Fugue in D Minor, and thrill to these powerful musical discourses on the centrality of order and beauty in creation.

Plato's highly structured perfect society remains an unattainable ideal, but that ideal lives in Bach's highly structured exquisite music. Six years after Bach's death, Mozart was born, and by the time he was six years old, this incredible prodigy had already written and performed a number of sublime compositions. Indeed, Mozart's music seems to have been transcribed directly from Plato's realm of pure beauty. Mozart's Concerto in A Major for Clarinet and Orchestra, for example, is a wonderful musical expression of the Platonic quest for wisdom. As you listen to the compelling dialogue between the clarinet and the orchestra you cannot help but feel closer to the essence of truth and beauty.

ONWARD TO BRUNELLESCHI

The Greeks manifested their profound love of wisdom through their architecture. The Parthenon in Athens, designed and built by Phidias, the supreme architectural genius of his day, was a monument to the patron goddess of Athens, Pallas Athena. Born, according to Greek myth, from the head of Zeus, she represents supreme godlike wisdom.

The Plato principle of deepening your love of wisdom is the wellspring of your journey through the breakthrough thinkers in this book. Plato's influence pervades all the geniuses you are about to encounter. The Platonic quest for wisdom, goodness, truth, and beauty is the vital force of our civilization and the personal secret of a fulfilling life and enduring youth.

After the fall of the Western Roman Empire, Europe endured a thousand years in which the love of wisdom was severely constrained by dogma. Our next revolutionary genius is, for many, the least familiar of our luminaries. Yet he changed the world forever by designing and constructing a temple of wisdom that became the locus of the transformation of consciousness known as the Renaissance.

Filippo Brunelleschi

(1377–1446)

Expanding Your Perspective

The discovery of the individual was made in early
fifteenth century Florence. Nothing can alter that fact.

—ART HISTORIAN KENNETH CLARK

Have you ever stood underneath the spire of one of the world's great Gothic cathedrals? Can you imagine how it would make you feel? If your experience is anything like mine, sensations of awe,

Initially I thought he would be the most difficult because there was no material on him other than an abstracted profile wrapped in a turban that looked as if it belonged on a Roman coin and, of course, his famous death mask. But I wanted him alive, and found that the lack of a reliable likeness fired my imagination.

After I looked at Renaissance portraits for a few days, Brunelleschi emerged as a compilation of images. A 1430 portrait, attributed to the Master of Flémalle, entitled Man, *supplied the elaborate*

humility, and personal insignificance may come to mind. I remember my first visit to Chartres Cathedral in France; as I stepped into its soaring nave, my mind and spirit rocketed upward even as I felt physically dwarfed by its towering vaults, and I was instantly overwhelmed by the upsweep of the sacred. Soon thereafter I visited Florence and stood underneath the magnificent dome of the Cathedral of Santa Maria del Fiore, designed and built a few hundred years later. Surrounded by this heavenly umbrella, I was more inspired to stand tall than to fall to my knees, and I began to understand in a new, more visceral way the essence of everything I'd read about the rebirth of individual power and potentiality in the Renaissance.

This contrast, far from accidental, was the product of our next genius, Filippo Brunelleschi, designer and builder of the dome of Florence's cathedral, or "Duomo," the supreme embodiment of the literal and figurative expansion of perspective that we call the Renaissance. In building his dome Brunelleschi replaced the medieval precept, expressed in the belittling proportions of Gothic cathedral architecture, that all power is vested above. He created instead a space that celebrates the individual's participation in heavenly glory.

Although less well-known today than Leonardo's *Canon of Proportion* and Michelangelo's *David*, Brunelleschi's creation is a uniquely palpable expression of the Renaissance's celebration of the divine power of the individual. But Brunelleschi's genius does not end with the revolutionary design for the Florence Duomo. The engineering and construction of the dome, which one architecture historian has declared the fifteenth-century

turban, but the features were not right. I needed to imagine the Brunelleschi profile with its strong aquiline nose as if it were turned around. For this, I looked at a number of Raphael portraits, which capture both intensity and naturalness.

My interpretation of expanding your perspective meant a gaze that is seeing the completion of a great undertaking, set in a face that shows the steel-like resolve and guts that make it happen.—Norma Miller

technological equivalent of putting a man on the moon, is itself a testament to the power of the individual—specifically, Brunelleschi himself, for whom the completion of the dome was a long-fought and hard-won personal triumph. And his insights into the lost classical wisdom of perspective and proportion not only facilitated a visual expression of the times' empowerment of the individual, but exerted an influence on all of the arts of the Renaissance that can not be overstated.

CHALLENGING THE SKY

As for how beautiful the edifice is, it is its own witness . . . it can be confidently asserted that the ancients never built to such a height nor risked challenging the sky itself . . .

Brunelleschi's genius was so commanding that we can surely say that he was sent by heaven to renew the art of architecture.

—GIORGIO VASARI,
LIVES OF THE ARTISTS (1568)

THE ORIGINAL RENAISSANCE MAN

Filippo Brunelleschi, known to his friends as Pippo, was, like Leonardo da Vinci, the son of a prosperous notary. But unlike the majestically beautiful Leonardo, Pippo was, as described by Vasari, "insignificant to look at . . . standing no more than 5'4", possessing a receding chin and hooked nose." Although Brunelleschi may have appeared insignificant, he was the seminal figure of the Renaissance.

The Renaissance looked back to the classical times of Plato and Aristotle for inspiration, with Plato held in particular awe by the avant-garde as the supreme exemplar of the love of wisdom. A true Renaissance man would cultivate that love within a multiplicity of pursuits, developing an interest and ability in a wide range of endeavors. As artists, inventors, designers, and engineers, they embodied both the emerging Renaissance consciousness of the potential of the individual and the ideal of the neo-Platonic magus, the wise man whose mastery of the secrets of the arts and sciences allowed him to harness and control the environment.

BRUNELLESCHI: MICHELANGELO'S HERO

In the Middle Ages artists were anonymous; all credit for their creative works went directly to the Supreme Creator. In the Renaissance artists began to sign their works, and individuals like Leonardo, Michelangelo, and Raphael became superstars. The reverence in which these great individuals of the Renaissance were held is illustrated by the scenes after Michelangelo's death in 1564 when the entire populace of Florence wanted to see his body. All of the painters, sculptors, and architects of the town, as well as the common people and the ruling Medici family, turned out to accompany his coffin to its last resting place. The magnificent decorations that they made for his funeral had to be left in place for weeks afterward to satisfy the crowds of thousands who had flocked to see them.

Before he died Michelangelo was asked where he wished to be buried. His last wish was that he be interred at the Church of Santa Croce, near the Florence Cathedral, so that, as his soul rose to heaven, his last image of earth would be Brunelleschi's Duomo.

Brunelleschi was a prototype of the ideal Renaissance man. Originally trained as a goldsmith, draftsman, and sculptor, he later traveled to Rome to immerse himself in classical art and architecture. When Pippo and his protégé Donatello spent time in Rome between 1401 and 1420 studying the Pantheon and other ancient buildings, they were, at first, under suspicion as spies. Later they became known as the "treasure seekers"—which in a sense they were, although the treasure they harvested was intellectual rather than material. During this time Brunelleschi kept notes on his observations in a secret code that Ross King, author of *Brunelleschi's Dome*, compares to the mirror writing of Leonardo da Vinci.

The firsthand exposure to Roman and Byzantine styles resulted in more than aesthetic influences. That study, coupled with Brunelleschi's training in mathematics—which was itself enriched by his friendship with one of Florence's leading mathematical theorists and astronomers—gave Brunelleschi the background he would ultimately need to rediscover and expand the classical systems of perspective and proportions. From these beginnings Brunelleschi nurtured the vision and learned the skills that enabled him to design and construct what would stand as the largest dome ever built for the next five centuries.

DIVINO INGENIO:
CREATIVE PROBLEM SOLVING

In 1418 a competition was launched to find a design for the dome of Florence Cathedral, which had been started in 1296 but remained unfinished. Brunelleschi was no stranger to Florentine competitions; years earlier, in his goldsmith days, he had entered a competition for creating bronze doors for the Baptistery in Florence, in which seven contestants were asked to cast four trial panels. After a year's labor, only Brunelleschi and Lorenzo Ghiberti were considered worthy to execute the final commission—but Filippo withdrew his name from further consideration rather than share the commission with Ghiberti, who became his lifetime rival. Soon thereafter Brunelleschi redirected his focus to architectural space, which would bring him into competition with his rival in Florence once again.

The dome competition offered the winner a huge purse of 200 gold florins. Ross King explains why the prize was so rich: "The unbuilt dome of Santa Maria del Fiore had become the greatest architectural puzzle of the age. Many experts considered its erection an impossible feat. Even the original planners of the dome had been unable to advise how their project might be completed; they merely expressed a touching faith that at some point in the future God might provide a solution . . .

Why was construction of the dome considered a virtual impossibility? Well, the octagonal walls of the church were 180 feet high with an opening between them that was almost 140 feet wide! The thin walls, and aesthetic considerations, made the use of flying buttresses unthinkable. This vast chasm could only be bridged by going beyond the unthinkable, to the realm of pure genius.

Dozens of entries were received by the wardens of the cathedral, all of them based on the traditional technique of centering—the use of a central internal scaffolding and support system. But Brunelleschi entered a design so radical and bold that it was almost unimaginable. He proposed to eliminate the central support and use a double shell of herringbone brickwork to raise the dome through a mathematically precise balancing of opposing material forces.

In 1420 the greatest architects of the day assembled in Florence to review the entries, but when Brunelleschi's turn came to explain his ideas they laughed at his highly controversial plan. Brunelleschi got so heated in defense of his idea that people thought he was babbling; when he refused to leave the room, he had to be carried out forcibly. Wherever he went for some time thereafter people called out, "There goes the madman."

In the Renaissance the insult was also an art form. The flavor of Brunelleschi's disputes with his rivals and critics is expressed in the following excerpts from an exchange of abusive sonnets.

Giovanni Acquettini wrote to Brunelleschi:

> *O you deep fountain, pit of ignorance*
> *You miserable beast and imbecile,*
> *Who thinks uncertain things can be made visible:*
> *There is no substance to your alchemy.*

To which Brunelleschi replied:

> *For wise men nothing that exists*
> *Remains unseen; they do not share*
> *The idle dreams of would-be scholars.*
> *Only the artists, not the fool*
> *Discovers that which nature hides.*

Unwilling to concede even after such a profound setback, Brunelleschi soldiered on with renewed patience and focus. Though he found some hope in the realization that the judges had not yet understood his vision, he also had to endure the jealousy of other designers and the fickleness of the Florentine citizens. But Brunelleschi was supremely confident. He told the judges, "I assure you that it is impossible to raise it [the dome] in any other way. You may well laugh at me, but you must understand, unless you are obstinate, that it neither should nor could be done otherwise . . . *I can already envisage the completed vaulting* and I know there is no method or way of doing it other than as I am explaining."

Another meeting was called and Brunelleschi challenged the contending architects to explain how they would stand an egg upright on a flat piece of marble—the man who could do it would be intelligent enough to build the dome. The others all tried in turn and were unsuccessful. When it was Brunelleschi's turn, he took the egg and cracked its bottom on the marble to make it stay upright. All the architects complained that they could have done the same, to which Brunelleschi retorted that they could also build his dome, if they understood his plans.

In the end Brunelleschi triumphed; his plans were approved and he was awarded the commission. But his glory was muted when he was appointed as overseer, *capomaestro*, with three other men, including his hated rival Ghiberti. Nevertheless, Brunelleschi took the lead in building the dome. His mastery was such that ultimately he was able to convince the wardens that he alone held the secrets of the dome's completion. Filippo demonstrated that all his rivals were dispensable, and eventually their roles and recompense were reduced.

I can already envisage the completed vaulting . . .

—FILIPPO BRUNELLESCHI

~

FROM VISION TO REALITY

Of course, winning the commission and marginalizing his enemies were just the beginning; Brunelleschi would have to find a way to make his vision real. Massive slabs of marble had to be transported to his building site and then hoisted and balanced hundreds of feet into the air. To accomplish this, Brunelleschi had to manage a temperamental workforce while contending with his rivals' constant attempts to discredit and undermine him.

Only by keeping the big picture of the completed dome in the forefront of his mind could he endure the enormous difficulties and many setbacks that awaited him. One of the worst was the debacle of the *Badalone,* which in translation means "monster." Brunelleschi's sea monster was a giant ship, which he designed with the intention of filling it with marble for the dome and transporting it more cheaply than by other means. Although its exact design is not known, it was impressive enough to win Brunelleschi the world's first ever invention patent, granted in 1421. Seven years passed before it was ready to carry its first load of 100 tons of white marble from Pisa to Florence. The ship completed only twenty-five miles of the journey before sinking, taking its tons of precious marble to the bottom of the river. All attempts to rescue the valuable cargo were fruitless, and Brunelleschi suffered a considerable personal loss on the project.

Driven by his vision of the completed dome, Brunelleschi continued to experiment with more innovations to make his vision a reality. More successful was his amazing ox hoist, an ox-driven machine using pulleys and tubs to heave building materials aloft. A wooden platform was specially built for the oxen, who worked over twelve years to raise an estimated 70 million pounds of marble, bricks, and stones.

When Brunelleschi successfully finished the dome he was showered with praise primarily for his engineering skills. The words "engineer" and "ingenious" have the same root in the Latin word *ingenium.* Florentine city official Carlo Marsuppini praised Brunelleschi for his *"divino ingenio,"* which Ross King proclaims as "the first recorded instance of an architect or sculptor being said to have received divine inspiration for his work."

By sticking to his vision and making it real, Brunelleschi can be awarded another first that speaks to us today. "Before Pippo there was never anybody who could design and build—although today this is normal," renowned architect Piero Sartogo told me. "Before him it was trial and error and on-site experimentation. He was the first one in the history of humanity to truly design a building and then build it." In form and in execution, Brunelleschi's Duomo is without equal as a monument to the Renaissance notion of the empowered individual.

A NEW CONCEPT OF SPACE

The Duomo revolutionized the Renaissance perception of three-dimensional space, as defined by the architecture that creates and encloses it. "The Greeks made monuments but did not create space, and the Romans created space with the arch and dome, but relatively inefficiently," explains

Brunelleschi was not only the initiator of Renaissance architecture. To him . . . is due another momentous discovery in the history of art . . . that of perspective. . . . It was Brunelleschi who gave the artists the mathematical means of solving this problem; and the excitement which this caused among his painter-friends must have been immense.

—PROFESSOR SIR ERNST GOMBRICH, *THE STORY OF ART*

Sartogo. "Brunelleschi showed, in an incredible way, that less material could create more enclosure. He demonstrated that form is a structural element."

But Brunelleschi's groundbreaking impact on our perception of space wasn't limited to his work in three dimensions; perhaps even more influential was his use of perspective to indicate three dimensions in a two-dimensional format. "Brunelleschi invented the way of representing and controlling a three-dimensional object in space," says Sartogo. "Perspective was his tool."

Ross King defines perspective as "the method of representing three-dimensional objects in recession on a two-dimensional surface in order to give the same impression of relative position, size, or distance as the actual objects do when viewed from a particular point."

We're so accustomed to the use of perspective in visual representation that we take it for granted. But in the years leading up to the Renaissance, painters typically made no attempt to imply in their paintings the same depth of field with which they regularly surveyed their world. Aside from some experimentation by the pioneering thirteenth-

and fourteenth-century Florentine artists Cimabue and Giotto, who undoubtedly influenced Brunelleschi, most pre-Renaissance art depicts a flat field of vision noticeably different from the material world.

"Filippo is generally regarded as [perspective's] inventor, the one who discovered (or rediscovered) its mathematical laws," according to King. And once again this seemingly innocuous innovation in visual representation spoke volumes about the Renaissance's concept of the empowered individual. The use of perspective to create a more accurate representation of the world was tantamount to a painter's assertion of his own godliness; never before had artists been invested with the authority to re-create so closely the world God created. And the implication of a particular point from which the painted scene is being viewed—the perspective to which the vanishing point is oriented—suddenly instilled in the individual viewer more godlike powers of observation than medieval standards had bestowed on mere mortals.

Brunelleschi's biographer, Antonio Manetti, described the artist's inaugural attempt to create the illusion of genuine space on a two-dimensional board. Brunelleschi carefully measured one wall of the hexagonal Florentine Baptistery, then painted an image of it onto a wooden panel. He drilled a hole through the vanishing point of the painting on the panel and set a mirror in front of it. Spectators standing opposite the Baptistery in the doorway of Florence Cathedral, where the equipment was set up, could now peer with one eye through the back of the painting onto the mirror. The reflected picture conveyed the illusion that the painting and the Baptistery were one and the same and the viewer was seeing the real Baptistery.

Not surprisingly, the use of perspective, as revolutionary as it was at the time, hearkens back to the then-revered classical era, which had employed these same techniques centuries before. "The principle of the vanishing point," says King, who attributes its rediscovery to Brunelleschi, "was known to the Greeks and Romans but, like so much other knowledge, had long since been lost." There is also speculation that Pippo's critically timed stunt with the egg during the Duomo competition was also informed by his mastery of classical wisdom. Knowing that classical mathematicians and engineers had studied the phenomenal strength of the egg—which, despite its apparent delicacy, resists crushing when force is applied equally to its top and bottom—Brunelleschi was most likely inspired by the shape of the eggshell in his contemplation of the perfect dome.

Amid the ferment of artistic activity in Florence, Brunelleschi's innovations in perspective were speedily assimilated by other artists including Donatello, Masaccio, and Alberti, the last of whom scientifically codified the geometric formulas of perspective. They in turn dramatically influenced Leonardo, Michelangelo, and Raphael, who are responsible for so many of the images we now associate with the Renaissance, and to whom we owe a debt for how we see the world.

Martin Kemp, chairman of the art department at Oxford University and author of *Visualizations: The Nature Book of Art and Science*, credits Brunelleschi with "establishing a mode of depiction that was ultimately to affect the conveying of visual imagery in virtually every field of artistic, scientific, and technological activity. When we look into the implicit boxes of space behind the screens of our television and computers, we are distant legatees of Brunelleschi's vision."

THE NEW SELF

Even one of Brunelleschi's legendary practical jokes speaks to the newfound primacy of the individual in Renaissance Florence. While the breadth of his achievements may give the impression that he worked hard all the time, Brunelleschi, according to Ross King, "was well-known in Florence for his talents in mimicry, chicanery, theatricality, and the creation of illusions." Pippo was a great prankster, and his most famous hoax went down in local lore as the "tale of the fat carpenter."

Around 1409 Brunelleschi played an elaborate practical joke on a carpenter called Manetto, nicknamed *il Grasso*, or "the Fat Man," after Manetto insulted him publicly. In retaliation Brunelleschi persuaded a number of people to treat *il Grasso* as if he had metamorphosed into another well known Florentine called Matteo.

The hapless Manetto was then jailed for failing to pay a debt supposedly run up by Matteo, and the next day Matteo's two brothers were sent along to pay the fine. Everyone, including his fellow prisoners, was in on the joke except Manetto; even his brothers treated him as if he were Matteo. Then Matteo appeared and claimed to have been transformed into Manetto. So complete was the hoax that Manetto truly believed that he and Matteo had changed into each other.

The delight that Brunelleschi and his friends had in playing this trick, the fact that they were able to pull it off, and the way in which it became such a famous story at the time reminds us that the emerging role of the individual was on the minds of more than the artists of the time.

DOME—SYMBOL OF THE BRAIN

Why is the dome such a popular form? It resonates in the geodesic domes of Buckminster Fuller; the celebrated church of the Salute in Venice; the Hagia Sophia in Istanbul; the U.S. Capitol, National Gallery, and Library of Congress; Thomas Jefferson's Monticello; and St. Paul's Cathedral in London. It was the British government's choice as a landmark at the prime meridian Greenwich to honor the new millennium. Perhaps the answer, as then British poet laureate Ted Hughes speculated in an article for the *London Times*, is that the dome subconsciously represents the human brain—the seat of all emotion, knowledge, and learning, and the driving force for what distinguishes us from other animals and the rest of known creation. The two sides of this most intimate dome are, indeed, temples.

In the early spring of 1446 the "heavenly form" of the dome was complete. It was formally blessed by the archbishop of Florence, and great celebrations were held. Thus Brunelleschi was able to savor the fulfillment of his dream before a short illness claimed his life on May 15, 1446. He was laid to rest in his beloved cathedral in a tomb created from a simple slab of marble, like the ones he had hoisted for decades to construct his masterpiece. All Florence turned out to mourn his passing. The Latin inscription on his tomb read: *Corpus Magni Ingenii Viri Philippi Brunelleschi Fiorentini* ("Here lies the body of the great ingenious man Filippo Brunelleschi of Florence"), to which we might add: *quis nostram perspectivam ad infinitum expandavit* ("who expanded our perspective forever").

Summary of Achievements

- Brunelleschi was the seminal figure of the Renaissance. He exerted profound influence on Alberti, Masaccio, Donatello, Leonardo, Michelangelo, and Raphael.

- Brunelleschi was the first to achieve and communicate a full understanding of the principles of perspective in art and design.

- At Florence Cathedral between 1420 and 1436 he designed and built the largest dome ever known, only exceeded when twentieth-century building materials like steel and concrete became available.

- He pioneered the revival of classical architecture—neoclassicism—influencing Western building ever since.

- As an engineer he designed machines so ahead of their time that some were not improved upon until the nineteenth century, and so imaginative that some were later mistakenly attributed to Leonardo da Vinci.

- Originally trained as a goldsmith and engraver, he became the model of a Renaissance man—expert in painting and sculpture as well as architecture and engineering.

- He applied for and received the first ever patent for an invention. Patents made individual innovation profitable and inspired tremendous creativity.

BRUNELLESCHI AND YOU

Brunelleschi's story is not intended to inspire you to dash off and become an architect or create a giant dome. Rather, the example of the seminal innovator and creative problem-solver of the Renaissance can inspire you to find new ways to look at life's challenges—new perspectives—that can lead you to become the architect of your own future. Brunelleschi shows us how to create and maintain vivid images of our goals and dreams. He approached his monumental project with a clear picture in mind of what he wanted to accomplish. As he told the great assembly of architects: "I can already envisage the completed vaulting . . .

His triumph demonstrates the power of beginning with the end in mind. Brunelleschi crafted a detailed visualization of success and maintained this ultimate vision in the face of opposition and misfortune. By beginning your projects and plans in life with a vivid visualization of what you wish to achieve, and maintaining an expanded perspective in the face of adversity, you'll find it easier to believe in yourself and conquer the challenges of life. The *capomaestro* himself was inspired by the words of the great Roman imperial poet Virgil, who wrote, "For they will conquer who believe they can." If you internalize Brunelleschi's spirit, you'll conquer the "small stuff" that obscures the expanded perspective of your highest priorities and aspirations.

Please begin by reflecting on the self-assessment questions that follow.

BRUNELLESCHI:
EXPANDING YOUR PERSPECTIVE
SELF-ASSESSMENT

- ☐ When I begin a project I start with a visualization of its successful completion.

- ☐ I keep my priorities in perspective when I'm under stress.

- ☐ I have faith in my own ideas.

- ☐ I don't let setbacks throw me off course.

- ☐ Opposition strengthens my resolve.

- ☐ I can improvise when necessary.

- ☐ When I set a goal, I work with patience and dedication until it is successfully realized.

- ☐ I want to expand my intellectual perspective.

- ☐ I can think "out of the box" and then apply creative solutions to real life problems.

- ☐ I understand and appreciate the influence of architecture in my view of the world.

EXERCISES

THINKING LIKE BRUNELLESCHI/ EXPANDING YOUR PERSPECTIVE

ARCHITECTURAL AWARENESS

Besides the Duomo, Brunelleschi designed the magnificent Pazzi Chapel, the churches of Santo Spirito and San Lorenzo, and the Innocenti Hospital, which historian Daniel Boorstin hails as the "first true Renaissance building." In addition to his profound direct influence on Michelozzo and Michelangelo, Boorstin points out that Brunelleschi's legacy is celebrated "on every continent . . . and . . . in America in countless county courthouses and post offices, on the facades of ambitious community builders, in Monticello and on Capitol Hill." As the father of the modern concept of architectural space, Brunelleschi has monumental influence.

Of all the arts, architecture is the most influential in our daily lives. It surrounds us and affects us profoundly, for better or worse. Deepening your understanding and appreciation of architecture is a marvelous way to expand your perspective on culture and the quality of life.

ARCHITECTURAL ALL-STARS: YOUR TOP TEN

Start by constructing a list of your top ten favorite buildings in the world. Reflect on why you like each one. How does each structure affect you emotionally? Consider the way space is created, who used it in the past and why, and its function now. Aim to discover more about your favorite buildings and their architects. For example, the Parthenon in Athens is now a tourist attraction, famous the world over. However, two and half millennia ago it was the cultural and religious center of one of the world's greatest powers. Imagine the proud architect Phidias unveiling his creation to the leaders of Athens. Picture the awed foreign delegations at their first glimpse of this majestic structure. Relish Socrates, Plato, and Aristotle holding forth in the public areas, keeping their Athenian audience spellbound with sparkling oratory. Now use this technique whenever you visit a historic building and think about what you can learn from those who have used it in the past. Discuss and compare your list with your friends.

ARCHITECT PIERO SARTOGO'S CHOICES FOR THE TOP TEN STRUCTURES IN THE WORLD

1. Brunelleschi's Duomo.
2. Katsuro Palace, Kyoto, four centuries old but still entirely modern and of today.
3. Fallingwater, Frank Lloyd Wright.
4. The Piazza di Pienza, Rossolino.
5. Sant'Ivo alla Sapienza—Rome-Borromini (like the Parthenon and the Hagia Sophia, this church is dedicated to wisdom—*Sapienza*!).
6. The Mosque, Cordoba.
7. Utrecht House, Rotveld.
8. Eniteo in the Acropolis in front of the Parthenon, Phidias.
9. La Ville Savoie, Le Corbusier.
10. Laurentine Library, Florence, Michelangelo.

ARCHITECTURAL AGONIES: YOUR TEN ABOMINATIONS

After you've made a list of your favorite buildings, try making one of your least favorites. What are the most hideous, unharmonious, and awful structures you've ever seen? What makes them so bad? Check out the website www.bbvh.nl/hate/fprojects.html for an up-to-date discussion of the world's worst buildings that includes a top ten list of architectural abominations.

ARCHITECTURE AND AWARENESS: WHAT WERE THEY THINKING?

Architecture shapes consciousness and, of course, reflects it as well. Brunelleschi's Duomo is the perfect symbol of the Renaissance consciousness of individual power and potency.

Using a few keywords, write a quick description of your best guess about the consciousness of the people who used or created the following structures:

Cave

Treehouse

Tepee

Great Pyramids

Parthenon

Chartres Catheral

Center Hall Colonial House

Palace at Versailles

Japanese Ryokan

Fallingwater

U.S. Capitol Building

Guggenheim Museums in New York City and Bilbao

Empire State Building

Getty Museum in Los Angeles

Ask a friend to do the same quick word-association exercise and then compare your responses.

EXPAND YOUR PERSPECTIVE BY THINKING LONG-TERM

The *New York Times* recently featured a series focusing on the collapse of the dot.com market. One article profiled a newly unemployed advertising director who found himself holding thousands of worthless shares in his once high-flying Internet employer. He began spending afternoons consoling himself in a local tavern, pondering his suddenly uncertain future. "I'm just down on myself and the whole thing," he lamented. "I would have been an architect if I was smart." For many, tales of overnight Internet millionaires offered a tantalizing vision of an easier way, a fast track to success that seemed quite out of reach any other way. Contemporary culture places tremendous value on material success. An endless parade of infomercials offers many examples of great financial gain realized over short periods, with little apparent effort. But get-rich-quick dreams don't usually amount to much.

Even though we live in fast times and must learn to multitask we mustn't be seduced away from some of the classic ingredients to a successful life. Brunelleschi offers us a vital lesson in the value of good, old-fashioned persistence, dedication, and hard work.

Brunelleschi's exhaustive research in Rome was preparation for the project of a lifetime. Construction of the dome started in August 1420 and continued until just before his death in 1446. Such lengthy projects were typical in that time, and would seem little related to long-term projects in today's workplace, which seem lengthy at twenty-six days.

Still, great works take time even now, and focused, sustained concentration is vital for the best results.

Take some time to think about your world, your life, and your long-term goals. Using your notebook, express your reflections on the following questions.

How does short-term thinking manifest in the world around me? Use this
    question as a theme for a week. Look for examples in newspaper stories,
    conversations with friends and associates, and in television, radio and
    other media.

What's the longest amount of time I've ever invested in a project?

What are my long-term goals? Try a ten-minute stream-of-consciousness
    writing session on your most important personal and professional long-
    term goals.

ULTIMATE PERSPECTIVE

In the Museo dell'Opera del Duomo in Florence you can still see Brunelleschi's actual death mask. The *capomaestro* appears to be musing, perhaps
on another "impossible" challenge, with a haunting, wry smile on his face.
It's clear that Brunelleschi lived a life of passionate dedication to his highest ideals and priorities. Interviews with people at the end of life reveal,
almost without exception, that when they look back on their lives, their
greatest regrets stem from habits and behaviors that didn't flow from
their priorities. Almost universally, people wish that they could have
maintained throughout life the expanded perspective that the imminent
prospect of death inspires.

Most people wish they had spent more time with loved ones, more
time learning and exploring their passions, more time savoring the joys of
living. Imagining the expression on your own death mask allows you to
reflect on your life while you still have the opportunity to change it.

EXPAND YOUR PERSPECTIVE BY EMBRACING PROBLEMS

Brunelleschi was able to maintain a revolutionary vision while solving an endless stream of practical problems. And he would probably agree that life is an exercise in creative problem solving. Please don't wait to be happy until you get rid of all your problems, because that day will never come. Instead, cultivate true happiness by expanding your perspective about your problems. Viewed creatively, your problems can be sources of learning and awakening, opportunities to strengthen your character and compassion.

The word "problem" comes from the roots *pro*, meaning "forward," and *ballein*, meaning "throw." The words "solution" and "solving" come from the root *solvere*, meaning "to loosen." So "problem solving" is the art of throwing things forward by loosening up!

Write out a description of your biggest problem in both your personal life and your professional life. Then view it from the perspective of the *capomaestro* and note three things you can learn from each problem and how you can use it to your advantage in your long-term personal growth.

EXPAND YOUR PERSPECTIVE BY FINDING NEW TOOLS

When beginning a project most of us use tools provided to us by others or ones that we already have in our possession. Carpenters wield hammers, saws, and screwdrivers, and investment analysts use computers, specialized software, and financial models. But sometimes the tools we start with are inadequate for the task, and we grow frustrated with the limits placed on us by devices that are supposed to be helping us achieve our goals.

Brunelleschi offers a new perspective on this problem. He developed new tools to translate his dreams into reality: graphic tools for realistically depicting three-dimensional space, proportional and stylistic tools for making buildings after the fashion of the Romans, and structural tools for bridging the great open chasm that was the dome-to-be of the church of Santa

Maria del Fiore. Filippo's willingness to think creatively was essential to his genius. His approach can work for you too.

Write a brief description of the two most important projects in your life, either at home or in the office. Alongside each, list the three main obstacles or frustrations you have with your project. Consider the following questions with each project:

Is there some fundamentally different approach I can bring to this project?
What could I do or learn or have that would make a difference?
How could I make or obtain new tools to help me solve this problem?

Think well past the boundaries of what might normally come to mind.

Elizabeth, a music teacher at a special education school in Virginia, finds Brunelleschi's ability to create new tools particularly inspiring. She laughed as she described the abrupt departures of the two music teachers before her, one to work as a bank teller, and the other literally running screaming out the door. When she first walked into her new classroom, the children were standing on desks and escaping out windows. She was dismayed to find an assortment of instruments from the 1950s, such as broken ukuleles and plastic recorders, and an eight-track tape player. So, in the tradition of the *capomaestro*, she improvised.

First she rewrote the curriculum. Then, working within her limited budget, she purchased a used CD player and secured donations from local record stores to build a music library. She slowly replaced the classroom instruments, purchasing a used electric guitar and a drum set. Improvising further, Elizabeth began writing and directing musicals for the kids. She also worked with the shop and art classes to build sets and a stage, and bought costumes at local rummage sales. She describes the transformation of her classroom: "These kids come in with everything from autism to ADD, so there's no hope of getting through to them without creativity. I expanded my perspective immediately by reworking the curriculum so that it would be more appropriate to the real needs of the children. I knew right away that I had to get them involved and keep them participating, but that job couldn't be accomplished with the tools that were provided, so I found new tools to get the job done.

"The results were inspiring. The children became passionate about learning and their creativity was redirected from mischief to musicals. Of course, this was a lot simpler than Brunelleschi building an ox hoist to move tons of marble, but the idea of improvising to achieve a vision is the same."

EXPAND YOUR PERSPECTIVE BY REMEMBERING PRIORITIES

What are your most important priorities, and how do they inform the choices you make every day about how you invest your time? Do you ever feel that you are so busy and pressed for time that your sense of what's really important begins to fade? Remembering your most important life goals and priorities is a key to expanding your perspective.

Translating your life goals and priorities into effective daily actions requires distinguishing between different levels of priority and between priority and urgency. When you are running late for a meeting, your phone and fax are both ringing, and someone is knocking on your door, it is hard to maintain perspective. Everything seems to be happening too fast, and it's easy to fall into the trap of forgetting priorities and responding to the most pressing elements in your environment.

EXPAND YOUR PERSPECTIVE BY OUTWITTING YOUR RETICULAR FORMATION

Have you ever noticed that in the midst of a very important meeting everyone will stop and necks will crane to observe the coffee cart as it enters the room? Why does everyone turn to look at the coffee cart? Have you ever observed that after a minute or two you can easily tune out the repetitive noise of an air-conditioning system or the sound of a ticking clock? How does your brain tune out these noises? And why does your alarm clock wake you up in the morning?

The answer to all these questions is that your brain is hard-wired, through millions of years of evolution, to respond to sudden changes in the environment and to tune out repetitive stimuli. All these responses are coordinated by the reticular formation, a complex little-finger-size network of nerves in your brain stem. Without conscious intervention, the reticular formation will automatically orient you to attend to the most pressing elements in your environment, such as a knock on the door or the sound of a ringing phone.

The biggest time drain of daily life is investing energy in activities that are pressing but not "on purpose." Many meetings, phone calls, and other interruptions fall into this category. Of course, many pressing activities are also priorities: working on a major presentation with an imminent deadline, fixing a leak in your basement, or taking your child to the hospital after a nasty fall.

Many of our most significant priorities elude us, however, because they do not set off reticular alarm bells. We must discipline ourselves to use our higher awareness to invest appropriate time in nonpressing priorities, such as planning sessions, relationship building, and educational programs. Ironically, many people protest that they are too busy and stressed to attend seminars on time and stress management. Appropriate time invested in nonpressing priorities expands your perspective as it progressively frees you from crisis management.

You can make your life easier to manage by assessing your daily activities in a way that reflects the balance of pressure and priority.

Keep a record for the next week of the percentage of time that you invest in each of the following categories of activity:

Category 1. Pressing priorities: crises, emergencies, and time-sensitive projects.
Category 2. Nonpressing priorities: planning, cultivating relationships, creative thinking, education, and self-renewal.
Category 3. Pressing, low priority: many phone calls, meetings, reports, and interruptions.
Category 4. Nonpressing, low priority: reading junk mail, mindless television watching, and general trivia.

Many of us spend too much time in activities from category 1, 3, sometimes 4, and not enough in 2. Expand your perspective by minimizing 3 and 4 and balancing 1 and 2.

In addition to revolutionizing our awareness of space, Brunelleschi also pioneered the modern concept of time management. Biographer Manetti credits him with the invention of the first accurate spring clock, and his workers on the Duomo were among the first in history to be paid by the sixty-minute hour. Now, time management is a function of self-management, and the key to self-management is expanding your perspective, so you can remember and live your priorities. In addition to managing your tasks, be sure to *manage your perception of time*. If you allow yourself to be run by pressing events, you lose your center and time seems short. If you remember to pause, breathe, and shift out of a reactive mode your sense of time, and freedom of choice, expands.

Make remembering your priorities a priority. Remembering and reinforcing your priorities is the key to transforming your life goals and values into reality. The small choices and decisions that you make every day determine the quality of your life.

Try the following experiment. For the next week, start each day by reflecting for a minute or two on the question, "What is really important in my life?" Then, at the end of each day, invest a few minutes and ask yourself, "How well did my activities today reflect my highest priorities? What adjustments can I make tomorrow to find a truer alignment with what I believe is most important?"

BRUNELLESCHI AT WORK

For over twenty-five years Brunelleschi managed a motley workforce and optimized their productivity. Early in his tenure as *capomaestro* he faced labor problems. His masons and carpenters insisted on leaving their stations in the sky to take long lunches. Brunelleschi conceived a plan to provide lunch, with wine, served hundreds of feet in the air. This kept his workforce happy and focused on building the dome, and Brunelleschi actually turned a profit from the catering venture. (He also built "lavatories in the sky" for his workers' convenience.) In addition to improvising "win-win" management strategies, Brunelleschi was also a genius at investing in and inventing new technology, such as his amazing ox hoist, to achieve his goals. And he offers a superb example of maintaining the primacy of one's vision and mission in the face of everyday challenges.

Jim D'Agostino, former president of Lehrer, McGovern, Bovis, worked his way up from pouring concrete to running a billion-dollar construction management firm. Jim helped to build a significant portion of the New York City skyline and supervised the renovation of the Metropolitan Museum of Art.

He recently decided to expand his perspective by changing careers. He comments on the inspiration that Brunelleschi provides: "After college I returned to my family roots in the construction business. Although my background was in the masonry trades I was interested in all the components that went into a completed building. Fortunately, I was given the opportunity to interact with all the pieces—design, engineering, and supervision of the craftsmen—on the construction of my first high rise in the early eighties in Philadelphia.

"For me, Brunelleschi has always been a truly inspiring role model. As the first true 'design builder,' he was able to see the 'big picture'—logistics, engineering, materials, labor—and fit all the pieces together. This approach is very much in vogue today on large, complex projects.

"Brunelleschi's creative problem solving came from constantly building on his life experience as a goldsmith, sculptor, and draftsman, and acquiring knowledge from others while taking his own vision to ever-higher levels. This visionary approach, driven by continuous learning, is one that I strive for.

"As a Renaissance man, Brunelleschi was always seeking new challenges and approaches. He defines the essence of fulfilling one's potential through vision, persistence, and hard work. After thirty continuous years of hard work in all facets of the building business I am forming a new vision and sense of proportion. I feel good about leaving a field that I became quite knowledgeable about and venturing into new areas where I know little. My expanded perspective involves pursuing a balance between my interests as a communications consultant, ski instructor, whitewater river guide, sculptor, and worker in the winery business. All this, together with more family time, will hopefully allow me to grow in different, more harmonious directions."

LISTEN TO THE SOUND OF THE DOME

Brunelleschi's ingenious use of proportion deeply impressed the Flemish composer Guillaume Dufay (circa. 1400–74), who worked with the Papal choir at Rome. Dufay adapted the mathematical ratios on which the dome's construction is based into a piece of choral music, entitled *Nuper Rosarum Flores*, which was played at the completion of the dome on 25 March 1436. The ratios between the length of the nave, the width of the crossing, the length of the apse, and the height of the dome of the cathedral were all reflected in Dufay's beautiful and harmonious composition.

Recordings of Dufay's music are difficult to find, but you can also evoke the spirit of the capomaestro's legacy by listening to the Canon in D by Johann Pachelbel. Pachelbel's simple eight-note heavenly composition mirrors the octagonal structure of Bruneschelli's heavenly dome.

Experiment with listening to the music of Dufay or Pachelbel as you contemplate the Duomo. If you can't go to Florence to view the Duomo then find a photograph and place it in easy view. As you look at this supreme masterpiece, listen to the music and experience the Duomo from the perspective of sound.

Then, go back to the first two exercises on architectural awareness and imagine the sounds of the different structures you considered. Which ones are most harmonious? Experiment with "humming" the sounds of your office and your home. This kind of multi-sensory perspective is a secret of creativity and richer enjoyment of your world.

ONWARD TO COLUMBUS

Brunelleschi's friend, the mathematician and astronomer Paolo Toscanelli, helped Filippo develop the perfect geometry of the dome. Toscanelli also had a passionate interest in geography, cartography, and exploration. Once the dome was completed Toscanelli used it as the site of a number of experiments, the results of which led him to speculate that it might be possible to reach the Orient by sailing west. (Toscanelli's experiments included one in which he transformed the Florence Cathedral into a massive sundial by placing a specially crafted bronze disc at the top of the dome. Holes in the disc allowed sunlight to pass through and reach a stone gauge placed strategically in one of the chapels.) Toscanelli published maps and tables to support this revolutionary idea and wrote to a Portuguese friend suggesting that an expedition be organized to attempt it. This letter found its way into the hands of a visionary sea captain named Christopher Columbus. Toscanelli's letter, inspired by the observations he made from the top of Brunelleschi's dome, accompanied Columbus on all four of his voyages to the New World.

Christopher Columbus

(1451–1506)

Going Perpendicular: Strengthening Your Optimism, Vision, and Courage

History knows of no man who ever did the like.

—INSCRIPTION ON COLUMBUS'S TOMB IN SEVILLE CATHEDRAL

I magine that you have developed a theory that boldly contradicts long-held conventional wisdom. If accurate, your theory holds the potential to bring you unfathomable power, wealth, and glory; if not, the

Columbus seems to have been interpreted very differently in the various portraits I studied. For my interpretation, I made his gaze look right at the onlooker because courage takes meeting a challenge head-on! Optimism for me is a quiet and soulful emotion; and so Columbus has a soulful and thoughtful smile, not a transitory happy one. And the strong directional lines of his hat took shape from the image of the wind powering his sails.—Norma Miller

likely reward is humiliation, financial ruin, or even death. You're confident that your theory is correct, and can back it up with secret information that the opinion makers you are refuting have never seen. Proving your theory's accuracy, however, will require more manpower and financial resources than you can provide, leadership skills that will inspire your team to follow you literally to the end of the earth, and the willingness to risk your life and the lives of others to see it through. And of the handful of sources that can afford the level of backing you need, most have already turned you down.

This was roughly the situation facing our third genius, Christopher Columbus, as he tried to convince fifteenth-century monarchs that fortune could be found by sailing west across the Atlantic rather than following the well-traveled land route to the east. Conventional wisdom regarded the western reaches of the Atlantic as an ocean wilderness, leading to an unknown void—or worse. But Columbus, armed with insights passed down from the Brunelleschi circle in Florence, finally won the support of Ferdinand and Isabella, king and queen of Spain. And in 1492, on three ships funded by the Spanish crown and staffed with sailors who had put their lives in his hands, Christopher Columbus ventured fearlessly across the unknown waters of the Atlantic Ocean.

Was he crazy, as some have alleged? Was he simply following the route of the eleventh-century Viking explorer Leif Eriksson? Or was he in fact a visionary genius? One can make a good case that his later expeditions demonstrated the mark of insanity, but his behavior was dramatically different from that exhibited on the first, famous voyage. If he was in fact emulating Eriksson, it's unlikely that Columbus intended to do so, as his voluminous writings never mention the Viking. Whatever happened decades later—or centuries earlier—Columbus sailed west from the coast of Spain in September 1492 with all the earmarks of genius—not just because he dared believe that the earth was not flat, but because he was able to master the skills and knowledge necessary to realize his vision and prove it to the world.

THE UNITED STATES OF COLUMBIANA?

The continent that Columbus discovered doesn't bear his name. Instead it was named after Amerigo Vespucci, who was born in Florence in 1454. Vespucci explored Venezuela in 1499, and German mapmaker Martin Waldseemüller mistakenly credited him with the discovery of "America" after reading a fabricated account of his travels. As Sigmund Freud commented, "Success does not always go along with merit: America is not named after Columbus."

SAILING PERPENDICULAR FROM THE COAST

Columbus became the first man to navigate an Atlantic crossing from the Old World to the New by doing what none before him had dared attempt, setting course directly out into the ocean's vast uncharted waters rather than hugging the shore. All previous, failed efforts to cross the Atlantic had been made by sailors who clung to a limited zone of westerly winds along the European coast in order to ensure a means of return. Not so Columbus, who, according to Oxford University historian Felipe Fernandez-Armesto, "was the first to succeed precisely because he had the courage to sail with the wind at his back." Turning his back also on the safety of the coastline that previous explorers were reluctant to leave, Columbus sailed perpendicular to the shoreline, straight away from civilization as he knew it, even though he did not know what, if anything, lay ahead.

He did not rely only on blind faith, however. The Renaissance into which Columbus was born was characterized by revolutionary new ideas about the place of humanity in the universe; in both art and science a new

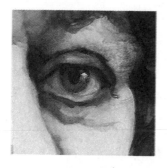

perception of distance, space, and perspective coincided with the introduction of both the microscope and the telescope. Columbus was part of a community of scholars and sailors who traded ideas about navigational tools, geography, and exploration. But none rivaled his ability to combine theoretical knowledge with practical skills—skills every bit as relevant to our own ventures today as they were five centuries ago.

The son of a weaver, young Columbus was expected to follow his father's trade, but at the age of fourteen he went to sea. It was a fateful decision that proved to be his inspiration: "from a very small age I went sailing upon the sea, which very occupation inclines all who follow it to wish to learn the secrets of the world," he later wrote. The European exploration of the seas had begun earlier in the century, with the Portuguese taking the lead. In 1415 they had begun to open up the west coast of Africa, though another seven decades would pass before Bartholomeu Dias rounded that continent's southernmost point, the Cape of Good Hope. In Columbus's time, the horizons of Europe were still limited to trading links with North and West Africa and the Middle East.

By the time he was thirty, in 1481, Columbus had already conceived the idea that it was possible to sail to Asia by traveling westward. He was encouraged by Brunelleschi's colleague Paolo Toscanelli, a Florentine physician and cosmographer, who had helped develop the perfect geometry of the Duomo. Toscanelli also had a passionate interest in geography, cartography, and exploration, and made observations from the top of the completed dome that led him to posit the possibility of reaching the Orient by sailing west. After publishing maps and tables to support this revolutionary idea, Toscanelli wrote to a Portuguese friend suggesting that an expedition be organized to attempt it. This letter found its way to Columbus, whose vision and optimism it fired for decades thereafter (and who carried it with him on all four of his voyages to the New World).

Columbus probably would not have known what to do with Toscanelli's insights if he hadn't already done such exhaustive research on his own. "Throughout this time," he later wrote, "I have seen and studied books of every sort; geography, history, chronicles, philosophy and other arts— whereby Our Lord opened my understanding with His manifest hand to the fact that it was practicable to sail from here to the Indies."

Essentially self-taught, as he never studied at a university or academy, Columbus made the most of the resources available to him. One notable influence was the 1477 publication of world maps derived from the *Geographia* of the Egyptian astronomer and geographer Ptolemy (90–168). In charting the world as it was known in his day—Europe, the North African coast, and Arabia—Ptolemy had mistakenly shown the continents as much closer than they actually were, leading Columbus to underestimate the distance he would have to sail.

Columbus was also influenced by medieval sources, including the fantastic travel books of Marco Polo and Sir John Mandeville, who had died in 1372. Marco Polo claimed to have traveled to China and stayed there for seventeen years in the late thirteenth century. But the overland route to China described by Polo made the trading of goods slow and expensive. Columbus was determined to find an alternative sea route that would be both swifter and cheaper. His ambition reinforced by "fables and stories" heard from fellow sailors, who claimed to have seen signs of land in the Western Atlantic, Columbus decided to test this bold theory in reality.

POWERS OF PERSUASION

Even before he began formulating his plans, Columbus was well on the way to gathering the vital practical experience he would need—on land and at sea. As a young man learning his trade, Columbus visited both

England and Ireland, and claimed to have sailed from Bristol to Iceland in 1477. He later boasted that "every sea so far traversed have I sailed." Not only was he an experienced sailor, but he was, in the words of Renaissance expert Sir John Hale, "an accomplished navigator and chart-maker and was familiar with the scholarly literature about cosmography."

The search for patronage for his intended voyage began in 1484, and would lead him to the seats of royal power of Portugal, England, and Castile. Fortunately, he presented a compelling figure at court. Gonzalo Fernandez de Oviedo's historical account, written in 1547, describes Columbus as "handsome and well-built, and of more than average height and strength. His eyes were lively and his features well proportioned. His hair was chestnut brown and his complexion rather ruddy and blotchy; he was well spoken, cautious and extremely intelligent. He had good Latin and great cosmographical knowledge; he was charming when he wished to be and very testy when annoyed." Like all of our geniuses Columbus was a great writer. Throughout his life he wrote letters campaigning for support, kept memoranda of his research, and made notes in the books he read. Among his voluminous papers he left an account of the many intellectual gifts that he combined to gain his aims; as was typical of the age, he ascribed the basis of his abilities to God's will. "He endowed me abundantly in seamanship; of astrology he gave me sufficient, and of geometry and arithmetic too, with the wit and craftsmanship to make representations of the globe and draw on them the cities, rivers and mountains, islands and harbours, all in their proper places."

Nevertheless, the maritime advisers of the monarchs he approached responded with suspicion, but Columbus used all his skills of communication and persuasion to convey his passionate belief in his vision of a new world filled with prosperity. He learned, for example, to speak with the accent and dialect favored by the aristocracy to enhance his rapport with intermediaries in the royal courts. He systematically gathered the information he had found in books and maps, later writing that he quoted the writings of many trustworthy authorities in his presentations, which he learned to tailor to his audience.

"I gave to the subject six or seven years of great anxiety," he wrote in his journal, "explaining, to the best of my ability, how great service might be done to our Lord by promulgating his sacred name and our holy faith among so many nations; an enterprise exalted in itself and calculated to enhance the glory and immortalise the renown of the greatest sovereigns. It was also requisite to refer to the temporal prosperity which was foretold in the writings of so many trustworthy and wise historians who related that great riches were to be found in those parts. And at the same time I thought it desirable to bring to bear upon the subject the sayings and opinions of those who have written upon the geography of the world."

Columbus's compelling vision and contagious optimism gave him the power to convert those in a position of authority to sponsor his adventure, and in Spain he persuaded two archbishops, the court astrologer, two royal confessors, the royal treasurer, and finally Queen Isabella of Castile herself to support his plans. Eventually, in 1492, King Ferdinand and Queen Isabella of the newly united Spain decided to finance Columbus, granting him considerable rights over any discoveries he might make. Colum-

Columbus was . . . a man of extraordinary vision with a defiant attitude to the art of the possible.

—FELIPE FERNANDEZ-ARMESTO

bus described their agreement as follows: "Your Highnesses ordained that I should not go Eastward by land in the usual manner, but by the Western way . . . in return you granted me great favours, bestowing on me the titles of Don and High Admiral of the Ocean Sea, and Viceroy and perpetual governor of such islands and mainland as I should discover and win, or should in future be discovered and won in the Ocean Sea, and that these rights should be inherited by my eldest son and so on from generation to generation." He was also to have a tenth of the profits of all spices, gold, and other riches—a reward rich enough to be one of the largest contracts on record at the time.

MANAGING TO
CHANGE THE WORLD

On Friday, August 3, 1492, Columbus sailed in command of the *Santa María,* the *Pinta,* and the *Niña*—three small ships with just 120 explorers on board. They reached the Canary Islands after a few days, where they reprovisioned and made repairs, and on September 6 Columbus struck out for the New World.

Columbus was prepared to forsake all physical comforts to achieve his ends. At the start of his captain's log for the first voyage he noted that "though all these things will be a great labor it is essential that I should neglect sleep and carefully watch my course." Even more essential was his leadership, and the courage that made it possible. Imagine being on board the *Santa María* after almost forty days in uncharted waters. Will you fall off the edge of the earth, after all? Will you ever be able to return home? Does the New World really exist? These questions haunted Columbus's crew, and in order to encourage them to continue, his own courage had to be monumental.

But leadership requires more than courage, and on his first Atlantic crossing Columbus developed a management ruse as cunning as it was effective. In addition to his own private account, he maintained a false ship's log in which he deliberately underestimated the number of miles sailed, so as to reassure the crew that they would still be able to return home. The crew took the bait, which ironically was less dishonest than intended; because his own real estimates were based on misinformation, the bogus version ultimately proved to be much more accurate.

On Friday, October 12, just over two months after they set sail, came the moment that would change the world forever, as Columbus made landfall at what is now called Watling Island in the Bahamas. After claiming the New World for Spain and Their Supreme Catholic Majesties Ferdinand and Isabella, Columbus sailed on to Cuba and Hispaniola, now known as Haiti, where he left a small colony of men. On this, his first voyage, he approached the local native populations with relative peace and harmony. Writing lyrically of his enthusiasm for the purity and kindness of the native peoples, he describes them as hospitable, gentle, and peaceful. His commands to his crew were firm: his men were to refrain from taking advantage of the aboriginals and to treat them with all kindness and respect.

Three months after reaching the New World he set out on the return voyage, arriving back in Spain on March 15, 1493. Carrying with him samples of gold and other treasures, as well as descriptions of the lands he had seen, he was received in great honor. Queen Isabella proclaimed the "importance, greatness and substantial nature" of his achievement and invited him to ride at the forefront of the royal entourage at ceremonies and in processions. Although he was to make three more voyages to the New World, this was his greatest moment, and his star would never shine brighter.

His unprecedented discovery suddenly reoriented the globe, with Spain now placed at the center of known civilization, the perfect position in which to become the hub of world communication. And the discovery of the New World was just beginning. As Columbus was blazing a new trail westward, the Portuguese explorer Vasco da Gama, though adhering to the time-honored pre-Columbian tradition of following the coastline around Africa and Arabia as closely as possible, reached India in 1498, paving the way for European expansion in the Far East. And in 1519–1522 Ferdinand Magellan, another Portuguese navigator, led the first circumnavigation of the world. These extraordinarily courageous men made global trade possible for the first time, and their achievements heralded four centuries of European expansionism.

Unfortunately, Columbus also led the way toward a view of the New World's native peoples that was terribly cruel and distorted. The most charitable thing we can say about Columbus's handling of the situation in his subsequent voyages is that it was tragically mismanaged, for which he has been justifiably excoriated by modern critics as well as by many of his contemporaries. But the tragedy and controversy surrounding the latter part of Columbus's career can't diminish the genius, determination, and bravery of his initial voyage, from which he still emerges as a unique, positive archetype of optimism, vision, and courage.

As Felipe Fernandez-Armesto writes: "That a weaver's son had died titular Admiral, Viceroy, and Governor; that he should have become the founder of an aristocratic dynasty and have established a claim to fame which has made and kept his name familiar to every educated person in the Western world: these are achievements which command the attention of any observer and the respect of most."

To many of his contemporaries Columbus had become a legendary figure, almost a deity—"like a new apostle" to a leading Spanish courtier, or "the sort of whom the ancients made Gods" to an Italian scholar. One Spanish royal historian described Columbus in his *Historia general y natural de las Indias* (1547) as "the prime mover of this great enterprise, which he initiated for the benefit of all now living and those who shall live after us." Thomas Jefferson, inspired by Columbus's vision and courage, kept a portrait of him at his estate at Monticello, where it still remains.

Columbus died in 1506 at Valladolid and was buried in a monastery near Seville. In 1536 his remains were reburied in Hispaniola, and in 1902 reached their final resting place in Seville Cathedral.

For centuries afterward many of the world's greatest poets, including Milton and Wordsworth, were inspired by his courage and vision. In his "Prayer of Columbus," for example, Walt Whitman writes:

> *O I am sure they really came from Thee,*
> *The urge, the ardor, the unconquerable will,*
> *The potent, felt, interior command, stronger than words,*
> *A message from the Heavens whispering to me even in sleep,*
> *These sped me on.*

Summary of Achievements

▲ Despite a lack of formal education he conceived the plan of his ocean voyage and successfully collected evidence to show that it was possible.

▲ He completed his epoch-making first voyage to the New World in 1492.

▲ Through his skill as a navigator he discovered the workings of the Atlantic Ocean wind system, so that contact between Europe and America was never broken again.

▲ He overcame opposition to make three more voyages and was the first to discover and describe the mainland of South America in 1498.

▲ He founded a noble family though his father was a cloth weaver—a self-made man of the age of discovery.

COLUMBUS AND YOU

In what ways do you hug the coastline of the familiar? In which area of your life might you benefit the most from "going perpendicular" to habit? Can you create a vision of a new world of possibility and inner richness? Can you back up that vision with the knowledge and experience needed to make it real?

Columbus serves as an archetype of optimism, vision, and courage in the face of uncertainty. He inspires us to face the unknown waters in our own lives, to leave the coastline of habit and to discover a new world of depth and possibility. He rose from humble beginnings through a powerful vision, personal optimism, and the Platonic love of learning, reading, languages, and cartography to become the icon of all explorers who travel in hope. As Whitman wrote:

> *And these things I see suddenly, what mean they?*
> *As if some miracle, some hand divine unsealed my eyes,*
> *Shadowy vast shapes smile through the air and sky,*
> *And on the distant waves sail countless ships,*
> *And anthems in new tongues I hear saluting me.*

Columbus calls on the explorer within you, inviting you to form a vision of possibility and to find the courage to embark on the journey to your dreams. Columbus is also a marvelous inspiration if you must sell an idea or find a sponsor for a project.

In the exercises that follow you'll have the opportunity to clarify your life vision and strengthen your optimism and courage to make it real. Please begin by considering the self-assessment questions that follow.

COLUMBUS: GOING PERPENDICULAR SELF-ASSESSMENT

- ☐ I have a dream or vision that sets the course for my life.

- ☐ I can persuade others to share my dream or vision.

- ☐ I can communicate my ideas clearly to others.

- ☐ I research my plans thoroughly.

- ☐ I take a positive view of my setbacks, misfortunes, and mistakes.

- ☐ I am an optimist.

- ☐ I take the word "impossible" as a challenge.

- ☐ I have the courage to pursue new ideas.

- ☐ I am willing to experience discomfort in the pursuit of my dream.

- ☐ I believe that my dreams will become reality.

- ☐ I use my practical knowledge to develop my ideas.

- ☐ I have a knack for calming people's fears.

EXERCISES

THINKING LIKE COLUMBUS/
GOING PERPENDICULAR

They all laughed at Christopher Columbus

when he said the world was round!

—George and Ira Gershwin,

from *Shall We Dance*, 1937

CULTIVATE OPTIMISM IN THE FACE OF ADVERSITY

Like many highly successful people, Columbus was extremely optimistic. Even after six weeks at sea with no sight of land, he maintained an unwaveringly positive attitude.

Optimism and resilience in the face of adversity—like that shown by Columbus—is the greatest long-term predictor of success for individuals and organizations. Individuals and organizations who view their setbacks in the context of progress are much more likely to continue in their efforts toward success. As psychologist Karen Horney discovered, most people actually succeed when they *commit* to do whatever it is they want to do in life.

Most of what people describe as failure in their lives, Horney discovered, is a function of withholding commitment. In other words, they give up prematurely and label the experience a failure. Shakespeare understood this when he wrote, "Our doubts are traitors and make us lose the good we oft might gain by fearing to attempt."

Columbus-like persistence is a critical key to success, and an optimistic attitude is the key to persistence. Dr. Martin Seligman, author of *Learned Optimism*, points out that pessimistic thinking tends to be self-fulfilling because it short-circuits persistence. His research, over more than two decades, shows that pessimists tend to give up when confronted by adversity, even when success might be right around the corner. Living under "Murphy's Law," they have "the knack for snatching defeat out of the jaws of victory."

The research also demonstrates that optimists perform better at work, at school, and in athletics. Optimists regularly outperform the predictions of aptitude tests. Their resistance to colds and other illnesses is superior, and they recover faster from illness and injury. And optimists make significantly more money. Seligman also discovered that pessimists are generally more accurate in their assessments of reality. Pessimists assume that optimists are people who do not yet have all the facts. Optimists really do seem to look at the world through rose-colored glasses. The results of numerous long-term studies demonstrate, nevertheless, that better results are obtained by erring on the side of optimism.

The core of optimism is explanatory strategy. In other words, when things go wrong, do you explain them in terms of your own fundamental incapacity thereby demotivating yourself and forestalling future attempts to succeed, or do you spin your interpretation of events in such a way as to encourage learning, adaptation, and renewed efforts at success?

▲ In your notebook make a list of the three most pessimistic people you have ever met (a pessimist is someone who, when faced with two unattractive alternatives, selects them both) and the three most optimistic people (an optimist is someone who, when faced with two unattractive alternatives, is thrilled to have a choice). Conjure up their images in your mind's eye and get a feeling for the effects their attitudes had or have on the quality of their lives.

▲ Do you know any talented people who've kept themselves in lesser positions in life because they avoided the risk of starting a new job, or going off on their own? Do you know anyone who seems overly optimistic to the point of delusion, a person who takes undue risks and often suffers the consequences?

- If the most pessimistic person you have ever met is a "1" and the most optimistic is a "10," what number rating would you give to yourself? Your spouse? Your mom and dad? Your children? Coworkers?
- In your notebook, describe the biggest challenge you faced—something that is now resolved—in the last ten years. Then describe the biggest challenge you face now. Starting with the challenge from your past, write out a sample of the internal dialogue that went on as you faced this challenge. Then do the same with a current challenge. Of course you can't change the past, but you can change your attitude toward it. Can you think of a more positive way to view your past challenge? Can you conceive a more optimistic way to look at the challenge you are facing now?

HOW TO LEARN OPTIMISM

You can learn to think—and succeed—like an optimist by changing your explanatory style, even if you are a confirmed pessimist.

"But," the pessimist protests, "according to the research I'll make less money, get sick more often, and be more subject to depression."

"And," the pessimist adds, "it's all my fault, it will never change, and it will completely, totally ruin my life."

The statements above reflect the key self-defeating elements of the pessimist's explanatory strategy. In other words, in the face of misfortune or bad news pessimists focus on the negative and then take it personally (it's all my fault), assume it's permanent (it will never change) and consider its influence pervasive (it will totally ruin my life).

When optimists confront misfortune or bad news they react differently. Optimists *don't take it personally*; they can see the influence of external factors in their problems.

Optimists view success and happiness as their normal state. They see negative events as *temporary glitches* on the path to inevitable progress. And optimists view negative events as *isolated phenomena*, insulated from other areas of their lives.

You can free yourself from the constraints of pessimism and achieve better results in life by consciously choosing a new, optimistic explanatory style. For example, imagine that you had spent years researching and developing a proposal for creating a new line of business (like Columbus), and you've finally gotten the opportunity to present it to the board of your company, and the board responds with an unequivocal no.

How would the pessimist respond?
How would the optimist respond?

Let's compare the contrasting "self-explanations" of the pessimist and the optimist:

Pessimist

1. It's my fault. My proposal was fundamentally flawed. I don't know why I bothered in the first place.
2. I'll never get another chance to present this. I blew it!
3. My life is ruined. I'm a failure.

Optimist

1. I probably could have given a stronger presentation, but the makeup of this board isn't conducive to what I'm trying to do.
2. New board members are elected in three months, I'll try again then, and maybe I can find a venture capital firm in the meantime. Either way I'll work out the glitches in the presentation so it'll be irresistible.
3. I'll use the lessons from this experience to improve everything I do, and my life is filled with so many other blessings that I can't let this little setback bother me.

Even if your first response to negative events continues to be pessimistic, you can begin achieving better results in your life—and strengthening your immune system—by practicing the discipline of optimistic self-explanation.

COASTAL AWARENESS

Before Columbus, most explorers hugged the coastline because they were uncomfortable with the uncharted waters and unfamiliar winds of the open sea.

The voyage of self-discovery begins with awareness of one's own "coastal" patterns and habits.

In your notebook, make a list of safe and comfortable habits from your everyday life. Aim to discover and jot down at least one "coastal" habit in each of the following areas.

Avoid judging these as good/right or bad/wrong, just look for behaviors that are habitual and that may have escaped your conscious consideration for a while:

The way you walk.
Your habits of listening.
Your attitude toward money.
The way you eat.
Your habits of speech.
The way you spend your free time.

If there was one "coastal" behavior you could change that would improve the quality of your life most dramatically, what would it be?

Columbus changed the world by "going perpendicular" to the coastline, straight out into the unknown. He dreamed of a new world and braved the deep to find it.

Look back on your life thus far and consider the times when you departed from the coastline of habit or comfort. Now note a few examples from your life experience of "going perpendicular." Examples might include things like:

Making a commitment.
Becoming a parent.
Changing careers.

Learning something completely new.
Traveling to unknown places.

Think about the anxiety or fear you may have felt before making a big change in your life.

What happened to that fear after you decided to act?

What's the greatest thing you've ever done? Did it involve "going perpendicular"?

If you could do anything, have anything, be anything, what would you choose?

If you could explore, learn, or know anything at all, what would it be?

If you could summon the optimism, vision, and courage of a Columbus, in what ways would you "go perpendicular" in your life now? Please spend a few minutes on a stream-of-consciousness writing exercise on the theme "finding my new world."

A few pleasant "perpendicular" possibilities for your consideration:

Learn to sail.
Climb a mountain.
Learn SCUBA or snorkeling.
Take a wilderness adventure course.
Attend a conference in a field outside your own.
Take a spin around the globe. Place a globe on your kitchen table and spin it around. Stop it at the places you have never been but would most like to visit. Ask your spouse, friends, or family to do the same. Then consider how you can make your greatest dreams of travel and exploration into reality.
Surf the Web. The Internet opens up unlimited new horizons for exploration. If you've never explored the Web, it's time to go surfing now. The

Web is as close as your computer, and you can find unlimited new worlds to explore. Make it a practice to visit a new website or subject at least once a week. Look for unusual, interesting, and extraordinary sites. Create a network with your e-mail buddies to share information on the most compelling sites. The Web is multiplying faster than you might imagine, and there's always something new to discover.

EVERYDAY COURAGE

The word "courage" is derived from *coeur,* which means "heart." Plato's student Aristotle noted, "Courage is the first of the human qualities because it is the quality which guarantees all others." In addition to Columbus's remarkable journeys, we are all familiar with stories of great courage like the heroism of New York City rescue workers after the attacks of September 11, 2001. We also marvel at the remarkable courage of individuals like Mother Teresa in the ghettos of Calcutta or Florence Nightingale among the wounded in the Crimea. But, fortunately, most of us are rarely faced with situations of such enormous drama. For us, courage is more of an inner drama, facing and moving beyond our fears to enrich our lives and the lives of those around us.

Twenty-seven years ago I traveled through Italy with six friends. We were on a slow, crowded, un-air-conditioned train somewhere south of Naples. The train pulled into a small station, and we saw an elderly couple waiting on the platform. They approached the train, and as the old woman mounted the stairs and looked inside at the seething, sweaty mass of seemingly rowdy young people, her face dropped and her body contracted. She turned around and gave her companion a look that said, "Please don't leave me on this train." The old man responded by looking at her with great gentleness, he said just one word: *"Coraggio."*

The old woman straightened up, her eyes afire, and she walked on the train as we all scrambled to help make her comfortable.

Think about the ways in your everyday life that you can "get on the train." It helps if you remember that courage is not the opposite of fear, but rather the willingness to forge ahead in the face of fear.

One of the best ways to strengthen your courage is to surround yourself with stories and examples of courage in everyday life. Courage is contagious and so is cowardice. Do you know, for example, older persons, perhaps grandparents, who left home and came to this country to seek a better life? If so, sit with them and ask to hear their story (it may take a little coaxing). Do you know people who have bravely faced illness or death and survived? Ask them to tell you their story. Do you know people who lost their business, faced bankruptcy, and recovered to become prosperous again? Ask them to tell you their story.

EXPAND YOUR DREAM

Some dreams develop in childhood, others begin later. Columbus was driven by a powerful dream, nurtured from childhood, of discovering a new world. Let his example inspire you to rekindle an old dream or help you find a new one. Consider these questions.

What is your dream?
Do you have a longing from childhood that is unfulfilled?
What holds you back from pursuing your dream?
How can you cultivate the optimism and courage to make your dream a reality?
What will your life look like when your dream is achieved?
Can you persuade others to share your dream, and perhaps to finance it?

Create a vivid picture of the result you desire. Involve all your senses as you visualize your dream becoming real. When you have achieved your vision, how does it feel? What do you hear, see, smell, or sense? As you vividly imagine and describe your desired outcome, you are instructing your unconscious mind to use all your resources to bring it into reality.

A dream becomes a driving and guiding force for living. It helps you align your daily choices and decisions with your broader goals and priorities. Like Columbus, remember to dream big.

Bobbi Sims, a professional speaker and author, comments on crafting her dream, "Before I wrote my first book, I dreamed it would be picked up by a publisher, and never had a doubt that it would happen. It did happen, but that was where my dream ended, because I neglected to focus on its success after publication."

Bobbi realized that she had limited herself by limiting the size of her dream. Now she dreams that her latest book will be a best seller. She enthused: "Expanding the size of my dream is incredibly energizing. It's inspired me to reprioritize my life, to discover talents I didn't know I had, and to access my deepest resources of creative power. I'm continually improving my manuscript until I know that it will be a bestseller!"

CULTIVATE A BIAS TO ACTION

Columbus is often criticized by people who say that he didn't really mean to discover America, but the fact that he was indeed looking for the Orient in no way diminishes the greatness of his achievement. Alexander Graham Bell started out trying to improvise a hearing aid and invented the telephone instead. The physicist who first discovered radio waves from the edges of the galaxy—and in the process became the father of radio astronomy—began by trying to develop an antenna to learn more about static on telephone lines. And the inventors of hugely successful products like Teflon and Post-it notes began by attempting to make something else. It's easy to criticize others while standing safely on the shore; instead develop a "bias to action." Try something new, begin working on making your dream come true today. As Shakespeare proclaims it: "Thoughts be but dreams 'til their effects be tried."

In your notebook list a few activities, goals, or projects that you've been considering, and then craft a plan for beginning at least one of them NOW!

COLUMBUS IN LOVE

Try this delightfully silly version of Columbus-inspired thinking. Get in the tub with your sweetie; splash around and immerse yourselves in the metaphor of charting new waters in your relationship:

What are your "coastal patterns" that interfere with intimacy?

How could you "go perpendicular" to some of your more challenging relationship issues?

Apply an optimistic explanatory style to the issues that arise. Explore the possibility of new routes. Then look each other in the eyes with depth and tenderness, and say a small way in which you'll start out on the uncharted waters of deeper intimacy.

COLUMBUS AT WORK

Sales is to business as wind was to Columbus's historic voyage—the practical driving force of success. Of course, Columbus would never have had the opportunity to set sail without extraordinary sales skills. The most successful salespeople possess Columbus-like optimism, as illustrated in Dr. Martin Seligman's studies of insurance salespeople from Met Life. He observed that the ability to remain optimistic in the face of frequent rejection was the most significant factor in sales success. Seventy-five percent of new insurance salespeople quit in their first few years because they couldn't handle the rejection. Seligman determined that new salespeople who scored high on his optimism scale outsold their colleagues by almost 40 percent in their first two years on the job. Encouraged by Seligman's initial findings, Met Life experimented by hiring some new sales agents based solely on their high scores on the optimism scale. This special "optimism squad" had all failed the normal screening process, but they outperformed their less optimistic but normally screened peers by over 20 percent in their first year and almost 60 percent in the second.

What's more challenging than selling life insurance? How about selling a new online investment research approach to investment professionals in the midst of the dot.com crash? Nina Lesavoy left a comfortable, "coastal" senior position at a traditional investment management firm to sail the turbulent waters of e-commerce. Despite torrents of chaos and ship-wrecks all around she continues to navigate successfully in dangerous waters. She comments: "My clients are among the smartest and most successful people in the world. But at the same time they haven't needed to change for thirty years. Technology is now offering them a way of doing business that they never dreamed of before, which is a scary thought for some. But despite the traumas in the birth of this 'new world,' it's clear to me that this is the future and that my clients will be much better off if they find the courage to change now. I love the fact that Columbus learned to speak the language and dialect of his potential allies in the court of Ferdinand and Isabella. This is what sales is all about—learning to speak your clients' language. I feel lucky every day that I can help people find solutions to some of their most important problems. I guess I feel that for my clients 'going perpendicular' is the wave of the future and that therefore our success is inevitable."

COLUMBUS: A NEW WORLD OF MUSIC

In *La Mer* (*The Sea*) Claude Debussy "went perpendicular" with unprecedented use of the whole-tone scale which, unlike traditional musical scales, has no tonal center. This music produces a feeling familiar to Columbus and his crew, the feeling of being afloat with no land in sight. Debussy was the first composer to successfully make beautiful music using this unorthodox scale in his compositions. Enjoy its sensual beauty and give in to the lost feeling as your ear searches for familiar musical territory. This sonorous piece, with its shimmering orchestral background, masterfully evokes the resonance of endless waves.

After an oceanic experience with Debussy, explore Antonin Dvořák's Symphony No. 9 in E Minor, also called the New World Symphony. Dvořák's masterpiece, this composition is a tribute to the unconquerable optimism of the human spirit. Through his use of dramatic and colorful orchestration Dvořák guides you to an exploration of new harmonic worlds. Listen to this inspiring music when you are gearing up your courage in order to "go perpendicular" to a habitual coastline.

ONWARD TO COPERNICUS

Edward O. Wilson applies the Columbus metaphor in his description of what separates great scientists from the norm:

". . . To be highly successful the scientist must be confident enough to steer for blue water, abandoning sight of land for a while. He keeps in mind that the footnotes of forgotten treatises are strewn with the names of the gifted but timid. If on the other hand he chooses, like the vast majority of his colleagues, to hug the coast, he must possess what I like to define as optimum intelligence for normal science: bright enough to see what needs to be done but not so bright as to suffer boredom doing it."

As Columbus set off to redraw the map of the globe, a young contemporary scholar, Nicolaus Copernicus, was bored by the "normal" approach to the science of his day. Talented and confident, he "went perpendicular" to the established assumptions of astronomy and redrew the map of the cosmos. In the process, he created the supreme model of the paradigm shift. Copernicus, navigator of the heavens, is a breakthrough thinker of the highest order and an inspiration for all of us who aim to embrace change with grace.

Nicolaus Copernicus

(1473–1543)

Revolutionizing Your Worldview

Then felt I like some watcher of the skies/When a new planet

swims into his ken; /Or like stout Cortez, when with eagle eyes/

He stared at the Pacific—and all his men/Looked at each

other with a wild surmise—/Silent, upon a peak in Darien.

—JOHN KEATS

What is the center of your universe? Are you sure? Have you ever moved it? Has anybody else ever moved it for you?

Twenty years before Columbus first returned from the New World, Nicolaus Copernicus was born on a flat, unmoving planet at the center of

The only available images of Copernicus depicted him in a way that made him look quite unreal, inspiring me to depict him as very human and very real. In my rendition of "revolutionizing your worldview" I wanted his look to convey something that was at the same time solid and in flux. And some of my friends commented that his head looks like a planet!—Norma Miller

the universe, around which the sun endlessly circled. A century after his death, that same planet was a rotating sphere orbiting around its sun, somewhere in a universe too vast to have a center. The planet hadn't changed, of course, but the paradigm for understanding it had turned inside out. A paradigm is a fundamental frame of reference for understanding the world. And the revolutionary genius of Nicolaus Copernicus offers the classic example of a paradigm shift.

The founder of modern astronomy, Copernicus was the first to present a compelling case for the heliocentric or sun-centered view of the cosmos, in his great work *The Revolution of the Heavenly Spheres*. The information was intellectual dynamite: heresy to the Church, which tried to suppress it, and a mandate for further inquiry to the scientists fortunate enough to hear of it during the work's slow initial dissemination. Although his ideas were by turns popularized, celebrated, ridiculed, and condemned after his death, Copernicus had not set out to court controversy or impose his beliefs on others. A spectacularly learned and insatiably curious independent thinker, he was troubled by what he considered a flaw in the prevailing cosmological paradigm; it was only by methodically and exhaustively investigating this flaw that he arrived at the unavoidable conclusion that an entirely new paradigm was required. Indeed, he cannily protected his work by limiting access to scholars and downplaying its revolutionary nature to its potential enemies, giving his vital ideas the opportunity to take root and grow. But by focusing on the ideas rather than their awesome implications, he was able to see his work through to its organic completion—a profoundly new way of looking at the world— thus setting into motion the events that ultimately brought him credit for reordering the universe.

Born into affluence in the Polish village of Torun, Copernicus was at an early age entrusted to his uncle, the Prince Bishop of Ermeland, for his education. Like many young men of the Renaissance, Copernicus traveled widely, visiting the best European universities to study their specialist subjects. At the University of Cracow he mastered mathematics, optics, and perspective; he then moved to the University of Bologna to study canon law, to prepare him for the career in the Church he was expected to pursue in his uncle's footsteps. In 1497 he was appointed to a lifetime post as cathedral canon at Frauenburg, the cathedral city of Ermeland. Significantly, though, Copernicus never definitively took holy orders, and throughout his life he avoided the religious conflicts of the Protestant Reformation and the Catholic counter-Reformation.

In 1501 Copernicus studied medicine at Padua, where he also attended lectures on astronomy. Two years later he became a doctor of canon law at Ferrara. In Italy he took the opportunity to learn Greek, a relatively new addition to the humanist curriculum. On his return to Poland he served as his uncle's scribe and doctor. He also took over many of his uncle's duties as prince bishop, becoming military governor, judge, physician, and reformer of the coinage. Although his medical skills made him a favorite among the diocese's affluent circles, he also acquired a reputation as something of a saint by offering free medical assistance to the poor.

THE QUEST FOR BEAUTY AND TRUTH

The speculations of a philosopher are far removed from the judgment of the multitude, for his aim is to seek truth in all things.

—COPERNICUS, PREFACE TO
THE REVOLUTION OF THE HEAVENLY SPHERES

As generous as he was with his considerable talents, Copernicus remained a restless intellect, and he began to ponder more seriously the problems of astronomy. Something about the prevailing explanations for, as he put it, "the motion of the spheres of the universe" didn't add up. "For a long time I reflected on the confusion in the astronomical traditions," he wrote. "I began to be annoyed that the philosophers had discovered no sure scheme for the movements of the machinery of the world, created for our sake by the best and most systematic Artist of all."

He was particularly drawn to inconsistencies of a complicated geometric scheme that had been devised to explain the motion of the planets and stars as they rotated about a fixed Earth. He intuited that the awkward mathematics traditionally used to justify the geocentric worldview could not be right, and began to think about the possibility that the Earth moved as well—even though the idea at first seemed absurd, as well as against Church doctrine. Contrary to critics' later charges, Copernicus didn't consider his work at odds with his faith in God as the supreme "Artist" who created the universe, and instead sought through science to better understand God's work rather than to refute His role in it. And glorious work it was; Copernicus saw the universe as an expression of the Platonic ideal of beauty, and elegantly described the movement of heavenly bodies as "the ballet of the planets." He floated these ideas in a short tract written sometime before 1514, but it was not widely circulated.

Eager to find support for the bold new vision he was beginning to glimpse, Copernicus set out to "read again the works of all the philosophers on whom I could lay hands to seek out whether any of them had ever supposed that the motions of the spheres were other than those demanded by the mathematical schools." As a scholar Copernicus was in an ideal position at Frauenburg, whose cathedral library contained many books for him to consult. Many of the classical writers who inspired him are still in print today, their eternal insights into the moral, ethical, and intellectual problems that we all face as relevant as ever. The relatively recent invention of the printing press also helped him broaden his inquiry; we know, for example, that Copernicus owned books by the Roman orator and statesman Cicero, the Greek historian Herodotus, and of course Plato, and that he also consulted books in other collections, including a Ptolemaic atlas printed in Ulm in 1486.

Almost 2,000 years before Copernicus, the ancient Greek astronomer and mathematician Aristarchus advocated a heliocentric model of the solar system. Forty years before Copernicus, Leonardo da Vinci wrote in his notebook (in capital letters for emphasis) *IL SOLE NO SI MUOVE* ("THE SUN DOES NOT MOVE"). But Aristarchus, Leonardo, and others—who knew that the earth wasn't still and flat—weren't able to present a fully developed, mathematically sound, explanatory model.

His exhaustive research paid off: Copernicus found his answer in the works of a small number of earlier philosophers who had suggested that the earth moved, although they could not explain the motion accurately. Realizing that such a revolutionary theory would remain meaningless without proof, Copernicus proceeded to build a solid case for the theory; using the best technology available to him, he observed the motion of the planets from his newly discovered perspective and produced extensive tables detailing his observations. All of this, his life's work, he summarized in *The Revolution of the Heavenly Spheres*, which he completed in 1530. But another thirteen years would pass before he brought his book to publication.

THE PRUDENT REVOLUTIONARY

'Tis much he dares; and to that dauntless temper

of his mind, he hath a wisdom that doth guide

his valour to act in safety.

—WILLIAM SHAKESPEARE, *MACBETH*

~

Imagine the seismic shock waves that Copernicus's discovery was just waiting to unleash. His ideas seemed to fly in the face of common sense; even today we still talk of the sun rising and setting, testament to how difficult it is to overcome the evidence of our eyes and to rid ourselves of the long ingrained geocentric terminology. Medieval and Renaissance popes, meanwhile, were not too keen on revolutions, and had repeatedly demonstrated their power both to suppress knowledge they deemed inflammatory and to punish the individuals who dared publicize it.

Copernicus was understandably wary of publishing his findings for many years, for fear of being scorned—or worse—by lesser minds. The boldness with which he formulated his theory was matched by prudence in its dissemination. As one modern account puts it, although he essentially "threw the final bomb into the celestial machinery . . . he did his best to make it look as if he was only oiling the rusty parts." He wrote in Latin, limiting his audience to men of science and other scholars with whom he chose to share it. And for years he resisted entreaties for publication made by friends and others who were fortunate enough to read one of the few extant copies. Finally, in 1539, a young German scholar visiting Copernicus in Poland as a pupil persuaded him to allow the manuscript to be prepared for publication. On May 24, 1543, he touched the first printed copy of his work. He died that very same day, never knowing the fate of his powerful ideas or the success or failure of his efforts to protect them.

He died knowing, however, that acceptance of his theory would cause people to reexamine their worldview—and that the Church would likely be the most resistant to such change. Still, Copernicus believed that his book would embellish religious faith, rather than challenge it, because it would allow the correction of the ecclesiastical calendar. Hoping that the pontiff would use his influence and judgment to uphold the work, Copernicus dedicated *The Revolution* to Pope Paul III. Though some detractors scoffed that, if he were right, then animals and people would fall off the earth, he generally succeeded in avoiding controversy largely because only serious scientists read his book. Of the several hundred copies printed, most ended up in the hands of mathematicians and astronomers, who made heavy use of them, spreading the word of a new way of understanding the universe.

It was only when his ideas were popularized that Church authorities began to take offense. While the greatest thinkers of the age accepted his argument, the traditional reactionary minds, led by the Inquisition, could not come to terms with such a dramatic paradigm shift. At first the Roman Inquisition recommended some changes to the work after acknowledging its usefulness in the calculation of the calendrical year. Then, in 1616, *The Revolution* was placed on the *Index Librorum Prohibitorum*, the official list of books banned by the Church authorities.

The heart of Copernicus's work, the assertion that the Earth circumnavigated the sun, remained a serious threat to the existing world order in the eyes of the Catholic Church, which continued to try to suppress it long after his death. At the same time Copernicus's intellectual heirs, most notably Kepler and Galileo (see box), worked equally hard to bring his ideas into the mainstream, using a new generation of telescopes and other instruments to compile more authoritative proof than Copernicus's tools could provide. In his absence, they became targets of the Inquisition's suppression efforts; Galileo's support for the Copernican cosmology led directly to his trial and condemnation by the papal Inquisition in Rome in 1632.

In the end, as we know, the Copernicans prevailed—but it took the Church more than 450 years from the date of the publication of *The Revolution* to recognize officially that Copernicus and his followers had been right.

KEPLER AND GALILEO: FOLLOWING IN THE FOOTSTEPS OF COPERNICUS

Johannes Kepler (1571–1630)

Copernicus believed that planets moved in perfect circles, but Kepler refined this by proving that their motion was in fact elliptical in *Mysterium Cosmographicum* (1596), the first openly heliocentric treatise to be published since Copernicus's death. Four years later he joined Tycho Brahe, the world's most famous living astronomer, becoming his assistant at the imperial court in Prague. When the eccentric Brahe died soon thereafter, Kepler was appointed court mathematician, astronomer, and astrologer to the Holy Roman Empire in his place. Kepler's main work, published in 1609, was entitled *Astronomia Nova*—the new astronomy—a fitting title. He later published *The Harmony of the World* (1619), in which he developed a theory of harmony in the areas of geometry, music, astrology, and astronomy.

With such chapter headings as "Musical Modes or Tones have somehow been expressed in the Extreme Planetary Movements" and "The Universal Harmonies of all six Planets may exist like Common Musical Counterpoint," *Harmony* makes clear that Kepler perceived remarkable comparisons between musical harmony and his scientific measurement of the heavens. As we saw with Brunelleschi, whose architectural calculations were turned into music by Dufay, the relationship between musical harmony and exact scientific measurement is extremely close.

Galileo Galilei (1564–1642)

Though Copernicus preceded him, Galileo is credited as the father of modern science by contemporary genius Stephen Hawking and many others. By the age of twenty-five he had become professor of mathematics at the University of Pisa, his hometown. It was there in the campanile, the famous leaning tower, that he conducted his revolutionary demonstration that heavier and lighter objects both fall to the ground at the same speed, shattering the long-held Aristotelian belief that heavy objects fall faster than lighter ones.

In 1592 Galileo took a post at Padua and pursued his interests in astronomy. He is believed to have come into contact with Copernicus's ideas as early as 1595; a copy of Kepler's *Mysterium Cosmographicum* found its way to him soon thereafter, as did the second edition of Copernicus's *Revolution*, printed in 1596 in Basel, which he annotated with his own hand.

Designing his own improved telescope, he was the first to recognize that the Milky Way consists of millions of stars, and in 1610 he discovered sunspots and the moons of Jupiter. Despite the great respect with which his work was received, in 1616 he was instructed by the Inquisition to stop teaching the Copernican cosmology. He accepted the command and was unmolested until the publication of his *Dialogue Concerning the Two Chief Systems of the World, Ptolemaic and Copernican* (1632).

This work followed Plato's structure of a conversation. In it Galileo did little to placate the Inquisition, putting the Jesuits' geocentric arguments in the mouth of the moron in the debate. The Inquisition, unsurprisingly, threatened him with torture unless he withdrew his opinions and put him on trial for breaking the ban of 1616. As a result Galileo did recant but was still sentenced to house arrest by the Inquisition. Nevertheless, he continued to pursue his interests and theories with passion, even after he went blind.

It was not until 1737 that Galileo was finally permitted a Christian burial by the Catholic authorities in the church of S. Croce in Florence, the last resting place of Machiavelli and Michelangelo. Over 250 years later, in 1992, the Vatican officially conceded that Galileo had not offended against Catholic belief.

TO BE A PHOENIX

Copernicus's world-shaking revelation that that the Earth was not at the center of all things led in some quarters to what is sometimes referred to as "post-Copernican depression"—a crisis of faith and an anxious search for meaning in the face of a dramatic paradigm shift.

This revolutionary effect on individual attitudes was poignantly expressed in an excerpt from the poem "The Anatomy of the World" by John Donne in 1611:

> *... The new Philosophy calls all in doubt,*
> *The element of fire is quite put out;*
> *The Sun is lost, and the earth, and no man's wit*
> *Can well direct him where to look for it.*
> *And freely men confess that this world's spent,*

When in the Planets and the Firmament
They seek so many new; then see that this
Is crumbled out again to his Atomies.

'Tis all in pieces, all coherence gone;
All just supply, and all relation:
Prince, Subject, Father, Son, are things forgot,
For every man alone thinks he hath got
To be a Phoenix, and that then can be
None of that kind, of which he is, but he.

Copernicus was the seminal figure in the "new philosophy" that inspired Donne's poem. He was the giant upon whose shoulders Kepler, Galileo, and ultimately Newton stood. Galileo himself credited Copernicus as the founder of modern science and applauded him "for making reason so conquer sense that, in defiance of the latter, the former became the mistress of belief."

The loss of the sense of certainty caused by Copernicus's reasoning was paralleled by the effect that Darwin's *Origin of Species* and Einstein's theory of relativity would later have on science, culture, art, and ultimately on the way we all see and understand the world. It requires a rational, reflective, and resilient mind to accept a Copernican, Darwinian, or Einsteinian revolution regarding our place in the universe, particularly when it conflicts with centuries, or even just a lifetime, of reassuring tradition.

Summary of Achievements

▲ Copernicus had the independence of mind to conceive of a different cosmology from that universally accepted for almost a millennium and a half since the time of Ptolemy of Alexandria (d. 170).

▲ Working almost entirely on his own, he assembled the evidence to show that his ideas were plausible—though they could not be fully proved with the observations then available.

▲ He convinced Europe's leading astronomers that he was right about the need for a new cosmology.

▲ He was finally proved correct, and heliocentrism was accepted, once better observations could be made with telescopes. Copernicus thus became the founding father of modern astronomy.

▲ His innovative ideas also meant that the lengths of years and months could be calculated more precisely than ever before.

COPERNICUS AND YOU

We all adopt paradigms to make sense of our experience and to define our sense of self. The process of personal growth involves learning to let go of models of the world that might have served us in the past but are no longer useful. As Jean Houston, author of *The Possible Human*, explains it, the path to wholeness requires us to "die to one story, one myth, in order to be reborn to a larger one. . . . Development involves giving up a smaller story in order to wake up to a larger story."

Copernicus shows us how to open our minds to a larger story. He stands as an inspiration for us to embrace new concepts and realities in our lives, even if they undermine everything that we have always thought to be true. He shows us also that our larger stories can sometimes start small—as small as that one troubling aspect of our existing paradigm that leads us to a whole new understanding.

Sometimes we change our paradigms, but sometimes they are changed for us, and Galileo and Kepler show us how expanding on change is a surer path to influence than resisting or denying it. As we live through this most exciting time of change and transformation, their ability to conceptualize a radically different universe speaks to us across the ages.

In the exercises that follow you will develop the ability to become more aware of your own paradigms and beliefs, and you'll experiment with challenging and maybe even changing them. Let's begin by contemplating the self-assessment questions that follow.

COPERNICUS:
REVOLUTIONIZING YOUR WORLDVIEW
SELF-ASSESSMENT

☐ My mind is open to new ideas.

☐ I am aware of my core beliefs and assumptions about the nature of things.

☐ I am willing to question my assumptions and beliefs.

☐ I am sensitive to others when presenting them with my ideas.

☐ I seek the truth in all things.

☐ I use my reason and logic to solve problems.

☐ I cultivate my memory power.

☐ I welcome and embrace change.

☐ I can lead a change process.

EXERCISES

THINKING LIKE COPERNICUS/
REVOLUTIONIZING YOUR WORLDVIEW

REVOLUTIONARY CONTEMPLATION

What would it take to revolutionize your worldview? How would your paradigm change if aliens from another galaxy established communication with Earth? What if you awoke one morning and read the following headline in your local paper: "Chinese Becomes Official World Language," or perhaps "Messiah Appears!"

Write a few thoughts in your notebook and/or discuss with a friend the discoveries, innovations, events, or changes in the world that would fundamentally shift your worldview. Aim to explore a few that you think might really happen and then conjure up some that seem farfetched. Contemplate the ways in which these revolutionary developments might affect your world.

Three dramatic paradigm changes are already in process and have begun to affect our lives: developments in bio-engineering, the evolution of the new economy, and the emergence of truly intelligent machines. Let's explore each one.

Genetics and Bio-engineering

The journal *Science* reported recently that Dr. Alain Fischer and his colleagues successfully treated two children for severe combined immuno-deficiency disorder exclusively through gene therapy. As *Time* magazine commented, "these 'bubble babies' are out of their bubble." At about the same time the human genome was decoded, ten years ahead of schedule. We are on the verge of a medical revolution that promises to extend human longevity and eliminate many diseases. It will also give us the power to alter our genetic makeup and "program" ourselves for desirable qualities. Moreover, animal cloning has been old news for a while, but when the first human is cloned the challenge to our view of ourselves will be profound. What are the ethical, political, and social implications of these extraordinary developments? What if you could live to be 150 years old? If you could bio-program your children to be stronger, taller, and smarter, would you do it?

The New Economy

As Don Tapscott, author of *The Digital Economy*, describes it: "Today we are witnessing the early, turbulent days of a revolution as significant as any other in human history. A new medium of human communication is emerging, one that may prove to surpass all previous revolutions in its impact on our economic and social life. Interactive multi-media and the so-called information highway, and its exemplar, the Internet, are enabling a new economy based on the networking of human intelligence."

Take some time to consider how the world may change as the new economy evolves. What will happen as billions of Chinese and Indians sign on to the Web and aspire to American-style standards of living? What will be the effects on our language, values, and culture as communication becomes faster and cheaper? What kinds of skills will be most marketable in this emerging world? How can you optimize your own chances of success and fulfillment?

Intelligent Machines

The most Copernican shift of all may be the one foretold in Ray Kurzweil's book, *The Age of Spiritual Machines*. Kurzweil is an information age innovator and pioneer of voice-recognition software. He explains that "Moore's Law," which posits that computing speed doubles every eighteen months, is now out-of-date. At the time of publication, computers are doubling in speed every twelve months. In other words, "the rate of exponential growth is growing exponentially!" Kurzweil predicts, "This trend will continue, with computers achieving the memory capacity and computing speed of the human brain by around the year 2020."

He adds, "The emergence in the early 21st century of a new form of intelligence on Earth that can compete with, and ultimately, significantly exceed, human intelligence will be a development of greater import than any of the events that have shaped human history." What if Kurzweil is right? What would be the implications for the nature of our work, human learning, government, warfare, the arts, and our concept of ourselves?

CONSCIOUS COMPUTERS?

When computers equal and begin to exceed the speed, complexity, and subtlety of the human brain, should they be viewed as conscious entities? Kurzweil points out, "This question actually goes back to Plato's time" and adds that the issue is far more compelling now because it is likely to happen soon.

REVOLUTIONIZE YOUR WORLD BY LETTING
GO OF A SELF-LIMITING BELIEF

Just as Copernicus revolutionized our view of the world, you can revolutionize your approach to learning by letting go of a self-limiting belief. Your beliefs set the boundaries of what you can and cannot do. A self-limiting belief shrinks the horizons of your personal cosmos. Just as Copernicus thought beyond the norms of his time, this exercise will help you think beyond yours.

Identify a belief you hold that may be self-limiting. A self-limiting belief is an idea or attitude about your own capability that prevents you from going for what you want. It could be something like "I'm not creative," "I can't sing," "I'm not good at math," "I can't be happy in love," "I'm not coordinated," etc.

Once the belief is identified, step into your objective mind and write out your answers to the following questions.

- When did I form this belief?
- What makes me think that this belief is true?
- How does this belief affect my behavior?
- If I let go of this self-limiting belief, how might it change my life?

Now map out a strategy for changing your self-limiting belief and replacing it with a "bigger story."

MEMORY POWER AND SOLAR SYSTEM ORIENTATION EXERCISE

Like all of our geniuses, Copernicus cultivated a powerful memory. This exercise will guide you to strengthen your memory power while orienting you in your cosmic environment.

In your notebook or on a scrap of paper take sixty seconds and list the planets of the solar system, in order from the sun. (This is a long-term memory exercise because you probably passed a test on the planets when you were in school.)

How did you do? Most people only get a few, although just about everyone gets "Earth"! Chances are that when you were in school you repeated the planets over and over again until you could hold them in your mind long enough to pass the test . . . and then they were gone.

Perhaps you were able to remember the planets because you learned an acronym memory system such as "My very eager mom just served us nine pizzas," in which the first letter of each word reminds you of the appropriate planet (Mercury, Venus, Earth, Mars, Jupiter, Saturn, Uranus, Neptune, Pluto).

An even more effective method for remembering the planets holds within it secrets of developing imagination and creative thinking as well as memory. Try this. Begin by imagining the sun and wondering just how hot it is. In your mind's eye you float up to the sun and plunge a giant thermometer into its core. The thermometer boils up and explodes and out into space shoots a glistening drop of MERCURY. Then an overwhelmingly beautiful goddess clad in robes of shimmering gossamer glides through space and catches this glistening drop, and she is VENUS. She descends to your backyard and plunges the glistening drop into your yard, which is located on the planet EARTH. Your neighbor is disturbed by all the commotion, he is angry and red-faced and stomping toward your house to fight because he's the god of war, MARS. Just before your neighbor gets close enough to cause trouble the king of the gods strolls regally down your street to save you, he's wearing a magnificent suit of golden armor and his name is JUPITER. On the breastplate of his armor the letters S, U, N, are emblazoned in vivid purple. S stands for SATURN, U stands for URANUS, and N stands for NEPTUNE. On the right shoulder of the king of the gods is a little Walt Disney laughing dog named PLUTO. If you did the exercise with enthusiasm and created vivid images in your mind's eye you'll find that it is almost impossible to forget the planets.

WALT WHITMAN (1819–1891)

When I heard the learn'd astronomer,
When the proofs, the figures, were ranged in columns before me,
When I was shown the charts and diagrams,
to add, divide, and measure them,
When I sitting heard the astronomer where
he lectured with much applause
in the lecture-room,
How soon unaccountably I became tired and sick,
Till rising and gliding out I wander'd off by myself,
In the mystical moist night air, and from time to time,
Look'd up in perfect silence at the stars.

EXPLORE THE HEAVENS

How many times a day do you remember to look up and appreciate the sky? Awareness of the heavens can revolutionize your everyday perspective and expand your overall awareness. Set aside a few minutes every evening to observe the phase of the moon and chart it through its complete cycle. Jot down your observations and reactions in your notebook.

A COPERNICAN WAY
TO WATCH THE SUN "SET"

Thanks to Copernicus we know that the sun doesn't actually set, but when you look out to the horizon at dusk the sun does appear to be sinking. So, to revolutionize your view of this cosmic dance, imagine "pinning" the sun to the wall of the sky. If you keep the disc of the sun pinned to its place, you can then watch the horizon move up toward it. Imagine that your part of the Earth is rolling away from the light of the sun and into the darkness of night. (that's what's actually happening). And then imagine that same roll exposing a friend in a more eastern time zone to more light.

Invest in a lightweight, portable telescope so that you can personally experience some of the thrill of discovery that fired Copernicus. Watch the sky at night—if you live in a city with ambient light that drowns out the stars, take a trip with your telescope into the countryside. Make a sketch in your notebook of the constellations you observe and the placement of planets and other heavenly bodies. Most importantly, as the Whitman poem suggests, open yourself to experience the pure, radiant wonder of the stars.

In the mid 1990s amateur astronomers observed a string of "titanic exploding diamonds," massively bombarding the giant planet Jupiter. This discovery of what has become known as the Schumacher-Levy comet was missed entirely by the professional astronomers who didn't expect to see it; the amateurs were looking with open eyes and minds.

TRY A COPERNICAN APPROACH TO TRANSFORMING
OUTDATED PROCESSES AND PROCEDURES

Copernicus is a wonderful role model for transforming outdated processes and procedures. Try the following exercise to revolutionize your world at home or at work:

- ▲ Identify a commonly used procedure or system that you believe could be improved.
- ▲ Collect enough data to have an accurate picture of the functioning of the current system.
- ▲ Make a short list of the weakest aspects of the system or procedure.
- ▲ Target those few negative aspects that have a major influence on function or efficiency.
- ▲ List the strongest positive features of the system, particularly noting those features that are used most frequently.
- ▲ Use your data to develop a new procedure or system that will improve the weakest aspects identified.
- ▲ Test how well your new system performs. Make sure that as weak aspects are improved, strong features are not weakened. If results are not satisfactory, make refinements or an improved new version until you have a new system that is clearly better than the current system in its overall function and results.
- ▲ Present your new system to other stakeholders with the same sensitivity that Copernicus used in introducing his revolutionary ideas.

Dr. Roy Ellzey is professor emeritus of computer science at Texas A&M University and a pioneer in the field of computer education. Ellzey also happens to be a great admirer of Copernicus. He comments on his application of the Copernican approach to transforming outdated processes and procedures: "In the early 1970s I became aware that the dominant curriculum model for computer science . . . was not preparing graduates very well for the rapidly increasing number of jobs in the field. Computer education at the time was devoted to understanding the machines and the theories behind them."

Ellzey responded by designing a new curriculum and writing a new textbook, focused on using computer technology to solve real world problems.

He comments, "Like Copernicus, I studied the existing model thoroughly, collected extensive data and information to create an alternate model. Tested the model, made improvements, sold the concept to upper management, and implemented with success."

Ellzey points out that his innovations were driven by the evolving new paradigm of information age business, but that the innovations themselves were simply examples of changing a model that was not appropriate to solve a growing problem. In his words, "Copernicus's monumental contribution to science and to our perception of the cosmos was a paradigm shift of the first magnitude. However, his methodology in developing a new model for the cosmos is valuable lesson for us all, and can be applied to a host of more mundane problems with rewarding results."

COPERNICUS AT WORK

Technological progress drives increasing global competition, pushing organizations to revolutionize their paradigms. Ma Bell is now ancient history, IBM has reinvented itself a number of times in the last few years, and the United States Post Office change its name to the United States Postal Service. My work with organizations over the last twenty years has involved guiding the development of new cultures to translate new paradigms into profitable practice. Since 1988 I worked with the treasury department at Amoco on these efforts, until Amoco merged with BP a few years ago. After the merger dust settled I was invited to facilitate a series of "innovation team" seminars for the BP Amoco Global Finance Group.

In our very first meeting the team experienced an epiphany that highlighted the truly Copernican nature of its mission. BP's effort to merge with Amoco and reinvent itself as an environmentally friendly, global energy services company was symbolized by new logo: a radiant green (for "sustainable development") and yellow (for "energy") helios. Everyone agreed that the new logo accurately symbolized the aspirations for the company. But then they thought about the old logos—Amoco's old logo was a torch and BP's was a shield—perfect symbols of the middle ages and an old paradigm way of doing business. The question arose: "How can we transform our shields and torches into radiant energy?"

The second meeting of the innovation team was launched by Group Vice President Tony Hayward. He acknowledged that one of the greatest challenges to implementing "helios-type" innovation was "shield and torch" performance management. As he put it, "We have wells in the North Sea that pump out 3,000 barrels a day and all the objectives in our performance contracts are written to assure that level of production. But our engineers believe that with experimentation some of those wells could possibly be pumping 12,000 barrels a day. Clearly, we've got to find a way to write innovative objectives into our performance contracts that support prudent, environmentally sound experimentation."

BP's finance innovation team is leading the effort to revolutionize its work processes and make the new paradigm a reality. As innovation team leader Tim Podesta comments, "Our ambition is double-digit growth which will require new ways of thinking and working. We must challenge current paradigms in the same way as Copernicus used technical and intellectual expertise to challenge the fixed idea that the Earth doesn't move."

Also Sprach Zarathustra by Richard Strauss was the theme music for the popular film classic *2001: A Space Odyssey.* It is a magnificent, intense evocation of the Copernican theme of "revolutionizing your worldview." Strauss was inspired by the genius of philosopher Friedrich Nietzsche. Nietzsche's work explored the quest for meaning in the face of the apparent emptiness caused by the death of old paradigms.

Another wonderful musical expression of Copernicus's vision is Gustav Holst's *The Planets.* Copernicus referred to his own work as a study of the "ballet" of the heavens. And in this majestic work, Holst provides the music to accompany the divine choreography. Holst evokes his perception of the emotion associated with each planet: Venus is dreamy and subtle, Mars is fiery and belligerent, and Jupiter displays perspective and good humor. Astronomers and musicians understand that creation manifests in cyclical, rhythmic patterns. As you listen to this heavenly piece of music be aware of the natural cycles around and within you. Savor the sky and the phases of the moon along with the flow of your breathing and the rhythm of your heartbeat.

CONFUSION ENDURANCE

At this point, if you've been experimenting with the exercises, you might be feeling a little disoriented, as if you were dropped into a strange city without a map. That dissonance is a sign that you are making progress. It means that you're embracing new information and allowing your mind to make unfamiliar connections, perhaps in opposition to beliefs you currently hold. As you continue to play with these new ideas, and strengthen your "confusion endurance," you'll be taking an important step in discovering your genius.

All of our geniuses possessed the ability to embrace the unknown. Indeed, the capacity to welcome uncertainty, be comfortable with ambiguity, and delight in paradox is one of the most distinguishing qualities of the finest minds.

ONWARD TO ELIZABETH

My parents recently celebrated their fiftieth wedding anniversary. It was a wonderful celebration overflowing with joy and love. But to get to that, my mom and dad had to weather a revolution that rocked their personal world in truly Copernican fashion. My mom had left college to marry my dad and raise my two younger brothers and me. She took care of the house and cooked great Italian meals while my dad worked. Both were operating from a set of beliefs about their appropriate roles in relationship and society. And then that traditional set of beliefs was turned upside down and inside out by one of the greatest social revolutions in history, the accelerating emergence of equal rights and opportunities for women. Mom went back to school, got her bachelor's and then her master's degree, and began working as a psychologist in a mental health clinic. Dad learned how to cook. It was a shock for the whole family, but fortunately everyone was able to adapt. Our next revolutionary genius, Queen Elizabeth I, was instrumental in launching the shift in perception about woman's capabilities that ultimately gave birth to the modern women's movement. She serves as a majestic role model for anyone who seeks to balance the best of masculine and feminine qualities while using power intelligently.

Queen Elizabeth I

(1533–1603)

WIELDING YOUR POWER
WITH BALANCE AND EFFECTIVENESS

Elizabeth . . . she shall be loved and feared. Her own shall
bless her: her foes shake like a field of beaten corn, and hang
their heads with sorrow. Good grows with her. In her days
every man shall eat in safety under his own vine what he
plants and sing the merry songs of peace to all his neighbors.

—WILLIAM SHAKESPEARE

Think for a moment about balance and power. Can you imagine
some situations in which it might be best to assert yourself, to be

I must confess that, as a woman, I was particularly interested in conveying her power and intelli-
gence while preserving her femininity. At first I thought the elaborate collar on her dress and the
pearls could only be used to distinguish her royalty and her era. I soon discovered that they went

141

bold, decisive, perhaps aggressive? Are there other situations in which it would be better to err on the side of sensitivity, to wait, to be patient, and to listen carefully before acting? How can you know the difference?

In a landmark study by Professor E. P. Torrance of Stanford University, the highest levels of creativity and general intellectual functioning were found in those subjects with a balance between sensitivity, usually considered a more "female" trait, and assertiveness, a trait traditionally associated with males. We live in an exciting age when these traditional patterns are undergoing a profound transformation. It is a time when all of us, men and women, need to find new models of excellence in the balanced use of our power.

Of course, you've probably noticed that nine of the ten geniuses we are studying are men; I know that I have (and I've had it pointed out to me more than once just in case I missed it!). I also know that I do not intend in any way to suggest that men are more capable than women. Rather, the last two millennia, during which all our geniuses lived and made their respective marks, were a more supportive and hospitable environment for men to cultivate, express, and be recognized for their genius than for women. I'm confident that if I were writing this 2,000 years from now, the genius dream team would reflect more parity between men and women. As it now stands, at least in terms of gender, our team is admittedly off balance, but no more or less so than the times that produced it.

It is fitting, then, that the sole female genius on our team has a lot to teach us about balance. Queen Elizabeth I was the first truly independent and successful woman in the realm of male politics. Britain's greatest monarch, she presided over the most remarkable flourishing of English culture at home and around the globe; it is as a direct result of the literary, military, scientific, and exploratory endeavors of the Elizabethan Age that

beyond that; as I got carried away with the collar it took on the meaning of her radiating intelligence and power, her pearls became pearls of wisdom and her curls a way of bringing these symbolic images together in a feminine fashion.—Norma Miller

English is now spoken so widely. Her ascension to the throne offended patriarchal thinkers, who argued that a woman could not wield power intelligently or effectively.

Yet her triumphantly successful reign forever changed the world's idea of women's capabilities, planting the seeds for the most powerful human rights movement ever: the empowerment of women.

On a large scale, Elizabeth made great strides to begin the process of righting the imbalance between male and female power. On an individual scale, she reached her great heights by wielding both—and can show us how we can maximize our own powers by making balance a priority.

I thank God that I am endowed with such qualities that

if I were turned out of the realm in my petticoat,

I were able to live in any place in Christendom.

—ELIZABETH I

ENTITLEMENT AND EMPOWERMENT

Elizabeth had to overcome tremendous adversity to attain her birthright. Before she was three years old her father, Henry VIII, ordered the execution of his second wife, her mother, Anne Boleyn, on trumped-up treason charges. Born a princess, Elizabeth was at once declared illegitimate by act of Parliament. It was not to be her last reversal of fortune; as Cambridge University historian David Starkey writes in *Elizabeth*, "from her birth in 1533 to her accession in 1558, she had experienced every vicissitude of fortune and every extreme of condition. She had been Princess and inheritrix of England, and bastard and disinherited; the nominated successor to the throne and an accused traitor on the verge of execution; showered with lands and houses and a prisoner in the Tower."

Still, Elizabeth was educated by the best humanist scholars of the time, who had all been influenced by Plato's educational ideas; so complete and effective was her education, and so dazzling her use of it, that she may well be considered the first personification of Plato's ideal of the philosopher queen. Her tutor Roger Ascham described her routine as beginning with reading from the New Testament in the original Greek, after which she read a selection of classical authors "to supply her tongue with the purest diction, her mind with the most excellent precepts, and her exalted station with a defense of the utmost power of fortune." It is no wonder, perhaps, that she soon gained the reputation for speaking with intelligence and quick-witted flourish in six languages—two of which were ancient.

On his deathbed Henry VIII named her as third in line to the throne, after her younger brother Edward and her older sister Mary. Edward later chose to ignore this, and at his premature death in 1553 he named his cousin Lady Jane Grey as his successor. But the young Lady Jane was no match for the resolve of Mary Tudor, who had Lady Jane executed in 1554.

In the same year Elizabeth was suspected of involvement in Sir Thomas Wyatt's plot to overthrow Mary Tudor. Although no evidence could be found against her, Elizabeth was sent to the Tower of London, a place of utter horror for her where her own mother had been executed and where the scaffold for Lady Jane's execution still stood. Later released into house arrest, Elizabeth was denied paper, pen, or ink, but she was still able to use a diamond to scratch a defiant verse into the window at Woodstock saying that although she was suspected to have committed treason nothing could be proved:

> *Much suspected by me,*
> *Nothing proved can be.*
> *Quod [said] Elizabeth the prisoner.*

When Elizabeth was brought the news that she had at last become queen, at her sister's death on November 17, 1558, she quoted the powerful words of Psalm 118 in Latin, *A domino factum est et mirabile in oculis nostris* ("This is the Lord's doing and it is marvelous in our eyes"). Elizabeth felt that she had been chosen to reign by God's will and saw herself as the rightful heir to the Tudor dynasty.

The fact that she had survived and ascended to the throne must have seemed like a miracle, but the challenges that awaited her were to provide a most extreme test of her talents. England was in a financial mess thanks to Edward and Mary's mismanagement, and the much richer and more powerful kingdoms of France and Spain were circling her like buzzards after a battle.

These two Catholic nations saw the Protestant queen and her realm as a constant thorn. Elizabeth also had the task of uniting a country torn by years of conflict between Catholics and Protestants. She favored a Protestant church settlement, but believed it could be achieved gradually and without persecution of her Catholic subjects for their religious beliefs. Nevertheless, in 1570 Pope Pius V excommunicated Elizabeth and theoretically deposed her in the eyes of Catholics. Over the years Rome issued numerous decrees calling for her demise. In 1580 the Vatican put out a "contract" on Elizabeth's life. As the papal secretary expressed it: "whosoever sends her out of the world with the pious intention of doing God service, not only does not gain sin but gains merit."

Elizabeth also faced tremendous opposition simply because she was a woman. John Knox, the Scottish author of *The First Blast of the Trumpet Against the Monstrous Regiment [Government] of Women*, had declared female monarchy to be against the will of God. "That God has revealed," wrote Knox, "that it is more than a monster in nature that a woman should reign and bear empire above man."

Considering that she was politically disinherited by the two men she loved the most, her father, Henry VIII, and her brother, Edward VI, it is no wonder that Elizabeth later resolved to rule alone. Elizabeth's advisers urged her to alleviate her political problems through a strategic alliance in the form of marriage. Indeed, at the start of her reign it seemed inconceivable to her councilors and to Parliament that Elizabeth would not marry, but whenever Parliament raised the question Elizabeth gave a forceful but charming riposte. Despite an array of powerful and attractive suitors, Elizabeth ultimately followed her intuition and remained the Virgin Queen. She knew that if she married she would lose her independence of action. Moreover, she endeared herself to her people by appearing to be "married" to the nation. And one cannot overrestimate the power of a virgin mother figure in her attempt to win the loyalty of her Catholic subjects.

BODY OF A WOMAN, HEART OF A KING

Elizabeth wielded her hard-won power by striking an ever-shifting balance between "male" and "female" characteristics. She certainly asserted her mastery of what Stanford professor Torrance would label her "sensitivity," as expressed in such traditionally feminine traits as empathy, compassion, patience, and openness to counsel. Yet on the side of masculinity—or "assertiveness"—she could be as bold, decisive, ruthless, and visionary as any king.

By cultivating both modes of leadership, she not only doubled the number of weapons in her arsenal, but she developed an unpredictability that kept her opposition guessing how she would decide her next move. Indeed, she often explicitly undermined the notion of traditional gender roles by referring to herself as a "king" or "prince." In 1588 during the great armada crisis, Elizabeth used this motif to brilliant effect, when she donned an armored breastplate and helmet—unheard of for a woman— to address her troops assembled to fight the Spanish invaders at Tilbury.

"I know I have the body but of a weak and feeble woman," she proclaimed to her legions, "but I have the heart and stomach of a king—and of a King of England, too." The subsequent defeat of the Spaniards ranked, of course, among England's most decisive military triumphs.

As effective as she was in her male posturing, Elizabeth was also unafraid to use an element of female vulnerability to her advantage by engaging in the rhetoric of love. In rectifying a minor problem with Parliament late in her reign, for example, she apologized to her politicians and reminded them that her power rested on their contentment: "Though God hath raised me high, yet this I count the glory of my crown—that I have reigned with your loves." Elizabeth did not just expect her subjects to love her, she was also prepared to love them in return—indeed, to remain for them their Virgin Queen, married only to the realm and to her people.

Balance was the watchword for so much of what Elizabeth did. In the area of financial management, for example, biographer J. E. Neale points out that "a sense of economy was inbred as well as inborn in Elizabeth . . . [who] believed in spending what she could afford and paying what she owed." Inheriting a sizable deficit from the reign of her two siblings, she was able to curtail expenses enough to liquidate her debts "without impairing the efficiency of government or casting the gloom of poverty over the Court, the splendor of which was the nation's pride and the monarch's dignity."

Timing—the balance of action and patience—was another strong suit. She had an uncanny gift for knowing the right time to act, a skill that was occasionally mistaken for indecision by her councilors and later by male historians. Some of her advisers, for example, felt that she was too slow to eliminate her greatest rival, her own cousin, Mary Stuart, Queen of Scots, who claimed the English throne with French backing. To neutralize this threat Elizabeth first tried negotiation, then sanctioned limited invasions of France and Scotland, which forced the Scottish queen to abdicate in 1567.

Elizabeth kept Mary under comfortable house arrest in England for twenty years, resisting the pleas of her council that she put her cousin to death. But after the exposure of yet another plot by Mary to depose Elizabeth, she finally signed the death warrant of Mary, Queen of Scots, in 1587. This was an agonizing decision for Elizabeth to make, but she came to realize that she could not rule the realm effectively if she did not eliminate this viper at her bosom. While keeping Mary alive and comfortable doubtless avoided unnecessary trouble from her Catholic supporters, Elizabeth resolved the problem shortly before another challenge would demand her full attention—the Spanish Armada the following year.

A master of political timing, Elizabeth revealed some of her thinking on the topic in a 1580 letter to a suitor, the Duke of Alençon, "I have used time, which ordinarily accomplishes more than reason does," she wrote. "I see well that many people go away repenting of having made rash judgments at the first stroke, without having weighed in a better balance the depth of their opinions."

TOLERANCE AND RUTHLESSNESS

Her handling of Mary demonstrates the balance Elizabeth struck between another vital pair of traditionally female and male attributes, tolerance and ruthlessness. In an age of brutal religious wars on the continent, Elizabeth was ahead of her time when it came to tolerance. As a Protestant she was faced with the task of reconverting the nation from the Catholicism of her sister Mary's violent reign. Unlike "Bloody Mary," Elizabeth did not rely on persecution, preferring to let time and moderation work on her side. Sir Francis Bacon later wrote that Elizabeth, "not liking to make windows into men's hearts and secret thoughts, except [when] the abundance of them did overflow into overt express acts and affirmations, so tempered her law."

Elizabeth was content to allow people to believe what they wanted in the privacy of their own souls, and she turned a blind eye to her subjects' Catholicism. Nevertheless, her overriding aim was to unite Catholics and Protestants through the common ground of their shared nationality. "If I should say the sweetest speech with the eloquentest tongue that ever was in man," she stated, "I were not able to express that restless care which I have ever bent to govern for the greatest wealth." She made great strides in uniting her people in their shared common opposition to foreign domination from the French and Spanish. J. E. Neale emphasizes that under her reign, "the beneficent idea of toleration was born."

At the same time, when necessary, she could be bold and ruthless in defense of her realm. When her tolerance was sorely tested by the dangerous revolt of northern Catholic earls in 1569, she acted fearlessly to secure her crown, eventually ordering the execution of her rebel kinsman the Duke of Norfolk for his role in fomenting the Northern Rebellion. Her Catholic subjects received harsh treatment again in the aftermath of the 1588 armada, which was essentially an attempt to overthrow Elizabeth staged by the world's most powerful Catholic ruler, Philip II of Spain. In the 1590s she was not above executing those who hid antigovernment priests in their homes.

Perhaps the sharpest example of her ability to be ruthless when necessary came shortly after the turn of the century, when her young favorite, the Earl of Essex, planned a coup against her. The coup failed, but Essex hoped to play upon the queen's female sensibilities. As Neale relates, "Elizabeth's supreme task—which had been accomplished painfully but successfully in the early decades of her reign—the eradication of sex prejudice in statesmen and courtiers—was beginning over again with the new generation. Essex could not help thinking of her as a mere woman, and an old and crusty one at that." Elizabeth played along with Essex, enough that he misinterpreted what he thought were signs of vulnerability. In fact, she had lured out a potential traitor. After the failed coup, he attempted to gain back his favor through the romantic gesture of sending Elizabeth a ring that she had once given him. Instead of restoring him to her good graces, Elizabeth had Essex and his henchmen executed.

I have a man's mind, but a woman's might.

—WILLIAM SHAKESPEARE, *JULIUS CAESAR*

~

MAJESTY AND MILDNESS

Elizabeth brought all her skills to bear with spectacular results on what may be the secret to her considerable success: her ability to cultivate and maintain a vast network of personal relationships. A master politician, she demonstrated in her relationships the same capacity for balance she exercised so effectively in other aspects of her life.

Elizabeth employed a full arsenal of complementary strategies with which she orchestrated a wide range of contacts, measuring trust against prudence, intimacy against authority, openness against protocol.

Her approach had a direct impact on her reign and the decisions with which she shaped it; Elizabeth listened to a wide range of advice from her councilors and courtiers and did not act until she had weighed all the pros and cons. In his *Fragmenta Regalia* published in 1641 Sir Robert Naunton complimented Elizabeth for balancing the different court factions: "the principal note of her reign will be that she ruled much by faction and parties, which herself both made, upheld and weakened, as her own great judgment advised."

During her forty-five years as queen, Elizabeth perfected a brilliant eye for talent, and she ruled with the aid of a carefully chosen group. She employed the two most intelligent politicians of the age, Sir William Cecil and Sir Francis Walsingham, as her closest advisers. As biographer J. E. Neale comments, "There was no greater tribute to the tolerance, sagacity and masterful nature of Elizabeth than her choice of such ministers as Walsingham. She chose them for their ability, their honesty, and their unshakable loyalty. Even in their intensity they were the expression of the England she was nurturing, and if like thoroughbreds they were hard to ride, she was the perfect horsewoman."

Elizabeth combined a towering mind and indomitable spirit with effervescent charm and exceptional intuition about people. According to one court observer, "If ever any person had either the gift or the style to win the hearts of the people it was this Queen . . . in coupling mildness with majesty as she did . . . all her faculties were in motion, and every motion seemed a well-guided action; her eye was set upon one, her ear listened to another, her judgement ran upon a third, to a fourth she addressed her speech; her spirit seemed to be everywhere, and yet so entire in herself it seemed to be nowhere else."

She coupled her majesty with mildness through a personal touch rare in the history of monarchy: she signed letters to key figures in her court, "Your Loving Sovereign"; she visited the estates of her nobles when they faced adversity, illness, or death; and she gave pet names to key courtiers that made them feel special: Sir Walter Raleigh was "Water," the Earl of Leicester, her "Eyes," and Sir Christopher Hatton, her "Lids." She brought the same personal touch to her common subjects. On one famous occasion she sampled food at a town banquet held in her honor without a taster and then asked for dishes to be sent to her private quarters, a compliment to the people that Neale describes as "unsurpassable."

In the intrigues of diplomacy, the French ambassador conceded, "she is the best hand at the game of living." Elizabeth used her interpersonal savvy to be the best-informed person in England and probably in all of Europe. Her adviser Lord Burghley described her "as the wisest woman that ever was, for she understood the interests and dispositions of all the princes in her time, and was so perfect in the knowledge of her own realm, that no councilor she had could tell her anything she did not know before."

Elizabeth nurtured personal relationships with the influential people in her sphere. And she used the information she gained from her network to cross-check the validity of advice she received. As Sir Christopher Hatton summed it up: "The Queen did fish for men's souls, and had so sweet a bait that none could escape her network."

Video et taceo (I see but say nothing).

And in return, she earned the outright adoration of her people, particularly in her final decades. The years after the tremendous victory over the armada—which was generally interpreted as a sign of divine favor—were the most glorious of Elizabeth's reign. "England had emerged from the Armada year as a first-class Power," observed Sir Winston Churchill. "Her people awoke to a consciousness of their greatness, and the last years of Elizabeth's reign saw a welling up of national energy and enthusiasm focusing upon the person of the Queen."

The "person of the Queen" was celebrated in the magnificent "Rainbow" portrait of Elizabeth, now at Hatfield House, in which she is depicted as the sun creating a rainbow, which she holds in her hand. The Latin motto on this picture says *Non sine sole iris* ("No rainbow without the sun"). She was careful to give her people what she thought they wanted as well, insisting that her youthful image be preserved to emphasize the eternal nature of royal power. In the 1590s Elizabeth ordered her Privy Council to destroy all portraits that showed her in old age; the "Rainbow" portrait, painted in 1601 when she was in her mid-sixties, depicts her as a young woman.

She was celebrated in literature as well. Edmund Spenser's national epic poem *The Faerie Queen*, published in 1590, was inspired by Elizabeth's struggles against her enemies. Spenser, renowned as the Virgil of the Elizabethan golden age, recounted the glories of Elizabeth's reign, representing her as Gloriana, whose regal beams are like the sun:

> *In widest Ocean she her throne does reare,*
> *That over all the earth it may be seen,*
> *As morning Sunne her beams dispredden cleare.*

Elizabeth died after a short illness on March 24, 1603.

Her funeral was a magnificent state occasion that gave her people one last chance to experience the power of Elizabeth's image. The historian John Stow, writing shortly afterward, recorded, "they beheld her statue and picture lying upon the coffin set forth in royal robes [and] there was such a general sighing and groaning and weeping, and the like hath not been seen or known in the memory of man."

An eyewitness to her passing described her death: "the most resplendent sun setteth at last in the west."

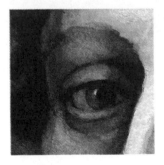

Summary of Achievements

- She began colonization of the New World. The state of Virginia is named in honor of Elizabeth, the Virgin Queen.

- She united the nation after eleven years of instability and bloodshed under Edward VI (1547–1553) and Mary I (1553–1558).

- She established the Anglican Church in 1559—the "Elizabethan Settlement."

- She repeatedly fought off threats from the two great superpowers of her age, France and Spain.

- The naval defeat of the Spanish in 1588 was her greatest victory, celebrated by the famous "Armada" portrait showing Elizabeth holding the world in her hand.

- The energies unleashed by her reign allowed the arts to flourish and led to the foundation of the British Empire.

- One of the longest ruling and most successful monarchs in history, she inspired the loyalty, love, and devotion of her courtiers and people for forty-five years.

- Elizabeth's reign planted the idea that ultimately led to a paradigm shift in beliefs about the abilities of women (see box).

ELIZABETH AND THE
LIBERATION OF WOMEN'S POWER

Elizabeth stands as an archetype of the liberation of feminine power. Her reign planted a seed in the mind of humanity about the capabilities and possibilities of women that culminated in the modern women's rights movements. Almost immediately after her death, Elizabeth's subjects described her reign as a golden age, and her achievements have continued to influence human consciousness through the ages.

Shakespeare recognized the impact of Elizabeth's genius. He undoubtedly drew inspiration from his own monarch in making his female characters powerful and multidimensional. The example of Elizabeth also influenced female writers such as Margaret, Duchess of Newcastle. One of the first critics to spot Shakespeare's ability to write convincingly about women, the duchess argued that the sexes were created with equal powers, but that women had been "usurped" by men. Her ideas were developed by Mary Astell (1668–1731), who established a reputation as a political philosopher and educator. Astell argued that the apparent inferiority of women was not natural but was acquired, and that its root lay in the narrow education given to girls at the time. She argued that a more liberal education would liberate women.

Later in the eighteenth century the great German writer Friedrich Schiller advanced the evolving perception of women with his play *Mary Stuart*. The play has two leading characters, Queen Mary Stuart of Scotland and Queen Elizabeth I. It deals with the agonies of mind suffered by Elizabeth before she ultimately decided she had to eliminate her rival for the English crown. This is the first play ever written in which the female characters dominate 100 percent of center stage.

As the nineteenth century dawned writing came to be seen as a suitable occupation for women, and female novelists assumed great prominence.

In *Pride and Prejudice*, for example, Jane Austen introduces her quintessential character, Elizabeth Bennet. Austen's powers are expressed through Elizabeth's depth, dimensionality, and independent thinking.

In addition to Austen the roll call of great names in the expression of this emerging consciousness is impressive: Mary Shelley, Frances Burney, George Eliot, Mary Wollstonecraft, Mrs. Gaskell, and Fanny Trollope. Their novels portrayed women as intelligent and powerful, and their publication corresponded with an acceleration in the call for women's rights. The first women's suffrage groups were formed in England, France, and the United States in the second half of the nineteenth century, and the word "feminist" entered the lexicon for the first time.

The paradigm shift initiated by Elizabeth's example gained further impetus from the contributions of outstanding women like Elizabeth Fry, Florence Nightingale, Sojourner Truth, Helena Blavatsky, Maria Montessori, Marie Curie, Mary Cassatt, Martha Graham, Margaret Mead, Golda Meier, Eleanor Roosevelt, and Margaret Thatcher. After women won the right to vote in Britain, the United States, and then elsewhere, the next great wave of women's empowerment broke after the end of the Second World War. It was heralded by Simone de Beauvoir's groundbreaking book *The Second Sex* and Betty Friedan's *The Feminine Mystique* (1963). Both women produced trenchant analyses of the subordinate role allotted to women in society. But it was the work of the Australian Germaine Greer that helped to complete the revolution in thinking about gender initiated by Elizabeth's reign. Greer's first major work, *The Female Eunuch* (1970), attacked the misrepresentation of women in a male-dominated society. Greer was a professor of English literature, and her writing on gender consciousness is underpinned by her speciality—an expertise on Elizabeth's England.

ELIZABETH AND YOU

What role does power play in your life? Are you comfortable being in charge, being the boss? How does your relationship to power affect your personal relationships? Would you like to gain more power? If you had more power, are you confident you could use it wisely?

Whether you are seeking to gain more power or simply to wield more effectively the power you have, and whether the sphere of influence in question is at home or at work, your power resides in your self-confidence and your skill in dealing with the people around you.

Elizabeth is a marvelous role model for anyone who seeks to use power intelligently. She defied stereotypes of a woman ruled by changing emotion more than principle and will, yet she made the most of her receptivity, empathy, and patience. By standing as a supreme example of the integration of traditionally "masculine" and "feminine" strengths, Elizabeth shows us the benefits of balance in all our relationships. Of course, Elizabeth is unsurpassed as an archetype of the liberation of feminine power—even if the full expression of that liberation was centuries away. In fact, it's still under way, and as time goes on it becomes increasingly evident that the integration of masculine and feminine principles is more than just a key to individual creativity and fulfillment: it is a social and cultural imperative. As intellectual historian Dr. Richard Tarnas concludes in *The Passion of the Western Mind*, we are on the verge of an unprecedented epochal transformation: "a triumphant and healing . . . reconciliation between the two great polarities, a union of opposites: a sacred marriage between the long-dominant but now alienated masculine and the long-suppressed but now ascending feminine."

You can increase your personal power and prepare yourself for that transformation by learning from Elizabeth. The exercises that follow will guide you to develop and expand your assertiveness and sensitivity in harmony. But first, spend some time contemplating the following self-assessment.

ELIZABETH:
WIELDING YOUR POWER
WITH BALANCE AND EFFECTIVENESS
SELF-ASSESSMENT

☐ I am comfortable wielding power.

☐ I am self-reliant and can keep important information to myself.

☐ I can wait patiently for the right moment.

☐ I am tolerant of other people's points of view.

☐ I am calm in a crisis.

☐ I am not easily intimidated.

☐ I try to study something new every day.

☐ I know how to delegate graciously at work and at home.

☐ I know how to reward the members of my support team.

☐ I am a sound financial manager.

☐ I have a strong sense of purpose.

☐ I am aware of my power and sensitive to the effects I have on others.

EXERCISES

THINKING LIKE ELIZABETH/WIELDING YOUR POWER WITH BALANCE AND EFFECTIVENESS

CREATE YOUR OWN COAT OF ARMS

Elizabeth knew the power of symbols and images and used them masterfully to influence her subjects and to inspire herself. The mythical phoenix was one of her favorite personal emblems. Like this bird of fable, she saw herself as rising from the flames of destruction and adversity.

In the Elizabethan Age a coat of arms was a sign of power and royal favor. Only a select few were granted the privilege of creating their own emblems (Shakespeare's father, for example, was originally denied permission to register his coat of arms, until his son's successes—and increasing wealth—won over the official registrars).

Now we are free to create our own symbols and to use them with pride. Just as companies create logos to strengthen their identity and influence in the marketplace, you can create your own personal logo to celebrate your own identity, which may then perhaps evolve into your own coat of arms.

Begin by expressing yourself through some creative doodling. Use a few pages from your notebook to play with images that inspire you. Don't try to create a finished product in your first session. Instead, let the idea of a personal symbol incubate in your soul for a day or two after your first creative doodling experiment. Keep your eyes, mind, and heart open to the world around you and look for images that capture your imagination and reflect something wonderful that resonates within you. Then experiment with another series of drawings and doodles. At the end of the second session craft the most compelling images into a rough-draft coat of arms. Then continue observing, doodling, incubating, experimenting, and refining your symbol until you feel that it's where you want it to be. You'll know it's "there" when you look at it and feel a frission of inspiration that reminds you of your ideals, purpose, and potentiality.

MASTER THE ART OF LISTENING

Elizabeth was a great listener. She surrounded herself with knowledgeable councilors and successfully used their advice. Of all the skills necessary for effective leadership, listening may be the most important. You can strengthen your Elizabethan listening prowess by experimenting with the following exercises.

Bad Listening

Begin by listing all the manifestations of bad listening you might encounter in the average week. Your list may include:

- ▲ Skeptical facial expressions.
- ▲ Finishing my sentences.
- ▲ Overaffirming—"Uh-huh, uh-huh, uh-huh."
- ▲ Stereotyping—"That's a typical [female, male, marketing, finance, liberal, conservative, etc.] perspective."
- ▲ Looking at his watch.
- ▲ Answering the phone.
- ▲ Constant fidgeting.
- ▲ Interrupting.
- ▲ Changing the subject.
- ▲ Continual self-referencing ("Oh yeah, the same thing happens to me all the time" or the classic "Well, enough about me, I'd like to hear from you; what do you think about me!").
- ▲ Giving unwanted advice.
- ▲ Failure to make eye contact.
- ▲ Gooey, invasive, pseudo-sincere eye contact.

▲ Leaving the room ("Please just carry on with what you're saying, I'll be back in a minute").

▲ Falling asleep.

After making your list, try this exercise with a partner. Tell your partner a real-life story, something meaningful that you'd really like to share. Your partner's job is to practice bad listening—to manifest as many of the non-affirming listening habits as possible. Your task is to persist in communicating your message. After a minute or so, switch roles.

When this exercise is practiced in a class setting, the results are always fascinating. Tension quickly fills the room, often manifested in near-hysterical laughter. Even though everyone knows it's only a game, a real fight could break out if the exercise is allowed to continue for more than two or three minutes.

Clearly, bad listening can be painful for everyone concerned.

The first phase of this exercise sets the stage for a deeper consideration of listening. Before completing the exercise—when you and your partner truly listen to each other tell these same stories—complete the following.

In your notebook, write the name of a friend, a family member, and a coworker with whom you've recently conversed.

Then ask yourself, "Who did the most talking?" and record your answers.

For each recalled conversation, estimate a ratio of listening to speaking for each of the speakers.

Overall, do you speak more than 50 percent of the time?

If so, experiment with listening more and speaking less.

Make the "art of listening" a theme for a week and observe yourself in conversations each day. Reflect on the following questions to get the most from your theme of better listening.

▲ How much energy and attention do you devote to preparing your response when someone else is speaking?

▲ Are you comfortable with pauses in conversations?

- Are you patient with people who are slow to get to the point?
- Do you listen attentively rather than focusing on what you're going to say next?
- Do you listen with the motive to understand?
- Does your body language show that you are really listening?
- Do you check out your understanding of what the speaker said to see if you heard her actual meaning?
- Are you able to read the feelings of the speaker as well as pick up the facts?
- Do you listen equally carefully during an entertaining conversation and a factual one?
- Do you make an effort to draw into the conversation people who are shy or noncommunicative?
- Do you acknowledge other people's experience and ideas before sharing your own?

Courage is what it takes to stand up and speak; courage is also what it takes to sit down and listen.

—SIR WINSTON CHURCHILL

To get the most from your "listening" theme, ask a friend, family member, and coworker to each give you constructive feedback on your effectiveness as a listener. Ask, "What could I do, specifically, to be a better listener?" Record their responses in your notebook as close to verbatim as you are able. Avoid discussing or arguing about the feedback, just listen to it and record it as objectively as you can. After your friend, family member, or colleague appears to have finished, ask, "Is there anything else?" Again, record their responses without discussion. If you can discipline yourself to listen and record without responding, you'll find that you've taken a great leap forward in your listening power.

TAKE THE POWER!

Elizabeth's confidence and inner power is delightfully expressed in a comment she made to a delegation of members of Parliament in 1567: "I thank God that I am endowed with such qualities that if I were turned out of the realm in my petticoat, I were able to live in any place in Christendom."

Elizabeth had a well-developed sense of personal power before she ascended the throne. Even as a little girl she trusted her intuition and believed in herself despite the loss of her mother, disinheritance, and imprisonment. She empowered herself with a vast array of knowledge, learned languages, developed exceptional "people skills," and was purpose-driven, all of which are needed to be successful today. One of the secrets of Elizabeth's extraordinary personal power was her powerful sense of purpose: she saw herself as protector of her realm, and this overarching purpose gave her tremendous strength in the face of opposition and adversity.

Do you have a sense of purpose or goal greater than yourself?

You can dramatically increase your sense of personal power by clarifying your sense of purpose. A number of the exercises in the other chapters have encouraged reflection on this clarity of purpose, because passion for a purpose is one of the most distinctive elements of genius. The next exercise is designed to help you further bolster this power-generating clarity. In no more than five minutes, please write a statement of your life purpose, in twenty-five words or less. By writing succinctly and quickly you'll cut through to the essence of your life's guiding principles.

Do this exercise as many times as necessary until you feel that you have developed a powerful, self-motivating purpose statement.

Personal Power Inventory

As sovereign, Elizabeth enjoyed a supreme position of power that she used with great wisdom. Her remarkable success was grounded, however, in the highly developed sense of personal power she brought to the throne. She always understood that her true effectiveness required give-and-take with a wide range of courtiers, military leaders, politicians, diplomats, and commoners, and she balanced that sensitivity to others with a profound belief in her own abilities that allowed her to assume the mantle, prerogatives, and symbols of power with absolute confidence.

Elizabeth equipped herself with the knowledge and strength necessary to lead before she became sovereign. Are you equipping yourself to take on more power?

Are you aware of your own power and the effect you have on others? Are you secure enough to empower others? Do you take full responsibility for that power? Many parents, bosses, teachers, and coaches underestimate the effect they have on their children, employees, students, and players, respectively.

As a theme for a day do a personal power inventory. In other words, aim to assess the power you wield to achieve your goals, to get your wants and needs met, and to influence others. Look especially for situations in which you may be underestimating your impact.

Of course, as part of your power inventory you'll no doubt become more aware of the situations and relationships in which you are subject to the power of others. Make a note of those that challenge you the most and then ask yourself, "What would Elizabeth recommend?"

Alexandra, a new partner in a law firm in Connecticut, reports that she has always been somewhat afraid of her own power. As part of her own personal power inventory she noted, "I have always seen powerful women as harsh and overbearing. Not only that, but power seemed to carry a heavy burden of responsibility. Looking at Elizabeth gave me a whole new way of thinking about power. She inspired me to rethink my beliefs.

"I'm becoming a more objective observer of power, and I'm especially sensitive to discerning who wields their positional power for self-gratification instead of for the good of the whole organization. I'm honing my focus on my own use of power. As a new partner, I'm starting to realize that I can be sensitive to others without apologizing for my own strengths. I'm becoming more comfortable with my position and my power and I'm committed to the idea of using it wisely."

FREEDOM FROM INTIMIDATION

Do you ever feel intimidated? Do you maintain your sense of self-confidence when you are with people who seem better educated, more eloquent, or more accomplished than you are? Do you sometimes feel your power sapping away as you walk to the front of the room to address senior people in your organization? Have you ever felt a bit queasy when walking into an elegant restaurant or entering a room filled with people who seem better-looking and better-dressed than you are?

Most of us can relate to at least one of the situations described above. And we can all call on Elizabeth's example to inspire us in the face of situations that may diminish our sense of personal power. Elizabeth was indomitable and impossible to intimidate, even as a little girl. When threatened she once responded: "I care not for death; for all men are mortal and though I be a woman I have as good a courage . . . as ever my father ever had . . . I will never be by violence constrained to do anything."

Of course, Elizabeth believed that she was chosen by God to rule, and this no doubt helped to inspire her self-belief. Nevertheless, even without a royal mandate, we can free ourselves from intimidation and access our personal power by embracing the scepter of responsibility. In other words, remember that you are free to choose your response to any situation and that "We teach people how to treat us."

EAT LIKE A RENAISSANCE QUEEN

Elizabethan recipe books make delightful reading—one recipe for roast pork starts "take a fair pigge and smite off his head"! In Elizabeth's time cheese, eggs, all manner of fresh salads, vegetables, and fruit were the popular fare, along with treats such as meat pies and fruit tarts.

Potatoes were rare and considered a delicacy, with a reputation as an aphrodisiac! Instead a plentiful supply of bread furnished carbohydrates and soaked up various sauces. Bread, or for banquets ground almonds, was

And lucent syrops, tinct with

cinnamon:

Manna and dates, in argosy

transferr'd

From Fez: and spiced

dainties, every one . . .

—JOHN KEATS

also used to thicken soups, stews, and sauces, and to make desserts.

You can add some Elizabethan Renaissance style to your next dinner party. Scatter your table with delicate sweet-smelling Elizabethan flowers such as violets and rose petals. Serve breads adorned with aniseed and caraway and spray the air with rosewater. Invite your friends to dress as courtiers or commoners, or perhaps as their favorite Shakespearean characters. Ask each guest to bring and be prepared to read a selection from a favorite piece of Elizabethan literature.

Here are some recipes that you can serve, inspired by Thomas Dawson's *The Good Huswifes Jewell* (1596).

"Groached" Salmon

The original recipe begins: "Take your salmon and boil him in fair water, rosemary and thyme; and in the seething [boiling water] put a quart of strong ale to it. And so let it boil till it be enough. Then take it from the fire and let it cool. Then take your salmon out of the pan and put it in an earthen pan or wooden bowl, and there put so much broth as will cover him. Put into the same broth a good deal of vinegar, so that it will be tart with it."

As a modern adaptation: put the salmon steaks or fillets on aluminum foil and then place them in an oven-safe pan. Instead of actually boiling the salmon, you can "groach" it—groaching is a combination of grilling and poaching. Coat your salmon with fresh herbs, rock salt, and whole peppercorns, then pour the ale (you can use white wine instead) over the whole thing and put it under the broiler. It will grill and poach simultaneously (hence, groaching). When it's perfect pink in the middle remove it and place it on a serving dish garnished with fresh herbs, and then drizzle some extra-virgin olive oil and a few drops of aged balsamic vinegar on top. Serve with Aphrodisia Potatoes (see next recipe).

Aphrodisia Potatoes

(Serves 8)

4 lbs. baking potatoes
½ cup whole milk
¾ cup sour cream
2 tablespoons fresh chives, chopped
1 tablespoon truffle oil
Salt, to taste
Pepper, to taste
Sprinkling of ground almonds

Wash and then peel the potatoes. Cut into one-inch cubes. Cook potatoes in boiling salted water to cover until tender, approximately 15 minutes. Drain. Return to pot. Mash with a fork or potato masher. Stir in remaining ingredients. Season to taste with salt and pepper, and garnish with ground almonds. Serve immediately.

ELIZABETH AT WORK

Professor John Kotter of Harvard Business School and many others have emphasized the importance of balancing the skills of leadership and management in the workplace.

Leaders, according to Kotter, guide the process of change, empower others to achieve important goals, craft the strategy for success, and nurture the vision and culture of the organization. Managers, on the other hand, focus more on monitoring performance, implementing tactics, setting budgets, and controlling costs. The success of great chief executives like Jack Welch of General Electric and Mary Kay Ash of the Mary Kay Company is, according to Kotter's research, attributable to the ability to integrate both of these modes.

Elizabeth is a supreme role model for anyone who holds or aspires to a senior position in an organization. She combined the best elements of leadership and management. Warren Bennis, author of the classic *On Becoming a Leader,* comments, "Managers do things right, Leaders do the right things." Elizabeth had an uncanny knack for doing the right things right.

As an inspiring leader, she rallied her subjects in the face of grave challenges. Her amazing speech to her troops at Tilbury—given in full armor astride a white charger—serves as a stirring example:

"Let tyrants fear: I have so behaved myself that under God I have placed my chiefest strength and safeguard in the loyal hearts and goodwill of my subjects. Wherefore I am come among you at this time . . . being resolved in the midst and heat of the battle to live and die amongst you all, to lay down for my God and for my kingdom and for my people mine honour and my blood even in the dust." When she concluded her gracious speech her soldiers roared their approval with a "mighty shout."

But Elizabeth's success in rallying her troops to victory at Tilbury might have been even more attributable to the words she spoke next:

"You have deserved rewards and crowns; and we do assure you, in the words of a prince, they shall be duly paid you."

One of the strongest elements in Elizabeth's successful reign was her ability to balance her visionary, inspiring leadership with an unrelenting emphasis on sound financial management. Her organization's "incentive and compensation" program was brilliantly crafted and administered with great dexterity. She insisted on getting good value in all her expenditures and was cautious and prudent without being mean and cheap.

Elizabeth also knew something that is essential for anyone in a position of power and responsibility to remember at all times: that everyone was watching her slightest move and that therefore only impeccable standards of behavior were acceptable. As she told Parliament: "We princes are set on a stage in sight of all the world; a spot is soon spied on our garments, a blemish quickly noted in our doings."

She once advised another queen, "if your subjects see your words so honeyed while your acts are envenomed, what can they think."

Of course, two of Elizabeth's management tools—Tower banishings and beheadings—aren't on the approved practices list of modern corporate human resource departments. But many workplaces are redolent, nonetheless, with all the intrigue of the Elizabethan court. Let the example of Queen Elizabeth I inspire you to monitor the alignment between your words and your actions as you gain power, and to wield your power with balance, effectiveness, and grace.

Debbie Dunnam, vice president for sales and marketing at Compaq Computer, comments on Elizabeth as a role model:

"Elizabeth's insights regarding the impact of her behavior on her 'employees' is something that, as a leader, I aim to remember every day. And her crisp remark about the importance of matching action with 'honeyed' words couldn't be more timely. As a woman in a relatively senior position, I'm most inspired by Elizabeth's balance of sensitivity and strength. It's clear to me that if Elizabeth had been too sensitive, she never would have survived. However, if she had been too ruthless, she would not have been able to lead her country forward in the great strides they took. That balance is essential in the environment I work in—it's an environment which moves incredibly fast. It often requires me to make split-second decisions and take immediate, decisive actions. But I've learned that Elizabeth's patience, perhaps the hardest yet most rewarding skill to acquire, is also crucial to me as a leader. She reminds me that sometimes it better to pause and consider multiple options and that time will occasionally provide the best, most creative solution of all."

ELIZABETH'S MUSIC:
TWO ASPECTS OF THE SOUND OF POWER

Elizabeth loved music and played a pianolike instrument known as the "virginal." One music critic at court commented that "she plays reasonably well, for a Queen."

Legend has it that Elizabeth's father, King Henry VIII, composed the beloved melody of "Greensleeves." True or not, this delightful composition is wonderfully evocative of the "Golden Age" of Henry's daughter's reign. The pure, unaffected melody, tranquillity of mood, and pastoral dignity of this piece is reflective of the best of things eminently English.

If "Greensleeves" represents the more informal and personal elements of Elizabeth's reign, Henry Purcell's Voluntary in D Major, written shortly after Elizabeth's death, captures the more formal, regal elements of her rule. This piece, with its solemn processional grandeur, is a musical expression of the pomp and power of the "Virgin Queen". It was chosen by Elizabeth II and Prince Phillip as the theme music for their wedding.

ONWARD TO SHAKESPEARE

Queen Elizabeth was a great lover of the arts and had a particular fondness for the theater. In the movie *Shakespeare in Love* Judi Dench portrays Elizabeth I as a champion of the artistic freedom of an emerging young actor and playwright named Will. Shakespeare biographer Park Honan tells us that Elizabeth "enjoyed theatre, and very nearly squashed proposals to ban plays . . . on Sunday . . . Her fondness for spectacle was shared by many, but she was the one who did most to ensure that her reign would be known for encouraging the drama."

We can be grateful to Elizabeth for nurturing the environment that allowed Shakespeare to develop and express his extraordinary gifts. Will Shakespeare was four years old when Elizabeth ascended the throne. As we've seen, one of the secrets of her successful reign over the next forty-five years was her exceptional degree of self-knowledge, complemented by her extraordinary ability to communicate with courtiers, councilors, and commoners. These two abilities—self-knowledge and interpersonal skill—combine to form emotional intelligence. How can you develop your emotional intelligence? Well, Shakespeare's works, and the lessons of his life, provide an endless source of discovery for this profoundly important genius quality.

William Shakespeare

(1564–1616)

Cultivating Your Emotional Intelligence

Thou hast been . . .

A man that Fortune's buffets and rewards

Has taken with equal thanks . . . Give me that man

That is not passion's slave, and I will wear him

In my heart's core, aye, in my heart of hearts

As I do thee . . .

—WILLIAM SHAKESPEARE, *HAMLET*

They say that youth is wasted on the young; I fear that Shakespeare is too. If you are like me, you had a hard time appreciating, in high school and college, how much Shakespeare had to say about the life

The conflicting material on Shakespeare again gave me more freedom of interpretation. To my mind, no one has better understood human nature. I wanted him to be very human; hence the lips

that lay ahead. As kids, we were doing well if we could see beyond the archaic language and stuffy formality to enjoy the lust, intrigue, passion, and humor on every page. As adults, of course, we are more aware that they are there—if we're wise enough to give Shakespeare a second chance. But many of us need help discovering that the life lessons of Shakespeare's magnificent array of unforgettable characters can be relevant to our own efforts to master life's most important skill: emotional intelligence.

A sense of self-mastery, of being able to withstand the emotional storms that the buffeting of Fortune brings, rather than being "passion's slave," has been praised as a virtue since the time of Plato. The ancient Greek word for it was *sophrosyne,* "care and intelligence in conducting one's life; a tempered balance and wisdom." Lately, in a term popularized by Daniel Goleman, we have come to know this ability as emotional intelligence. Like any form of intelligence, emotional intelligence can be studied, practiced, and cultivated; by doing so, we can bring direct benefits to our daily lives. No longer do we have to think of our demeanor or our "people skills" as vague, unquantifiable, or beyond our control. In fact, we can demystify it even further by seeing emotional intelligence as the combination of two distinct types of intelligence: intrapersonal intelligence, or getting along with oneself, and interpersonal intelligence, or getting along with others.

Shakespeare's work shows us how to cultivate both intrapersonal intelligence, by gaining insight into ourselves, and interpersonal intelligence, by enriching our understanding of others. Shakespeare's uncanny observa-

that are about to speak, the eyes that are reacting to someone. When I was finished, several of my friends commented that he looked sexy! Well, no one better understood the emotional intelligence of women and men, and our relationships to each other.—Norma Miller

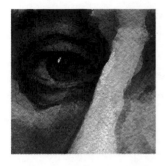

tions of human nature in all its complexity make his works a vast treasure trove for students of emotional intelligence.

Polonius's advice to his son Laertes in *Hamlet*, "to thine own self be true," expresses the essence of Shakespeare's program of self-knowledge development. But the program is anything but simple, for it involves a confounding study of every foible of ego, self-delusion, vanity, and pride. By offering a remarkable diversity of characters, roles, and relationships, the Bard guides us through a dazzling universe of human interplay. The sheer volume of characters who came from his pen—over 1,200—sets him apart from all other writers. "No one, before or since Shakespeare, made so many separate selves," writes Harold Bloom in *Shakespeare: The Invention of the Human*. More remarkable, that incomparable assortment of characters demonstrates a peerless sensitivity to the infinite possibilities of human nature—and reflects them back to us. "Our ideas as to what makes the self authentically human owe more to Shakespeare than ought to be possible," writes Bloom. "Shakespeare will go on explaining us, in part because he invented us." Shakespeare's approach to the "invention" of the self is invaluable for anyone who seeks to live a more authentic life.

Interpersonal intelligence is the ability to understand other people: what motivates them, how they work, how to work cooperatively with them. Successful salespeople, politicians, teachers, clinicians, and religious leaders are all likely to be individuals with high degrees of interpersonal intelligence. Intrapersonal intelligence . . . is a correlative ability, turned inward. It is a capacity to form an accurate . . . model of oneself and to be able to use that model to operate effectively in life.

—HOWARD GARDNER

THE ESSENCE OF THE HUMAN DRAMA

Shakespeare's legacy is enshrined in the narrative poems *Venus and Adonis* and *The Rape of Lucrece*, in his cycle of 154 sonnets first printed in 1609, and above all in the 36 plays collected after his death in the famous first folio edition of 1623.

The plays fall into four main categories: tragedies (such as *Macbeth, King Lear*, and *Romeo and Juliet*); comedies (*A Midsummer Night's Dream, A Comedy of Errors*, and *Twelfth Night*); romances (*The Winter's Tale* and *The Tempest*); and histories (both classical histories such as *Julius Caesar* and *Troilus and Cressida* and the great cycle of plays charting the then recent history of the Wars of the Roses, which starts with *Richard II* and ends with *Henry VIII*).

John Hemings and Henry Condell produced the famous first folio edition of Shakespeare's plays in 1623, seven years after Shakespeare's death. According to the editors, earlier efforts to publish Shakespeare and record him for posterity were simply pirate versions, which had mangled Shakespeare's brilliant verse. Their first folio is the true authoritative text. In their introduction they wrote: "as he was a happy imitator of nature, he was a most gentle expresser of it. His mind and hand went together and what he thought he uttered with that easiness, that we have scarce received from him a blot in his papers . . . his wit can no more lie hid, then it could be lost. Read him, therefore, and again and again."

Just as Elizabeth I initiated the eventual success of English as the primary world language, Shakespeare helped to shape and create that language. Shakespeare mobilized more than 20,000 different words, a full tenth of which had never been recorded before. His work lives in translation into more than fifty languages. Shakespeare has influenced not only the development of the theatrical tradition, but also the writing of poetry, essays, novels, and other forms of artistic endeavor, including opera, film, and ballet.

Because his appeal is timeless and universal his work is readily transferred to other contexts: twentieth-century New York forms the backdrop to the reworking of *Romeo and Juliet* in *West Side Story*, and a fascist regime features in Ian McKellen and Richard Loncraine's film version of *Richard III*. Ethan Hawke stars in a recent film version of *Hamlet* centered around turnover at "the Denmark Corporation." Themes of romance, betrayal, love, fear of gang warfare, and brutal tyranny unite past and present audiences on a global scale. Shakespeare's work celebrates the essence of our common human experience.

THE UNIVERSAL SELF

William Shakespeare was the supreme literary manifestation of the Renaissance, who knew, as Leonardo da Vinci did with his *Canon of Proportion,* that "Man is the measure of all things." But just as Leonardo's example lives far beyond the Renaissance, so does Shakespeare's. As Ben Jonson wrote, Shakespeare "was not of an age, but for all time."

According to Harold Bloom, it was Ben Jonson who "first saw and said where Shakespeare's eminence was located: in a diversity of persons." Indeed, Shakespeare's range of investigation into his concept of the inner self is dazzling in its breadth and depth. His characters come to life not so much as Protestants or Catholics, Danes or Englishmen, but as archetypes of consciousness.

Shakespeare is able to show us so much about ourselves because what he reveals of the self is universal and true. His plays are simple and accessible enough to be understood and enjoyed by masses of people from all continents. Yet they are so infinitely complex that scholars continue a never-ending quest to fathom his depths. Shakespeare still has much to tell us, and the emotional intelligence in his work has not yet been fully measured. If you are tired of Shakespeare, as Ben Jonson suggested, you are tired of life.

Even the father of the scientific study of emotions, Sigmund Freud, acknowledged his debt to Shakespeare, from whom he drew many of his case histories. (He maintained, for example, that the key to *Hamlet* was the Oedipal relationship between Hamlet and his mother, Gertrude, and that all earlier attempts to interpret the play were "differing and contradictory.") In fact, Shakespeare conveys the human drama so effectively as to foreshadow virtually everything that the father of psychoanalysis would later tell the world about the human psyche. Three centuries before him, Macbeth's question to his physician anticipates the very premise of the discipline Freud would create:

Canst thou not minister to a mind diseased;

Pluck from the memory a rooted sorrow;

Raze out the written troubles of the brain;

And, with some sweet oblivious antidote,

Cleanse the stuffed bosom of that perilous stuff

Which weighs upon the heart?

—WILLIAM SHAKESPEARE, *MACBETH*

Shakespeare provides a monumental guide for understanding the inner drama of your own emotional life. He knew that mental fears could be crippling and called our doubts "traitors." Deservedly famous is the revelation of Lady Macbeth's guilty conscience in the famous sleepwalking scene, in which she declares that "all the perfumes of Arabia will not sweeten this little hand." Through his female characters who take on male disguise, such as Viola in *Twelfth Night* and Rosalind in *As You Like It*, we see the tension between our sense of identity and the images we present to the world. Shakespeare also offers insights into overcoming our self-imposed mental limitations. "There is nothing either good or bad," he wrote "but thinking makes it so." Similarly Octavius Caesar advises Cleopatra after she had been taken captive with the following words: "make not your thoughts your prisons." And responding to his mother's inner conflicts, Hamlet offers profoundly useful advice that speaks to the essence of changing a habit of body and mind:

Gertrude: O Hamlet, thou hast cleft my heart in twain.

Hamlet: O throw away the worser part of it

And live the pure with the other half.

Good night. But go not to my uncle's bed.

Assume a virtue if you have it not.

. . . Refrain tonight,

And that shall lend a kind of easiness

To the next abstinence, the next more easy;

For use almost can change the stamp of nature,

And either lodge the devil or throw him out

With wondrous potency.

—WILLIAM SHAKESPEARE, *HAMLET*

OBSERVING EMOTION:
BALANCE AND PROPORTION

Shakespeare was clearly an immensely receptive, accurate, yet unobtrusive observer of people's actions and emotions. His genius lay in the ability to observe the fullest range of human experience and emotions and to express them in the most compelling way.

So powerful were his observation skills, noted Margaret Cavendish, Duchess of Newcastle, one of the first critics to try to analyze the universal appeal of Shakespeare's plays, that he was able to enter the mind of any character, regardless of gender. "So well hath he expressed in his plays all sorts of persons as one would think he had been transformed into every one of those persons he hath described," she wrote in 1664. "Nay one would think that he had been metamorphosed from a man to a woman, for who could describe Cleopatra better than he hath done, and many other females of his own creating?"

Shakespeare's plays range across the entire spectrum of human emotions, which he described with a precision that could be rooted only in careful observation—both of his own emotional life and that of others. As a result, he evoked these emotions with unprecedented intensity and dimensionality. He was able to capture both the most tender of human feelings, such as the love of a parent for a child, and the most brutal, as any viewer of his blood-soaked tragedies can attest.

His fascination with the human psyche involves all ages. In Jaques' great speech in *As You Like It,* he identifies the Seven Ages of Man: the "mewling and *puking*" infant followed by the "whining schoolboy with his satchel and shining morning face, creeping like snail unwillingly to school," the lover "sighing like a furnace," the soldier "jealous in honor, sudden and quick in quarrel," the justice "full of wise saws," old age "a world too wide" and finally senility and "second childishness." All seven of these ages came under examination in his work, and his tragedies in particular explore some of these ages in detail. Thus we can see Hamlet as the young man, Othello as the lover, Macbeth as the soldier and politician, and Lear as the old man.

These plays show us how we come to grief because of the frailties of the human ego, through lack of balance, perspective, or proportion in our personal affairs. For Hamlet, the ability to see and analyze every side of every question is perverted into a creeping paralysis of the will, an inability to act decisively. For Othello, intense love is warped into insane jealousy, while Macbeth's honest aspirations to become a leader metamorphose into a nakedly ruthless drive to power. Finally, Lear's justifiable pride in the achievements of his reign subsides into petulance and ultimately howlingly impotent tirades of self-pity. Shakespeare shows us that it is only through the abandonment of egotism and a conscious decision to embrace balance that we can resolve the conflicts in our lives. Nowhere is this more magnificently evident than in *The Tempest, The Winter's Tale,* and *Cymbeline,* the late plays of reconciliation that many critics regard as Shakespeare's most sublimely profound works.

Drawing on his acute observation of the human soul, Shakespeare was able to bring new, revealing light to the great universal dramas in human life—from the nature of love and forgiveness, to the essence of political power and of relations between men and women, to the inevitability of death—and our reaction to it:

> *Ay, but to die,*
>
> *And go we know not where;*
>
> *. . . The weariest and most loathed worldly life*
>
> *That age, ache, penury, and imprisonment*
>
> *Can lay on nature, is a paradise*
>
> *To what we fear of death.*
>
> —WILLIAM SHAKESPEARE, *MEASURE FOR MEASURE*

and

To die, to sleep;

To sleep: perchance to dream: ay, there's the rub;

For in that sleep of death what dreams may come?

When we have shuffled off this mortal coil,

Must give us pause.

—WILLIAM SHAKESPEARE, *HAMLET*

Just as he awakens the cold fear of death, Shakespeare luxuriates in his celebration of love in all its complexities and splendor. He presents love as an eternal tide in an ocean of loneliness; we cannot read Shakespeare, truly know the essence of his work, without glimpsing some measure of the redemptive power that love holds in our own lives. Shakespeare presents it as the ultimate force of transformation, and he brings to bear on the vicissitudes of mortal existence like an Elizabethan Rumi. In *The Comedy of Errors*, Antipholus speaks to Luciana as if she were a goddess of love:

Teach me, dear creature, how to think and speak.
Lay open to my earthy gross conceit,
Smothered in errors, feeble, shallow, weak,
the folded meaning of your words' deceit.
Against my soul's pure truth why labour you
To make it wander in an unknown field?
Are you a god? Would you create me new?
Transform me, then, and to your power I'll yield.

STUDENT OF THE SOUL

Love, self-knowledge, people skills . . . these were certainly not the names of courses offered in the august halls of Oxford or Cambridge, already the great English universities by Shakespeare's time. Although none of Shakespeare's working papers survive, it is clear that he never attended either university. The greatest body of work in the English language was not the product of a great formal education. Shakespeare's education was indisputably informal—welcome news to anyone today who sets out to read him outside the halls of academia, to be sure, but also an inspiring reminder that one need not receive the finest formal education to leave a lasting mark. Shakespeare's school—as for many of us— was life itself, a fitting method for mastering the intricacies of emotional intelligence.

But how did Shakespeare develop the mastery of language to express his exquisite insights into human nature? We know that he received a level of education that was typical in the grammar schools of the time, where the emphasis on the new humanist learning would have given him a grounding in the study of classical myths, history, and Latin. And he lived in an age when sensitivity to language was much more refined than it is today. Yet he was probably not an outstanding student at school; he would have been encouraged to seek a university education if he had been, and as his friend Ben Jonson later acknowledged, he knew "small Latin and less Greek."

Park Honan, author of the definitive biography of the Bard, offers a journey through Shakespeare's known life that explains much about his development as a writer and a student of the soul. He describes the young Shakespeare as "a smart, enthusiastic lad who had fled from pedantry, but prized what he had learned," and indeed made the most of it with "a remarkable, assimilating mind." Two of Shakespeare's elder siblings died at birth in plague-ridden Stratford, and young William was raised with special care and intense love by his mother, Mary. It is not unlikely that this influenced his extraordinary sensitivity to nuances of emotion, his apparent freedom from the macho-egotism of contemporaries like Marlowe and Jonson, and his Olympian gift of empathic understanding. Honan sheds light on young Will's theatrical orientation by explaining that the youth of Stratford was exposed to many of the finest theatrical touring companies of the day, including those sponsored by the nobility of Leicester, Warwick, Berkeley, and Essex.

Though "hungering for books and learning," according to Honan, Shakespeare vigorously pursued the kind of education that could only be found through life itself. His marriage to an older woman when he was just eighteen was motivated in part by an "urge to purchase experience." And by age twenty Will Shakespeare likely "had known more domestic complexities and responsibilities and probably a more intense emotional life than some people have known at 40."

Nevertheless, so perceptive and sublime is his work that debate has long raged about whether a man of Shakespeare's education and background could truly have been the author. At least four other possible candidates have been put forward as secret originators of the Shakespeare canon—Edward de Vere, Earl of Oxford (1550–1604), Sir Francis Bacon (1561–1626), Christopher Marlowe (1564–1593) and Elizabeth I. All of these "alternative Shakespeare" theories emerged years after the death of the great man, springing from the argument that little is known about Shakespeare's private life and education—and the more modern prejudice that what is known could not lead to such greatness.

We do know all his major life events, which were recorded at the time: his birth and christening on April 26, 1564, in Stratford; his marriage to Anne Hathaway in 1582, the births of his daughter Susanna and of a twin boy and girl, Hamnett and Judith; and finally his death on April 23, 1616. We also know that Shakespeare's father, John, was at one point relatively prosperous—he was an alderman, or town councilor, in Stratford—but later fell on hard times. Other documents chart Shakespeare's involvement in lawsuits and his gradual acquisition of a sizable amount of property in his hometown and London.

We also know, from the many contemporary references to him from his times, that Shakespeare's mastery of the subtleties of emotional intelligence extended beyond his works into a remarkable ability to get along with others. From 1595 he owned a share of and acted with the Lord Chamberlain's Men, who later became the King's Men in 1603 when James I took the throne. Shakespeare is the only major playwright of the period to have had such a long-lasting relationship with one company of players. Shakespeare also worked successfully with John Fletcher, who may have had a hand in writing *Henry VIII, Two Noble Kinsmen,* and a lost play, *Cardenio,* with him. Shakespeare also collaborated with four other writers to create the play *Sir Thomas More* in the 1590s.

THE ART OF GLOVE MAKING

Shakespeare's work is filled with many references to the details of the Warwickshire countryside where he was raised and to his father's craft of glove making. Of the scores of references to gloves in his work, perhaps the most famous example is Romeo's exultation: "O, that I were a glove upon that hand."

Freud theorized that better documented men have been claimed as the author of Shakespeare's work because there is a "need to acquire affective relationships with such men, to add them to the fathers, teachers, exemplars whom we have known or whose influence we have already experienced, in the expectation that their personalities will be just as fine and admirable as those works of art of theirs which we possess." One could also argue that the academic establishment—which has never been known as a hotbed of emotional intelligence—felt a need to claim Shakespeare as its own, which has had the unfortunate effect of making it easy for the rest of us to miss his relevance to our nonacademic lives.

Harold Bloom surmises: "By reading Shakespeare, I can gather that he did not like lawyers, preferred drinking to eating, and evidently lusted after both genders. But I certainly do not have a clue as to whether he favored Protestantism or Catholicism or neither, and I do not know whether he believed or disbelieved in God or in resurrection. His politics, like his religion, evades me, but I think he was too wary to have any."

The case for an alternative Shakespeare is never as convincing as it needs to be: Elvis is dead, Oswald shot Kennedy, and Shakespeare wrote Shakespeare.

Yet his genius remains mysterious. As Norrie Epstein suggests in *The Friendly Shakespeare,* "Neither a sensitive consumptive like Keats nor a 'man's man' like Hemingway, Shakespeare does not readily lend himself to romantic mythmaking. In his infinite complexity, he resembles one of his own ambiguous creations."

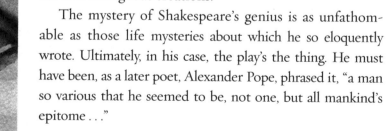

The mystery of Shakespeare's genius is as unfathomable as those life mysteries about which he so eloquently wrote. Ultimately, in his case, the play's the thing. He must have been, as a later poet, Alexander Pope, phrased it, "a man so various that he seemed to be, not one, but all mankind's epitome . . ."

Summary of Achievements

- Shakespeare is the greatest writer of all time. Only Homer—whose output is much smaller and whose themes are less wide—comes close. Shakespeare scores over Dante, Austen, Borges, Rumi, Virgil, Racine, Milton, Schiller, and Goethe by the sheer breadth and universality of his writing.

- A verbal virtuoso, he displayed a truly astonishing range of vocabulary, and crafted thousands of words, phrases, and concepts that have entered the mainstream of the English language. Shakespeare outdoes the Bible as a source of linguistic expression in English. So many phrases we now regard as clichés, because they have become so popular, were actually freshly minted formulations from the pen of the Bard.

- The vast emotional sweep of his drama and poems paved the way for the development of modern-day psychoanalysis. Freud frequently turned to Shakespeare to illustrate and explore his theories.

- He exerted a commanding and enduring influence on world cultures, which looks set to persist into the twenty-first century and beyond.

- He rose to literary and social prominence in his own day from humble beginnings and without a university education.

- Shakespeare's majestic history cycle, ranging over nine plays from *Richard II* to *Henry VIII,* is the quintessential English epic, on a par with Homer for the Greeks, Virgil for Rome, or Dante for Italy.

SHAKESPEARE AND YOU

All the world's a stage,

And all the men and women merely players:

They have their exits and their entrances;

And one man in his time plays many parts . . .

—WILLIAM SHAKESPEARE, *AS YOU LIKE IT*

〜

One hardly needs to point out the value of developing one's emotional intelligence, for which Shakespeare provides such eloquent guidance. Its importance cannot be overstated; our traditional measure of intelligence, or IQ, contributes "about 20 percent to the factors that determine life success, which leaves 80 percent to other forces," writes Daniel Goleman. But that 80 percent needn't be left to chance, he points out. "Emotional life is a domain that, as sure as math or reading, can be handled with greater or lesser skill, and requires its unique set of competencies."

Shakespeare helps us play the many parts we are called upon to play in the multitasking, multimodal lives many of us lead. Our ever-accelerating pace requires a flexibility of mind that adapts gracefully to many different "scenes" and "stages." As players in the theater of the self, we can learn to call on our own inner troupe of actors to play the parts we need according to the audience of the moment. If schizophrenia is a splitting and disconnection of our inner troupe, then "polyphrenia"—a word coined by Jean Houston to refer to the coordinated performance of our inner ensemble—may well be the expression of our full intrapersonal intelligence.

A few lines from *The Tempest* provide a haunting reminder of the timelessness of our task of learning from the geniuses who came before us.

Full fathom five thy father lies;
Of his bones are coral made:
Those are pearls that were his eyes:
Nothing of him that doth fade,
But doth suffer a sea-change
Into something rich and strange.

The father—a deceased genius—has drowned. In death he does not disappear, but transforms into something "rich" (like coral and pearls) and "strange," as in unknown. In a time of profound change, the past doesn't vanish altogether. Rather, it transforms into something rich—new values and meanings—and strange—the unfamiliar, what we can't yet know or do not recognize.

Our survey of revolutionary genius mines the pearls and coral of the past to unleash its transformational power to guide you through your own sea changes now. Transformation is strange—we cannot undergo profound change without being somewhat foreign to ourselves. In a symbolic sense, you "fade" to your familiar self to create a new one, ready for the future that awaits you.

SHAKESPEARE:
CULTIVATING YOUR
EMOTIONAL INTELLIGENCE
SELF-ASSESSMENT

☐ I understand my own emotions and how they affect my behavior.

☐ I am sensitive to the emotions of others and understand how their experiences affect their behavior.

☐ I can analyze my doubts and fears and strive to overcome them intelligently.

☐ I take delight in the richness of language.

☐ I make time to give my imagination free rein.

☐ I enjoy reading and listening to poetry.

☐ I thrill to the drama of everyday life and the experiences it offers me.

☐ I am sensitive and empathic in interactions with the opposite sex.

☐ I see myself as a work in progress.

☐ I am aware of the different roles I play.

☐ I am a team player; I can blend into a group and bring out the best in everyone.

☐ I can laugh at myself in almost any situation.

EXERCISES

THINKING LIKE SHAKESPEARE/
CULTIVATING YOUR EMOTIONAL INTELLIGENCE

Leonardo da Vinci's *Mona Lisa* is so famous that it can be difficult to fully appreciate and understand her mysterious beauty and eternal allure. The secret, of course, is to begin by leaving aside preconceptions and looking at the painting with fresh eyes.

The exercises in this chapter are designed to guide you to a fresh experience of the mysterious beauty and eternal allure of Shakespeare's amazing portraits of the human soul. The best way to cultivate your emotional intelligence through the genius of Shakespeare is to immerse yourself in his works and let him speak to you directly.

READ THE PLAYS/ATTEND LIVE PERFORMANCES/
WATCH THE MOVIES

> *. . . the plays read me better than I read them.*
>
> —HAROLD BLOOM

In Shakespeare's day many people made a habit of reading a book of the Bible every month as a method of religious self-improvement (this remains an excellent idea). You can do the same with the works of the Bard. Read one of Shakespeare's plays every month. As the editors of Shakespeare's famous first folio advised, "Read him, therefore, again and again."

Harold Bloom explains that after the Bible, Shakespeare's works have more influence than any other work. He refers to the Bard's collected works as "The Book of Reality" and points out that after Jesus, Hamlet is the most well-known character in human consciousness. "No one prays to him," Bloom assures us, "but no one evades him for very long either."

Each Shakespeare play offers a master class in emotional intelligence and the lack thereof. As you read each play approach it with the following questions in mind:

What can I learn from this play that will help me know myself better?

What can I learn from this play that will help me understand others better?

(It's useful to think of specific people you might wish to understand better.)

Complement your reading by attending live performances of Shakespeare's masterworks. Live performance is my favorite way to experience the magic of Shakespeare, but it's also the most fraught with risk, as production and performance quality vary dramatically. Nevertheless, even bad Shakespeare is good, and great Shakespeare is amazing. Remember, however, to hold the two questions in mind throughout your audience experience.

I recently attended a Royal Shakespeare Company performance of *Henry V* at the Barbican Theatre in London with a dear friend who is suffering through a painful divorce from a man who refuses to pay his share of their child's support. She's a classic "woman who loves too much": kind, generous, and focused on the needs of others but prone to neglect her own needs. She recoiled from the adversarial nature of the legal process, and her reluctance to fight put her in danger of receiving an unjust settlement. In Act II, Scene 4 a royal adviser says, "self-love, my liege, is not so vile a sin as self-neglecting." As this line was uttered we looked at each other and knew that Shakespeare was speaking directly to her situation. Then Henry delivers the incredible oration to his troops before the Battle of Agincourt. Again we looked at each other: just as Henry inspired his army to battle against the superior French forces, so my friend was feeling the birth of fire for the battle she needed to fight. "Once more into the breach" has become her motto—and isn't it wonderful poetic justice that her deadbeat husband just happens to be named Francois?

Of course, if you are reading *Henry V* you'll want to see a live production, but even if one isn't available to you, you can always rent the video of the movie. Many of the plays are available in more than one movie version, and if you can muster the stamina, it's highly rewarding to do a comparative appreciation exercise with multiple versions (particular comparisons recommended at www.discoveryourgenius.com).

UNDERSTANDING AND ENJOYING SHAKESPEARE: THE MEDIUM IS OFTEN THE MESSAGE

Listen to the rhythm of the lines to "feel" the meaning. You don't have to understand every word to get the gist of a line and you don't have to understand every line to get the gist of a scene. When Richard of Gloucester says, "Instead of mounting barbed steeds to fright the souls of fearful adversaries" or Juliet Capulet cries out, "Gallop apace, you fiery-footed steeds," the pace and placement of the syllables recreates the beat of horses' hooves and expresses the rumbling passions they feel. The sluggish pace and tone of Macbeth's repetition of "Tomorrow and tomorrow and tomorrow" communicates his sense of ennui and emptiness, and the witches' bubbly incantation is clear enough even without a detailed understanding of all the specific ingredients in their evil gruel.

Of course it is also a good idea to read a synopsis before attending a performance, and to familiarize yourself with key terms. Keep Michael Macrones' *Brush Up Your Shakespeare* next to your bed and read a passage or two each day to deepen your understanding and enjoyment.

ENJOY A SONNET A DAY

Shakespeare's sonnets are a microcosm of his genius—his masterpieces in miniature—and they illuminate the themes and structures of his plays. The sonnets are Shakespeare's chamber music as opposed to the symphonic scale of his major plays.

Complement your sonnet reading with audio appreciation. You can get numerous compact disc and audiotape recordings of all the sonnets. For the last few months I've had the tape of the sonnets in my car. I play them over and over again as I drive and find that they not only lessen the likelihood of road rage, but as they wash into my consciousness, I seem to become more sensitive to nuances of language and emotion in my life every day.

Be sensitive to the rhythm of each fourteen-line sonnet. What images and special linguistic effects does Shakespeare deploy? How does the sonnet affect you? What emotions does it evoke? How does each sonnet speak to your inner world?

THE SOUL'S IMAGINARY SIGHT

The following sonnet with its reference to "a journey in my head" and "my soul's imaginary sight" offers an intriguing insight into the workings of Shakespeare's powerful imagination. Please read it (best to read it aloud a few times) and note your reactions.

Sonnet 27

Weary with toil, I haste me to my bed,
The dear repose for limbs with travel tired;
But then begins a journey in my head,
To work my mind, when body's work's expired:
For then my thoughts, from far where I abide,
Intend a zealous pilgrimage to thee,
And keep my drooping eyelids open wide,
Looking on darkness which the blind do see:
Save that my soul's imaginary sight
Presents thy shadow to my sightless view,
Which, like a jewel hung in ghastly night,
Makes black night beauteous, and her old face new.
Lo, thus, by day my limbs, by night my mind,
For thee and for myself no quiet find.

CHOOSE A SONNET FOR
SOMEONE YOU LOVE

This is a marvelous exercise to do with your significant other. (If you are seeking a significant other, the sonnets will make the search more informed.) Light some candles and perhaps some incense, play some Elizabethan Renaissance music in the background, and then take turns reading a few sonnets that you have specially chosen for your love. Use the sonnets to express and explore new depths and delights of communication in your relationship.

LEARN BY HEART

When Will Shakespeare was a lad in Stratford's grammar school he spent hours memorizing the classics. His daily lessons had to be recited from memory the next day, "without booke." At the end of each week, Will and his classmates were expected to know what they had been taught "by heart, perfectlie."

When he entered the world of the theater, his early memory training served him well. Like actors today, Shakespeare had to keep an extensive repertoire in his memory. In addition to his few significant roles, he might, in the course of a season, play up to a hundred small parts.

Although memorization has been out of fashion as an educational strategy for some time, it is nonetheless a marvelous means for developing your mental power and enriching your understanding. Learning by heart can give you a more intimate and complete appreciation of Shakespeare.

Choose a favorite passage, soliloquy, or sonnet and commit it to memory. You'll enhance your enjoyment dramatically.

My friend Forrest Hainline III is a very successful attorney, aikidoist, and author. He comments on learning by heart:

"When I was a student at Notre Dame, I became comfortable and competent at analyzing poems. For me, the *Summum Bonum* was best served by analyzing Browning's use of the dash, Shakespeare's iambics, and Joyce's 250-word sentences. I didn't realize, however, that I was cataloguing trees and missing the forest.

"One day, my poetry professor announced that the major semester examination would be a hundred-question objective test. We would actually have to memorize the poetry we were studying. I was furious. With all the arrogance of a successful college literature student, I went to his office and breathlessly demanded a defense of his preposterous idea. How could he conceive of giving such an infantile exam? My professor smiled and asked me this, 'Forrest, in twenty, thirty or forty years, would you rather have made a few poems a part of your soul, part of the warp and woof of your being? Or would you rather not remember, and not have any need or desire to remember, the interpretation you gave to a poem no lines of which you can recall?'

"His words cut right through my bravado and arrogance. This was a moment of humility and enlightenment. I went back and inhaled all the semester's poems. I read them aloud, over and over, until they became part of me. When the exam came, my friends were furious because I ruined the curve. I remember the poems today.

"Of course, I'm familiar with the Bard's critique of my profession, but nevertheless, I invoke him on a regular basis to persuade judge and jury."

LINGUISTIC AND EMOTIONAL INTELLIGENCE: HAND-IN-GLOVE

For the Bard, emotional intelligence and verbal intelligence went hand-in-glove. Of course, it's possible to have highly developed linguistic intelligence without great emotional intelligence. Nevertheless, you'll find that if you cultivate your own emotional intelligence, you'll be able to manifest it more effectively as you deepen your appreciation for the subtleties and delights of language. The following exercises will guide you to a more Shakespearean appreciation of the joy of words.

Learn More About the English Language

Thanks largely to Elizabeth and Shakespeare, English is the primary world language today. It is one of the richest languages in the world, because the English have had contact with so many different societies. Two thousand years ago England was invaded by the Romans, and over the next millennia by Germanic tribes and by the Normans in 1066. As a result Latin, German, and French words feature prominently in modern English. The English later colonized countries across the globe and adopted words from these cultures as well. English has absorbed so many words from other cultures that it has more synonyms than any other language.

Learning about the roots, history, and development of words over time will give you a much richer appreciation of the subtleties of the everyday language you use.

Here is a simple and delightful way to begin enriching your appreciation of English.

List Your Ten Favorite English Words

Why do you like them? Is it the sound, the feel, the meaning, or perhaps an association with a pleasant memory? Look them up and learn about the derivation, synonyms, and usage for each one. (If you consult the full twenty-two volumes of the *Oxford English Dictionary* in a library or on CD-ROM, you will also have the bonus of learning when your words were first used and in what context. Are they Shakespearean or modern?)

From the Sacred to the Profane

After listing the most beautiful words you know, have fun making a list of ten rude, lewd, and naughty words. Even the rudest words have a fascinating history. According to Geoffrey Hughes, author of *Swearing: A Social History of Foul Language, Oaths and Profanity in English*, the word "fart" is probably Anglo-Saxon in origin and was first recorded in 1250. Hughes recounts a story told by the seventeenth-century antiquarian John Aubrey in his *Brief Lives*, about the Earl of Oxford, Aubrey de Vere (one of the famous alleged "Shakespeares"), who made a low bow before Queen Elizabeth I and "happened to let a fart." In shame he traveled abroad for seven years hoping it would be forgotten, but "on his return the Queen welcomed him home and said, 'My Lord, I had forgot the fart.'"

Master the Art of the Insult

In addition to naughty words you can also enrich your appreciation of English by enjoying the pleasure of the articulate insult. Although it's best to use your emotional intelligence and burgeoning linguistic artistry to cultivate harmonious interactions with all, it is always prudent to have a few elegant but devastating ripostes in your verbal arsenal. And, of course, Shakespeare was the master here as well.

Top Ten Shakespearean Insults

1. Go thou, and fill another room in hell.
2. Thou clay-brained guts, thou knotty-pated fool, thou whoreson obscene greasy tallow-catch.

3. Thou slander of thy heavy mother's womb! Thou loathed issue of thy father's loins!
4. You are as a candle, the better part burnt out.
5. Out, you green-sickness carrion! Out, you baggage!
6. Such a dish of skim milk . . .
7. Thou elvish-marked, abortive, rooting hog!
8. He has not so much brain as ear-wax.
9. Would thou wert clean enough to spit upon!
10. Oswald: What dost thou know me for?

    Kent: A knave, a rascal, an eater of broken meats, a base, proud, shallow beggarly, three-suited, hundred-pound, filthy-worsted-stocking knave; a lily-livered, action-taking, whoreson glass-glazing super-serviceable finical rogue, one-trunk-inheriting slave; one that wouldst be a bawd in way of good service, and art nothing but the composition of a knave, beggar, coward, pander, and the son and heir of a mongrel bitch; one whom I will beat into clamorous whining if thou deniest the least syllable of thy addition.

    ("Broken meats"—leftovers; "three-suited"—a servant's wardrobe; "action-taking"—litigious (a grave insult from the Bard!); "glass-gazing"—narcissistic; "super-serviceable"—meddlesome and servile; "finical"—foppish; "one-trunk-inheriting"—Elizabethan for white trash; "bawd" and "pander"—pimp; "addition"—name).

Swearing in the Renaissance had a rich complexity, combining exuberant creativity and severe restraint.

—GEOFFREY HUGHES, SWEARING: A SOCIAL HISTORY

Become a Logodaedalus

A logodaedalus is an inventor of words and phrases—a wordsmith. *Logos* is the Greek for "word," and Daedalus was the famed artificer of Greek myth who fashioned the wings for his son Icarus to fly. Shakespeare was the logodaedalus par excellence. He invented words and they stuck—"porpentine" for porcupine, for example—much more expressive. And the phrase "hoist with his own petard!" (blown up by his own bomb—creating the concept of the explosion from the root of the French word "to fart") has an immortal ring to it.

In his book, *Mother Tongue: The English Language*, Bill Bryson comments that as an inventor of words and as a phrase maker, there has never been anyone to match Shakespeare: "Among his inventions: one fell swoop, in my mind's eye, more in sorrow than in anger, to be in a pickle, bag and baggage, vanish into thin air, the milk of human kindness, remembrance of things past, the sound and the fury, to thine own self be true, to be or not to be, cold comfort, to beggar all description, salad days, flesh and blood, foul play, tower of strength, to be cruel to be kind, and on and on and on. And on."

BECOME AWARE OF YOUR "ROLES" AND PLAY THEM WELL

Through the immortal lines of Jaques, the philosophical idler in *As You Like It,* Shakespeare says:

> All the world's a stage,
> And all the men and women merely players;
> They have their exits and their entrances,
> And one man in his time plays many parts.

What roles do you play in your life every day, and how well do you play them?

In your notebook, write a few lines to express each role you play in life: then note your reflections on how well you play each role. Which is your best part and where are you weakest? Reflect on the theatrical nature of life, and the ensemble with which you perform. Life is theater: will it be good theater or bad?

I am re-reading—and with immense enjoyment—all of Shakespeare's plays, with Harold Bloom's Shakespeare as my excellent guide.

—92-YEAR-OLD PETER DRUCKER'S STRATEGY FOR MAINTAINING HIS EDGE AS THE WORLD'S LEADING MANAGEMENT EXPERT

Stacy Forsythe is a professional opera singer, linguist, Renaissance woman, and gifted teacher of voice, movement, and drama. She shares some notes on this exercise from her genius journal:

"My roles include wife, aunt, teacher, student, artist, daughter, sister, and friend. I play most of my roles fairly well. I would say that I'm best in the teacher role . . . But my greatest challenge is to maintain balance between the various roles I play . . . In much the same way that a director lays the foundation for a theatrical performance, I've learned to develop criteria for selecting the players and inventing the specific life choreography that supports my personal 'script,' for a successful life. I think it is of essential importance that the 'roles' I play every day are motivated by authentic emotional or spiritual desires . . . Tipping the scales toward life as 'good theater' involves learning to live like a good actor, defining my roles in a way that is true, genuine, and authentically inspired."

SHAKESPEARE AT WORK

In more than twenty years of work with companies around the world, the best leaders I've met display qualities of intrapersonal and interpersonal intelligence that the Bard describes to perfection, including:

- ▲ Consistency in the face of change and crisis like Shakespeare's Julius Caesar, who is "constant as the northern star, of whose true fixed and resting quality there is no fellow in the firmament."
- ▲ "Empowering" ourselves and others. As Shakespeare puts it, "our remedies oft in ourselves do lie, which we ascribe to heaven."
- ▲ Providing inspiration. He tells us: "strong reasons make strong actions."

- Resilience in the face of adversity. In *Timon of Athens* Shakespeare tells us that the truly valiant "can wisely suffer, the worst that man can breathe, and bear his wrongs carelessly on the outside like clothes."
- An exquisite sense of timing, expressed exquisitely: "There is a tide in the affairs of men, which taken at the flood leads on to fortune; omitted, all the voyage of their life is bound in shallows and miseries."

Great leaders also combine sensitivity and empathy with toughness and a bias to action. They communicate powerfully in big meetings and also work one-on-one. Of the many marvelous leaders in the "book of reality," *Henry V* offers a most relevant example for these qualities of modern leadership.

Henry is one of Shakespeare's master communicators. In the first scene of the play the Archbishop of Canterbury marvels at Henry's skills in oratory, which are such that when he speaks, "mute wonder lurketh in men's ears." According to Shakespeare scholar David Bevington, King Henry's versatility as a rhetorician applies to all the vital disciplines of kingship: Henry can "reason in divinity," "debate of commonwealth affairs," "discourse of war," handle "any cause of policy," and in all such matters speak in "sweet and honeyed sentences."

Henry is as adept at communicating on an intimate, personal level as he is at speaking to huge crowds. On the eve of the Battle of Agincourt, in which Henry's army is severely outnumbered, the king goes from campfire to campfire, comforting his troops, "thawing cold fear." The English, outnumbered ten to one, proceed to rout the French the next day. Imagine what your organization could achieve with that kind of leadership.

And we know that Shakespeare himself was a success in the workplace. We have evidence of his prosperity and of the esteem in which he was held by his contemporaries. Shakespeare's own "emotional intelligence" was the key to his ability to get along in the rough-and-tumble world of the Elizabethan theater. Emotional intellingence is a frequently overlooked key to success in the the world of work now.

Consider the following:

▲ Egon Zehnder International, a leading executive search firm, conducted a study of over 500 senior executives and concluded that "emotional intelligence was a better predictor of success than either relevant previous experience or high I.Q."

▲ American Express Financial Advisers trained over 3,500 people in "emotional competencies." More than 80 percent reported strong personal and professional benefits as a result.

▲ The United States Air Force found that by screening and selecting recruiters based primarily on their emotional intelligence they tripled their success rate and realized a short-term gain of more than $3 million.

▲ Sale agents at L'Oreal hired on the basis of emotional intelligence outsold their colleagues hired on the traditional basis by almost $100,000 per year and had a turnover rate in the first year that was more than 60 percent lower than the traditional group.

SHAKESPEARE: MUSIC IS THE FOOD OF LOVE

The greatest composers and musicians combine extraordinary technical virtuosity with exceptional emotional intelligence. Music touches our hearts and expresses the range of our emotions in a unique and seemingly magical way. So it's not surprising that Shakespeare, the master of emotional intelligence, has provided continuing inspiration for composers since his death in 1616. One catalogue of Shakespeare-inspired music lists more than 21,000 compositions based on his works. Siblieus's delightful *Tempest,*

Shostakovich's brilliantly garish *Lady Macbeth*, Tchaikovsky's compelling fantasy overture to *Romeo and Juliet* and Mendelssohn's magical *Midsummer Night's Dream* (which includes the universally recognized Wedding March) are among the most notable.

But two works stand out as perhaps the greatest of the great Shakespeare-inspired music: Giuseppe Verdi's majestic opera *Otello* and Serge Prokofiev's unparalleled ballet score for *Romeo and Juliet*. Shakespeare's unique capacity to communicate the personal and universal, simultaneously, is alive in both of these musical masterpieces.

ONWARD TO JEFFERSON

His life was gentle, and the elements so mix'd
in him that Nature might stand up and say to
all the World "This was a man!"

—WILLIAM SHAKESPEARE, *JULIUS CAESAR*

What a piece of work is man! How noble in reason!

How infinite in faculty! In form and moving how

express and admirable! In action how like an angel!

In apprehension how like a God! The beauty of the World!

The paragon of animals!

—WILLIAM SHAKESPEARE, *HAMLET*

Our next genius visited Shakespeare's birthplace at Stratford-upon-Avon in 1786, and the Bard would probably agree that he fit the descriptions above. As President John F. Kennedy quipped to a distinguished gathering of Nobel laureates:

"I think that this is the most extraordinary collection of talent, of human knowledge, that has ever gathered together at the White House, with the possible exception of when Thomas Jefferson dined alone."

Thomas Jefferson

(1743–1826)

Celebrating Your Freedom in the Pursuit of Happiness

Almighty God hath created the mind free.

—THOMAS JEFFERSON

Why did you buy this book? To improve your station in life? Learn a little history? Explore a new direction for your spiritual journey? Most of us take for granted that these options are available to us. But such was not always the case. The geniuses we have studied thus far all lived and worked in societies in which social standing was determined by class, education was a privilege for a few, and religious beliefs were subject to government approval.

Our next genius helped change all of that with a few simple yet powerful words: "We hold these truths to be self-evident, that all men are created equal, that they are endowed by their creator with certain inalienable rights. That among these are life, liberty and the pursuit of happiness." In

Jefferson's strong facial structure and steadfast gaze are intended to convey his strength of vision and clarity about the "self-evident" truths of life and liberty as his wry, enigmatic smile suggests the pursuit of happiness. —Norma Miller

what may be the most magnificent act of revolutionary genius ever formulated by the human mind, Thomas Jefferson put into words the essence of a political philosophy that would soon enshrine the freedom of body, mind, and spirit as the world had never seen. By declaring and protecting the rights of the individual, the new American system not only represented the supreme step forward for the Renaissance ideal of the self, but also unleashed the potential for human creativity on an unprecedented scale.

Advocate of education and champion of religious freedom, Thomas Jefferson personifies the revolution in physical, mental, and spiritual liberation that began in the English colonies of America and swept much of the Western world. Though he by no means worked alone, the author of the Declaration of Independence was the architect of the turning point in human history that makes possible so much of what we pursue today. He speaks to all of us still, and indeed was cited on the same day by both Presidents Bill Clinton and George W. Bush in their respective farewell and inaugural addresses. "He always has something to say to us, and the nation always seems ready to listen," writes historian Daniel Boorstin. "While the folk figure of Benjamin Franklin has tended to become quaint and sententious, and George Washington towers over us, marbleized, monumental, and superhuman, Jefferson somehow has remained relevant to our national crises and grand concerns." For both a broad and lasting legacy of liberty and a life that honored the principles he championed, he remains relevant to our individual concerns as well, standing as an inspiring guide to any of us who use our freedom to "pursue happiness."

I have sworn upon the altar of God eternal hostility against every form of tyranny over the mind of man.

—THOMAS JEFFERSON

∿

THE ENLIGHTENMENT IDEAL

The third President of the United States was the third child of Peter and Jane Jefferson, born in Albermarle County, Virginia, on April 13, 1743. When Jefferson was age fourteen, his father died and Jefferson came into a substantial inheritance, which helped him establish himself in business and politics. In 1760 he entered the College of William and Mary, where he read Plato in Greek, Cicero in Latin, Cervantes in Spanish, and Montesquieu in French. He immersed himself in Shakespeare, Milton, and Dante, played the violin, and studied philosophy, science, mathematics, and, ultimately, law.

Jefferson's captivating brilliance and charm brought invitations to dine on a regular basis with the governor and a circle of Renaissance men who nurtured and encouraged his talents and ideas. His thirst for knowledge was legendary. As one of his contemporaries noted, "I never knew anyone to ask so many questions as Thomas Jefferson."

Biographer Saul Padover presents a vivid picture of the brilliant young man: "Standing well over six-feet . . . [he] was lean, bony, rough-hewn and broad-shouldered, but surprisingly slender . . . The cheeks were lean and the jaw square and firm, but the wide-winged nose was somewhat feminine and inquisitive. Quizzical hazel eyes, set deep, were flanked by bushy temples. He danced gracefully, and his walk had the lightness of one seasoned in the forest. His voice . . . was soft . . . like his eyes."

An avid reader of the Enlightenment philosophy expressed in the works of Francis Bacon, Isaac Newton, and John Locke, he was familiar with the emerging ideal of universal human rights and individual freedom—and no doubt aware that it still existed only as an ideal. In the late eighteenth century England and France were still ruled by kings, China and Japan by "divine" emperors, Russia by an imperial tsar, and Turkey by an all-powerful sultan. Despite the famous English Magna Carta of 1215 and the English Bill of Rights of 1689, no nation on earth fully protected the rights and freedoms of the individual citizen.

Jefferson had a natural sensitivity that led him to be, as one biographer phrased it, "stirred by injustice and indignant at persecution." When he attended a rousing revolutionary speech by Patrick Henry in 1764, Jefferson began to hone his focus on what was to become the central theme of his life: freedom. At this time Jefferson adopted the personal motto, "Resistance to tyrants is service to God."

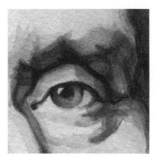

From 1767 to 1774 Jefferson thrived in the practice of law, married his beloved wife, Martha, and began to design and build his magnificent home in Monticello. Although he appeared quite happy to pursue the life of a Virginia country gentleman, Jefferson could not ignore the oppressive nature of British governance of the colonies. Heeding the voice of his ideals, Jefferson joined the Virginia House of Burgesses, where he drafted "A Summary View of the Rights of British America" and helped lead the call for the First Continental Congress in 1774.

After drafting the Declaration of Independence at age thirty-three Jefferson went on to serve in the Virginia House of Delegates and then as governor of Virginia from 1779 to 1781. Against great odds he managed to pass the first bill establishing religious freedom, and in concert with George Washington, John Adams, Alexander Hamilton, Benjamin Franklin, and other extraordinary individuals, helped to throw off the yoke of British domination.

In 1781 Jefferson was ready to leave politics behind and enjoy the pursuit of pure truth, beauty, and happiness at his estate in Monticello. "Domestic life and literary pursuits were my first and my latest inclinations," he wrote. "Circumstances and not my desires led me to the path I trod." When his country called again, Jefferson left domestic life to serve as ambassador to the courts of Europe from 1784 to 1789 and then as the first U.S. Secretary of State under George Washington from 1790 to 1793. After serving as John Adams's vice-president from 1797 to 1801, Jefferson was elected the third president of the United States of America, serving two full terms before he left office in 1809.

JEFFERSON AND THE CONFLUENCE OF AMERICAN REVOLUTIONARY GENIUS

In 1787 the convention to establish the first Constitution of the United States of America took place in Philadelphia. The Founding Fathers faced the problem of balancing individual freedom and equality with the responsibilities of citizenship in building a new nation. This challenge was addressed by Plato in his consideration of the ideal state in *The Republic*, and was raised again during the Renaissance rediscovery of classical political thought and rebirth of emphasis on individual freedom and empowerment. From then on political systems evolved that could support the rights of the individual, but it was not until the American Revolution that the Renaissance "discovery" of individuality became enshrined in the founding document of a nation.

In the words of Jefferson himself, the men who gathered in Philadelphia were "an assembly of demi-gods." Although Jefferson and John Adams were absent on diplomatic service abroad—their trip included a visit to Shakespeare's birthplace in 1786—the Constitutional Convention was attended by Benjamin Franklin, James Madison, Alexander Hamilton, and of course, George Washington. Their grand endeavor led to the creation of the most prosperous and freedom-conscious nation the earth has ever witnessed.

This confluence of constructive genius in the former British colonies ranks with the Academy of Plato in Athens and the courts of the Medici in Florence. Although Jefferson reigns as a most prominent and enduring influence from this period, his achievements took place in a ferment of freedom brewed by his revolutionary brethren. Let's take a closer look at three of the most noteworthy.

George Washington

George Washington, the military leader of the American Revolution, became the first president of the United States in 1789.

Under Washington's leadership the American army with French help forced the surrender of British General Cornwallis at Yorktown in 1781. On September 3, 1783, the peace treaty that guaranteed the independence of America was signed with Great Britain. Joseph Ellis calls Washington "America's one and only indispensable character." Ellis explains, "Washington was the core of gravity that prevented the revolution from flying off into random orbits, the stable center around which the revolutionary energies formed." Ellis refers to Washington as an American combination of Zeus and Moses and cites a popular toast to the first president: "the man who unites all hearts."

Washington was a genius of military and political leadership and a paragon of integrity. The story that he confessed to cutting down a cherry tree with the words, "Father, I cannot tell a lie," is probably apocryphal. On other occasions, however, he did summon up the famous phrase. In his farewell address to the people of the United States in 1796 Washington advised: "labour to keep alive in your breast that little spark of celestial fire called conscience."

John Adams

It was Adams who delivered the votes that put Jefferson's Declaration into play. The second president of the United States was a devoted patriot, inspired statesman, and seminal figure of American independence. Through his brilliant diplomacy in Europe Adams succeeded in securing vital loans for the new republic, and he laid the foundations of cooperative relations with France and other nations. Adams also served as a loyal vice-president to General Washington, casting the still unsurpassed record of thirty-one tie-breaking votes on behalf of his party and president. Renowned for his honesty, practicality, and volcanic temper, as well as his tender, passionate, and creative collaboration with his beloved wife, Abigail, Adams stands as one of the great original Americans.

Benjamin Franklin

Benjamin Franklin was, like Jefferson, a multifaceted genius, a journalist, scientific experimenter, inventor, diplomat, and Enlightenment thinker. Franklin's achievements are astonishing. Although he came from a humble background and his formal education ended when he was ten, Franklin's zeal for freedom, learning, and life changed the world. Franklin started his working life as a printer. In 1729, aged just twenty-three, he bought the *Pennsylvania Gazette*. Driven by a fierce spirit of individual enterprise and gargantuan zest, he became the original American paragon of success. He founded and wrote *Poor Richard's Almanack*, in which he regularly advised readers on how to be successful. Franklin also conducted a famous experiment in electricity, which earned him election as a Fellow of the Royal Society in London. He proved that lightning and electricity are identical and demonstrated the distinction between positive and negative charges.

Franklin invented bifocal glasses, an efficient stove, and a lightning conductor to protect buildings. He also charted the routes of storms over North America and the course of the Gulf Stream.

During his many years in Paris, where he was greatly admired, Franklin obtained French support for America in the War of Independence and at the same time helped export egalitarian notions of freedom and brotherly love; one can sense his spirit in the motto "Liberté, Egalité, Fraternité" that guided the French in overthrowing their own form of despotism in 1789. When Jefferson later called on French foreign minister Count Vergennes, the count asked whether he had come to replace "le Docteur Franklin." Jefferson responded, "No one can replace him, sir. I am only his successor."

In *Founding Brothers* Joseph Ellis comments, "What Voltaire was to France, Franklin was to America, the symbol of mankind's triumphant arrival at modernity." Ellis says of Franklin: "The greatest American scientist, the most deft diplomat, the most accomplished prose stylist, the sharpest wit, Franklin defied all the categories by inhabiting them all with such distinction and nonchalant grace."

FREEDOM TO LIVE

The nation that Jefferson and the Founding Fathers created came closer to the ideals of universal human rights than any on the planet; the claim that equality was a God-given attribute broke the hold that monarchy and class systems had exerted on societies for centuries, and finally freed citizens to make their own place in the world. But how real was the liberty when it was not available to the victims of the most inhumane affront to individual rights, the cruel and despotic institution of slavery?

No one can deny that slavery was a national scourge, a tragedy that blighted the national ideals of liberty for decades. Jefferson's participation in it is shockingly irreconcilable with the ideals he championed. But whatever criticisms are justifiably made of his character and of the way he lived, his role in laying the groundwork for the eventual elimination of slavery cannot be denied.

Jefferson grew up in a slaveholding family and had about fifty slaves in his own right at the time he inherited another one hundred and thirty-five from his wife's father's estate. He kept these and others throughout his life and, unlike George Washington, who freed all his slaves, Jefferson liberated only five, and not until after his death. By all accounts Jefferson treated his slaves with kindness, but he knew that slavery was wrong and struggled mightily with this moral cancer. The third panel of the Jefferson Memorial in Washington, D.C., expresses Jefferson's sense of shame about slavery: "Indeed I tremble for my country when I reflect that God is just, that his justice cannot sleep forever. Commerce between master and slave is despotism. Nothing is more certainly written in the book of fate than that these people are to be free."

Jefferson's opposition to slavery was sincere, but he also accepted, reluctantly, that the time to free the slaves had not yet come. As he wrote in a letter to Edward Coles in 1814, "the hour of emancipation is advancing, in the march of time. It will come . . . It is an encouraging observation that no good measure was ever proposed, which if duly pursued, failed to prevail in the end." And elsewhere he expressed his frustration with the abomination of slavery: "There is nothing I would not sacrifice to a practicable plan of abolishing every vestige of this moral and political depravity."

One of the greatest achievements of his second term of presidency was the prohibition of the expansion of the slave trade. However, the nation had to wait for a further half century before slavery was finally and effectively abolished by Abraham Lincoln, and still another century after that before

They created the American republic, then held it together through the volatile and vulnerable early years by sustaining their presence until national habits and customs took root . . . they got us from the short run to the long run.

—JOSEPH ELLIS IN
FOUNDING BROTHERS

Martin Luther King and President Lyndon Baines Johnson conclusively established civil rights for all black Americans. Despite his participation in the national shame of slavery, Thomas Jefferson laid the foundations for the achievements of Lincoln, Johnson, and King. As Lincoln declared before issuing the Emancipation Proclamation, "All honor to Jefferson!"

FREEDOM TO LEARN

Jefferson's education was a critical building block of the intellectual revolution that preceded the military uprising, and he continued to view education as the key to the lasting success of the American experiment. He pioneered the introduction of free public education for all citizens and believed that a lifetime of learning was an intrinsic element of a happy life. As he noted, "Enlighten the people generally, and tyranny and oppressions of body & mind will vanish like evil spirits at the dawn of day."

As the supreme expression of his lifelong devotion to education, Jefferson created the University of Virginia, the first institution of higher learning established outside the framework of the church. He hoped to create a center to cultivate the judges, legislators, scientists, architects and statesmen "on whom public prosperity and individual happiness are so much to depend." He proposed a wide-ranging curriculum that included anatomy, astronomy, ancient and modern languages, botany, chemistry, ethics, fine arts, geography, government, grammar, history, law, mathematics, rhetoric, and zoology.

Biographer Saul Padover explains that from 1818 Jefferson "lived only for the University of Virginia. The institution was to be the crowning glory of his life, and upon it he lavished all his energies, his talents, his hopes. He turned himself into a one-man construction plant, a one-man architectural firm, a one-man apprentice school, and a one-man planning board. He did everything himself. He raised money. He drew up the architectural plans. He procured the workmen, including the importation of sculptors from Italy. He prepared all the details of construction. Since there was a shortage of skilled labor, he also taught brick-layers how to work and carpenters how to measure."

Jefferson's love of reading and learning was also a lifelong personal passion, and he considered his collection of almost 10,000 books his most prized possession. "Books constitute capital," he wrote in a letter to James Madison. "A library book lasts as long as a house, for hundreds of years. It is not an article of mere consumption but fairly of capital, and often in the case of professional men, setting out in life, it is their only capital." When the British burned the national library in Washington, D.C., in the War of 1812, Jefferson sold his collection to the nation, forming the core of what is today perhaps the greatest library in the world, the Library of Congress.

> *I cannot live without books.*
>
> —THOMAS JEFFERSON

THE SAGE OF MONTICELLO

Jefferson biographer Saul Padover tells us, "The years of struggle and turmoil had given him an immense reservoir of moral strength. Time, like fire, having purified whatever weaknesses lurked in his character, he could face the opinion of his contemporaries and the judgement of history with equal serenity. Well past middle age, he was now that most rare of human species, a balanced and harmonious man capable of viewing the world with detached compassion and serene wisdom. Few men in history ever achieved such philosophical balance and spiritual harmony as Jefferson did in his later—his post political—years."

JEFFERSON THE LOVER

Much controversy has been raised about Jefferson's amorous activities in the years after his wife's death in 1782. But to know his spirit and character it may be of more value to understand just how much he adored and cared for his wife in the ten years they were together. United originally through a common delight in music, Thomas and Martha Jefferson shared a profound, joyous love and a deep, mutual commitment. They produced six children together, although three were to die before their mother. When Martha was dying one of the surviving Jefferson children described the ministrations of the family patriarch:

"As a nurse no female ever had more tenderness nor anxiety. He nursed my poor mother . . . For four months that she lingered he was never out of calling . . ." When his beloved wife died Jefferson was inconsolable, his grief was so extreme that friends and family feared he might never recover.

Although Jefferson was still young, and noted for his charisma with women, he honored the deathbed promise he made at Martha's request and never remarried. But later, while serving as ambassador in Europe, Jefferson fell in love with Maria Cosway, an elegant and beautiful Anglo-Italian artist and musician. The marvelous letters they exchanged express a deep affection and poetic love. As he wrote to her:

"I wish they had formed us like birds of the air, able to fly where we please . . . Yet if I had it [the power to wish himself anywhere], I question if I should use it but once. I should wish myself with you, and not wish myself away again."

Of course, Jefferson's most controversial relationship is the one that he may have had with a slave at his home of Monticello. Sally Hemings was a beautiful African-American woman who served as a nanny in the Jefferson household. DNA tests show that Jefferson could have been the father of her son. In the book *Jefferson's Children: The Story of One American Family*, Shannon Lanier presents the case for his descent from the union of Thomas and Sally.

FREEDOM TO BELIEVE

As difficult as it is to imagine today, in the years following Jefferson's death his beloved Monticello fell into disrepair. A national treasure might have been lost had it not been purchased in 1834 by Uriah Levy, a Jewish American who aimed to restore it as a tribute to Jefferson's legacy of freedom of religion. It stands today as a fitting monument to our right to worship God in whatever way we choose.

"Almighty God has created the mind of man free," Jefferson wrote, the touchstone of his passionate conviction that no external authority or government should have the right to impose beliefs on anyone. Religious freedom was a basic human right for Jefferson and he was particularly proud of his Bill for Religious Freedom enacted in Virginia in 1786 after a decade of campaigning.

Drafted in 1777, a short year after the colonies' break from a global empire that had shed centuries of blood over religious beliefs, Jefferson's first Bill for Establishing Religious Freedom read as follows:

"We the General Assembly of Virginia, do enact that no man shall be compelled to frequent or support any religious worship, place, or ministry whatsoever, nor shall be enforced, restrained, molested, or burdened in his body or goods, nor shall otherwise suffer, on account of his religious opinions or belief; but that all men shall be free to profess, and by argument to maintain, their opinions in matters of religion, and that the same shall in no wise diminish, enlarge, or affect their civil capacities."

Before Jefferson's pioneering efforts, church and state were interwoven and citizens were subject to official discrimination if they did not submit to the dominant religious authority. Jefferson saw domination of society by religious organizations as another form of tyranny over the human mind. He referred to himself as "a real Christian, that is to say, a disciple of the doctrines of Jesus." And he believed "the precepts of Jesus, as delivered by himself, to be the most pure, benevolent, and sublime which have ever been preached to man."

He had far less faith in man's ability to manifest those precepts himself; he felt that organized religion had a tendency to turn these sublime teachings into their opposite. As he wrote in a letter to Charles Thompson in 1816: "They have compounded from the heathen mysteries a system beyond the comprehension of man, of which [Jesus], were he to return on earth, would not recognize one feature." For Jefferson, freedom was a gift from God and deeds rather than dogma measured goodness. "For it is in our lives, and not from our words," he wrote in a letter to Mrs. Samuel H. Smith in 1816, "that our religion must be read."

THOMAS JEFFERSON'S "RELIGION"

"Adore God. Reverence and cherish your parents. Love your neighbor as yourself, and your country more than yourself. Be just. Be true. Murmur not at the ways of Providence. Above all things lose no occasion of exercising your dispositions to be grateful, to be generous, to be charitable, to be humane, to be true, just, firm, orderly, courageous, & compassionate. Consider every act of this kind as an exercise which will strengthen your moral faculties & increase your worth . . . From the practice of the purest virtue you may be assured you will derive the most sublime comforts in every moment of life, and in the moment of death."

Thomas Jefferson died just past midday on the Fourth of July, 1826, exactly fifty years to the day after the signing of the Declaration of Independence. At the same time, the last of the Founding Fathers, John Adams, lay on his deathbed in Quincy, Massachusetts. Adams couldn't know that his Virginian compatriot had already breathed his last.

With his last breath Adams spoke the words: "Thomas Jefferson still lives."

Indeed he does, though not without controversy. Pulitzer Prize–winning biographer Joseph Ellis, echoing others, has accused Jefferson of being "the chief beneficiary of romanticized versions of history." Critics cite especially Jefferson's tendency toward sophisticated self-delusion and unrealistic idealism. Ellis calls him "the American Sphinx," highlighting how the alleged contradictions and inconsistencies of his character remain hidden behind his idealized memory. Like all our geniuses, Jefferson wasn't perfect and he made major mistakes. But as Jefferson himself noted, "error is the stuff of which the web of life is woven: and he who lives longest and wisest is only able to weave out the more of it."

Jefferson's life was marked by heartbreak and tragedy; he outlived not only his beloved wife but also five of his six children. Yet he was often described as radiating a quality of compassion and unconditional love. A few hours before he died, Jefferson bade goodbye to his only surviving child, his daughter Martha. He placed a tiny casket-shaped box in her hand containing the following, which can only be described as the words of an openhearted man:

A Death-bed Adieu from TH.J. to M.R.

Life's visions are vanished, its dreams are no more;
Dear friends of my bosom, why bathed in tears?
I go to my fathers: I welcome the shore
Which crowns all my hopes or which buries my cares.
Then farewell, my dear, my lov'd daughter, adieu!
The last pang of life is in parting from you!
Two seraphs await me long shrouded in death;
I will bring them your love on my last parting breath.

Summary of Achievements

- Jefferson drafted the Declaration of Independence—the most inspiring statement of human rights ever penned.

- He helped frame the Constitution for Virginia and served as governor from 1779 to 1781.

- In 1783 he secured the adoption of the decimal coinage in Congress.

- He became president of the United States in 1801.

- With assistance from James Madison, he authored the Virginia Statute on Religious Freedom, which became law in 1786 and remains in effect today. This statute served as a model for the statement on religious freedom found in the First Amendment to the Constitution, but was even stronger in its position on separation of church and state.

- He presided over the prohibition of the expansion of the slave trade.

- He founded the University of Virginia in 1819; it began operation in 1825.

- He negotiated the greatest real estate deal in history—the Louisiana Purchase, which doubled the size of the young country and effectively ended the prospect of foreign domination of American soil.

- He introduced superior strains of rice to farmers in South Carolina and pioneered the introduction of olive oil, macaroni, Parmesan cheese, raisins, vanilla, and fine wine to the American table.

JEFFERSON AND YOU

Above all things, and at all times, practise yourself

in good humor; this of all human qualities is

the most amiable and endearing to society.

—THOMAS JEFFERSON

~⁀

Thomas Jefferson lives as an inspiration for anyone who dreams of life, liberty, and the pursuit of happiness. As he noted:

"Mine, after all, may be an Utopian dream; but being innocent, I have thought I might indulge in it till I go to the land of dreams, and sleep there with the dreamers of all past and future times." Jefferson worked for his dreams, and struggled with his demons, in a way that still lights the path to true individual freedom.

For Jefferson, the patriot and statesman, the pursuit of happiness begins with freedom and opportunity for all. But there's more than work to Thomas Jefferson. In Italy they have la dolce vita, the sweet soulful life, in France there's joie de vivre, the art of joyous living; but what is the modern American equivalent? "Miller time" just doesn't have the same ring of sweetness, soulfulness, and joy. Yet for anyone interested in living a richer, fuller, more beautiful life, Thomas Jefferson, regarded as "one of the greatest epicures and connoisseurs of the art of living, of his day," offers a delightfully American inspiration. On a personal level, his approach to happiness included such pursuits as the cultivation of family and friendships, reading, the appreciation of music, gardening, walking, and sharing good food and fine wine.

In the exercises that follow we will explore these Jeffersonian approaches to celebrating your freedom in the pursuit of happiness.

JEFFERSON:
CELEBRATING YOUR FREEDOM
IN THE PURSUIT OF HAPPINESS
SELF-ASSESSMENT

- ☐ I am aware of and value the freedoms I have in my society.

- ☐ I understand and embrace the responsibilities that come with freedom.

- ☐ I actively protect the rights and freedoms of other people.

- ☐ I cherish and support intellectual freedom.

- ☐ I regard education as a fundamental human right.

- ☐ I regard religious freedom as a fundamental human right.

- ☐ I strive to overcome negative habits and to refine my character.

- ☐ I nurture my friendships.

- ☐ I savor the joy of living every day.

EXERCISES

THINKING LIKE JEFFERSON/
CELEBRATING YOUR FREEDOM
IN THE PURSUIT OF HAPPINESS

*Encourage all your virtuous dispositions, & exercise
them whenever an opportunity arises, being assured
that they will gain strength by exercise as a limb
of the body does, & that exercise will
make them habitual.*

—THOMAS JEFFERSON

Thomas Jefferson believed in cultivating inner as well as external freedom. With Ben Franklin, he launched the American tradition of self-help. The following annotated thoughts from Jefferson are offered to inspire your own personal quest for freedom. Read, reflect, and then make your own notes on this sage advice.

THOMAS JEFFERSON'S
TEN-POINT PLAN FOR PERSONAL IMPROVEMENT

1. Never put off till tomorrow what you can do today. (Jefferson rose before sunrise each day to get a head start on his massive to-do lists.)

2. Never trouble another for what you can do yourself. (Jefferson believed in the spirit of personal as well as political independence and thought that it began with the ability to solve one's own problems.)

3. Never spend your money before you have it. (Jefferson learned this the hard way by violating this advice repeatedly and suffering the consequences.)

4. Never buy what you do not want because it is cheap; it will be dear to you. (Jefferson loved life and saw material objects as means to experience rather than as ends in themselves.)

5. Pride costs us more than hunger, thirst, and cold. (At the center of power for many years, Jefferson witnessed the disastrous effects of egotism and believing one's own publicity on many powerful people.)

6. We never repent of having eaten too little. (Jefferson's extraordinary vitality was in part a function of his healthy diet and his practice of leaving the table before he was full.)

7. Nothing is troublesome that we do willingly. (As a natural optimist, Jefferson was able to choose to see the best in all life's circumstances. This was his way of saying, "To get what you choose, choose what you've got.")

8. How much pain has cost us the evils which have never happened. (Jefferson reminds us that worry is pointless. His optimism helped protect him from anxiety about the future.)

9. Take things always by their smooth handle. (Jefferson was an elegant man with a talent for finding the path of least resistance.)

10. When angry, count ten, before you speak; if very angry, a hundred. (As a man of the Enlightenment, Jefferson championed the voice of reason and understood the great power of words to cause harm as well as good.)

PLAY MENTAL SPORTS

Thomas Jefferson and Benjamin Franklin were both avid chess players, and Franklin wrote and published the first American book on chess. He likens the game to life itself: "The game of chess is not merely an idle amusement; several, very valuable policies of the mind, useful in the course of human life, are to be acquired and strengthened by it, so as to become ready on all occasions. For life is a kind of chess . . ."

If you already play chess, you will understand what Franklin meant. If you do not, then buy a chess set and beginner's book (or a program for your computer) and get started. Playing chess will develop your logical thought processes and strategic and tactical thinking skills, and strengthen your memory power as you get older.

JEFFERSON'S SECRETS OF HEALTH AND HAPPINESS

Take a Holistic Perspective on Health

Although many members of his family suffered from ill health, Jefferson himself was blessed with great vitality and well-being throughout his life. He developed strong opinions on the secrets of good health and healing. Professor Garrett Ward Sheldon of the University of Virginia notes, "Jefferson shared the common eighteenth-century suspicion of physicians, joking that if a doctor was visiting the neighborhood, buzzards would immediately begin circling above it." For Jefferson, the Hippocratic principle "first do no harm" was the most important element in medicine. He believed in the power of the body to heal itself and wrote that "nature and kind nursing" were the best prescription for most ailments. Jefferson referred to the outdoors and the shining sun as his "great physician." As Professor Sheldon emphasizes, "He believed in what today we would call holistic medicine—integrating physical with emotional and spiritual."

Jefferson emphasized that prevention was the key to good health. His program of preventive health care included exercise, diet, rest, the cultivation of friendships, and harmony with nature. Before exploring these elements of the Jeffersonian approach to wellness, take some time to contemplate the extent to which you practice holistic health now. Consider these questions and note your responses in your notebook:

What habits of mind or body do I now practice that may have a negative effect on my health in the long run?

What is my attitude about health and wellness? Am I an optimist or pessimist? How can I cultivate a more optimistic attitude about my own health?

What habit or activity could I do, or stop doing, that would have the single greatest benefit for my health and well-being?

Take Long Walks

Walking is the exercise of choice for history's greatest geniuses, and Jefferson was one of its most enthusiastic advocates. When in residence at his beloved Monticello he walked through the Virginia countryside for an hour or two each day. And even while away in Paris, Philadelphia, or New York he took the time to go for an extended stroll daily. Jefferson believed that walking strengthened the whole body and sharpened the mind; and he practiced the classical wisdom of *solvitas perambulatorum*—solving problems in the process of physical exercise.

Next time you are struggling with a problem or creative challenge, try the Jeffersonian strategy of *solvitas perambulatorum*—go for a long walk, preferably in the countryside or perhaps in a city park, and see if the problem solves itself. A long walk is also a wonderful way to resolve problems with a significant other or with colleagues at work. A group of chemical engineers from Du Pont successfully implemented after-lunch walks around their building as a regular part of their team approach to problem solving. Even if you don't solve your most important problems by walking you'll find it to be an easy way to stay in shape and strengthen body and mind.

Of all exercise walking is best . . . No one knows,

till he tries, how easily a habit of walking is acquired . . .

I have known some great walkers . . . and I never knew

or heard of one who was not healthy and long-lived.

—THOMAS JEFFERSON

Enjoy a Healthy Diet

A healthy diet was another essential element of Jefferson's program for vitality and well-being. He advocated liberal servings of fresh vegetables and whole grains and viewed meat as a condiment. Jefferson promoted a low-fat, high-fiber diet, and viewed wine as an integral element in facilitating good digestion. Jefferson would be appalled by junk food and would be an advocate of what we now call whole foods. He also believed that hard liquor and tobacco were poisonous and recommended abstinence.

In your notebook, record everything you eat for the next few days. Then consider the following questions.

Is your diet wholesome and balanced?
What percentage of your diet is fresh versus processed or frozen?

If you could reduce or eliminate one thing from your current diet that would
    improve your health, what would it be?
If you could add or increase one element in your current diet that would
    improve your health, what would it be?

Take Long Vacations

If you visit France or Italy in the month of August you'll notice that almost
all the residents are away on vacation. One of the delightful customs that
Jefferson adopted from his time abroad was the European notion of an
extended vacation from the stresses of life. Professor Sheldon explains that
Jefferson "insisted, as president, on taking a two-month summer vacation
in the mountains of Virginia, to escape the stresses of executive work and
the unhealthful heat and humidity of Washington, D.C." Most of us can't
afford, of course, to take a two-month vacation, but we also can't afford, in
the long run, not to take a real break on a regular basis.

Try the following exercise with your friends or family.

Take a large sheet of paper and in the center sketch an image that suggests the theme of "an ideal vacation"—perhaps some waves and a beach,
or a snow-covered mountain, or maybe the Eiffel Tower—just get started by
drawing a "creative doodle" that symbolizes a place you'd like to be. Now
imagine that you had three weeks and unlimited funds to implement an
ideal vacation. Sketch out the elements of your dream retreat.

Where would you go?
Who would you like to go with you?
What activities would you most enjoy?

After you've allowed your imagination to roam free, compare your ideas
on a dream vacation with the ideas of your friends or family members. Then
combine all the best elements of your dream vacation and discuss how you
could make it a reality.

Savor the Beauty of Nature

Jefferson loved nature and experienced it as evidence of God's love of humanity. He frequently expressed the joy of creation in poetic rhapsodies inspired by the beauty of the Virginia countryside: "Where has nature spread so rich a mantle? Mountains, forests, rocks, rivers! With what majesty do we ride above the storms! How sublime to look down into the workhouse of Nature, to see her clouds, hail, snow, rain, thunder . . . And the glorious sun when rising, as if out of a distant water, just gliding the tops of the mountains, and giving life to all nature!"

Jefferson's favorite way to savor the beauty of nature was through gardening, as he noted:

No occupation is so delightful to me as the culture of the earth, & no culture comparable to that of the garden. Such a variety of subjects, some one always coming to perfection, the failure of one thing repaired by the success of another, & instead of one harvest, a continued one thro' the year. Under a total want of demand except for our family table. I am still devoted to the garden. But tho' an old man, I am but a young gardener.

Cultivating your own garden is one of the most delightful Jeffersonian exercises in nature appreciation. Even if you live in an apartment in the city, you can experiment with growing some simple herbs as a way to get started.

Nurture Friendships

Just as a garden requires regular attention and plenty of care, so, Jefferson believed, do our friendships. Andrew Burstein, author of *The Inner Jefferson*, refers to friendship as "a prime social relation, universally understood to be an important source of entertainment and emotional fulfillment, an intellectual outlet, a desirable instrument for acquiring images of all that exists beyond the self. It can offer a convenient (and sometimes crucial) sounding board for one's own thoughts, more powerful than family by its voluntary nature."

Jefferson spent many hours each morning keeping up his correspondence with friends all over the world. In his last years he renewed his correspondence with John Adams, and the letters between the two are a treasure of American history and a moving testament to the value of reclaiming old friends.

- ▲ In your notebook, make a list of friends with whom you may have lost touch. Make a phone call or send a letter or e-mail to open the possibility of renewing the bond you once felt.
- ▲ Then make a list of the friends who are active in your life now. Under each name write a few things you could do to nurture or strengthen the friendship. Program reminders of your friends' birthdays and anniversaries into your computer or Palm Pilot. Experiment with giving generous gifts and writing notes that let your friends know just how much you care.
- ▲ Jefferson emphasized the importance of friendship in the "sunshine of life" but also in its "shade." Reach out to dear ones in your life who are suffering through adversity. Make a list of friends who are struggling with illness, financial problems, divorce, or other challenges, and then seek ways to be of service.

I find friendship to be like wine . . .
ripened with age, the true restorative cordial.

—THOMAS JEFFERSON

∽

A JEFFERSONIAN WINE EXPERIENCE

Thomas Jefferson was ahead of his time when it came to extolling the virtues of wine: "I rejoice," he wrote in 1818, "at the prospect of a reduction of the duties on wine. . . . No nation is drunken where wine is cheap . . . Its extended use will carry health and comfort to a much enlarged circle." Jefferson filled his wine cellar at Monticello with the great wines of the world, including Bordeaux from France and Barolo from Italy. Washington, Madison, and Monroe all relied on him for oenological advice.

For Jefferson, wine was a key element in "the pursuit of happiness." In addition to recognizing its health benefits he appreciated fine wine as an aesthetic treasure and as a catalyst for conviviality. A true connoisseur, Jefferson emphasized the importance of quality over quantity. He served small amounts of the best wines he could find and took time to savor their color, aroma, "feel," taste, and aftertaste.

Try a Jeffersonian-style wine tasting. You might begin, for example, with a comparison of a wine from his native state of Virginia with a wine from his beloved France.

Try, for example, the white Viognier wine made by Guigal in France's Rhone Valley with the version made by Horton in Virginia (both should be easy to find at a good wine store for under $20—a 750 ml bottle of wine offers ten tastes, so the cost is only $2 per person). Viognier is an unusual and exotic white wine with a faint aroma of roses and fresh peaches. It goes particularly well with salmon, and if you don't mind mixing genius metaphors, it would be ideal with the "groached" version in the recipe in the chapter on Elizabeth I.

Next, move on to a comparison of red wines. Jefferson was a great champion of America's westward expansion and would be thrilled with the international success of California wineries. Honor this expansive and fruitful Jeffersonian dream by trying a California Cabernet, perhaps a bottle of Monticello "Jefferson" Cabernet Sauvignon from the Napa Valley. Compare this treasure of American winemaking with a classic Bordeaux from France.

As you enjoy, consider a toast to the Founding Fathers and their legacy of freedom, and remember the words of Ben Franklin: "Wine is proof that God loves us and loves to see us happy."

WRITE A DIALOGUE BETWEEN YOUR HEAD AND HEART

While in Paris Jefferson found himself enamored of a charming and beautiful Anglo-Italian socialite named Maria Cosway. She touched him deeply and set off an inner conflict about the extent to which he should pursue their friendship. He attempted to work through this conflict by writing a letter in the form of a dialogue between his head and his heart.

His head counseled caution:

Head: "Consider what advantages it presents, and to what inconveniences it may expose you. Do not bite at the bait of pleasure till you know there is no hook beneath it. The art of life is the art of avoiding pain."

But his heart yearned for tenderness:

Heart: "Friendship is precious . . . We have no rose without its thorn . . . when I look back on the pleasures of which it is the consequence, I am conscious they were worth the price I am paying."

Do you, like Jefferson, have conflicts in your life between your head and your heart? In your notebook, list possible areas of inner conflict. Then choose one of the issues that divides you internally and explore it, in the manner of Jefferson, by writing a dialogue between the parts. Although you may not find an immediate resolution, the process of inner dialogue can guide you to the greater self-awareness that is the touchstone of inner freedom.

Karen is a CPA at a public firm. She's proud of her work and feels that she has the potential for becoming a partner. She works long hours, and in the few months prior to April 15 she rarely escapes the office. Her husband is supportive and takes time away from his own demanding job to contribute to the care of their infant son.

But with the birth of their second child, Karen found that the conflict between her career aspirations and her parenting priorities was increasing.

She addressed the issue with a dialogue between her heart and head, recorded in her genius notebook. She generously agreed to share the following excerpt with us:

"My eight weeks of maternity leave are nearing completion. I can't bear the thought of leaving my baby in the arms of another and marching back into the office. Just thinking about it makes my heart ache. The conflict is keeping me awake at night, so I'm trying this 'dialogue' between my head and my heart.

"Head: There is no way that you can afford to quit your job, even for a few years.

"Heart: But my children will only be this young for a short time. They are more important than anything.

"Head: Agreed, that's why they need to be fed and clothed.

"Heart: But they need me, most especially while they're young. And I can't stand the thought of the babysitter hearing their first words and seeing their first steps.

"Head: Ah, so it's about what *you* will be missing, not about what the *children* will miss!

"Heart: It's about both! They need me, but I need to be with them too. I want to enjoy this time in their lives. They're only little for such a short time.

"Head: The bottom line is you just can't afford to quit. You cannot live off your savings, and you have bills to pay. And you always pay your bills, you're an accountant, for goodness sakes!"

"Heart: But I'm also a mom and I want to be with my kids. I have every intention of paying my bills, and I intend to find a way to do both."

Of course, Karen's dialogue didn't magically yield a breakthrough idea. But as she listened to both her head and heart, she eventually found her way to an acceptable solution. She worked out a plan with her firm that allowed her to do more work at home in a more flexible schedule. As she commented, "The dialogue process helped me lay out the situation, making it possible to consider it in a more objective but also more creative fashion."

READ THE DECLARATION OF INDEPENDENCE

Read it a few times aloud and notice how it makes you feel.

What does the Declaration of Independence mean to you?

Consider committing it to memory.

As you contemplate this magnificent document, you might also consider the following questions:

What freedoms do you enjoy?

Do you take your freedom for granted?

Are there freedoms you desire that are prohibited?

Are there freedoms desired by others that you would deny?

What sacrifices have others made to preserve and protect your freedom?

What sacrifices would you be willing to make to preserve and protect the
  freedom of others?

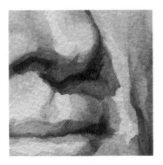

JEFFERSON AT WORK

Thomas Jefferson was, as one biographer called him, "an executive beyond compare." His visionary, humanistic, and effective leadership style makes him a wonderful role model for anyone who aspires to lead. These are some of the elements of his approach that you may wish to emulate.

Choosing the Best People

Some executives go through their careers bemoaning the lack of quality people. Others actually seek out second-rate associates to enhance their own stature. The best leaders, of course, surround themselves with the best people, and in this regard Jefferson is a role model par excellence. He once said: "If I had a universe to choose from, I could not change one of my associates to my better satisfaction." His associates, men like James Madison and Albert Gallatin, were gifted leaders in their own right. As Professor Garrett Ward Sheldon observes: "[Jefferson's] leadership style required a certain character of 'follower.' Independent, responsible, competent, Jefferson chose colleagues who were equal to him intellectually, morally, and circumstantially. . . . Jefferson abhorred yes-men and intellectual weaklings; he didn't want inferior disciples, but equal colleagues."

Modeling Openness and Collegiality

Even though most organizations are working overtime to break down unwieldy hierarchies and encourage a democracy of ideas, rigid, authoritarian leadership styles are still shockingly prevalent. Open communication and collegiality are key ingredients in optimizing intellectual capital in a competitive environment. And, in contrast to that of his predecessors, whose more formal and imperial leadership style often created internal discord, Jefferson's administration was marked by the kind of harmony and loyalty that any modern executive would envy.

Jefferson achieved that harmony and loyalty by nurturing a friendly, open collegiality that brought out the best in his extraordinarily gifted team. For the first few hours of each working day, for example, he left the door to his office open, inviting a free flow of communication. Acting more as facilitator than boss, he encouraged lively debate and a thorough exchange of views among his leadership team. Thomas Jefferson married informality and charm with professionalism and commitment to excellence.

As Professor Sheldon notes, "He ran cabinet meetings as gatherings of friends, not bureaucratic committees. The only rules were those of open, honest discussion, fair play, and mutual respect . . . He did not 'pull rank'; he did not threaten or bully or intimidate or manipulate others. He respected their free will and judgement . . . because of his democratic leadership style, [he] 'commanded' only the loyalty and respect of his associates."

Acting with Politeness and Grace

A CEO of a global technology company made headlines recently because his rude e-mail to all employees was posted on the Internet, causing the company's morale, and stock price, to plummet. Politeness and grace are leadership qualities that never go out of style, and Jefferson is a marvelous exemplar of both. Thomas Jefferson combined the courtly elegance of a Virginia gentleman with a down-to-earth soulful quality that made it difficult for anyone not to like him. His unfailing politeness and genuine humility were reflections of the respect he held for his colleagues, opposition, and fellow citizens. His affable manner was balanced with a natural dignity that made him a quietly charismatic commanding presence. Tirades and tantrums were not in his repertoire. He met disagreement, conflict, and controversy with an attitude of respect and fair play, seeking solutions that fulfilled common interests and purposes.

Team Building

Have you ever attended a corporate conference where every moment seemed to be scheduled with a formal activity? Or perhaps you've been exposed to a team-building exercise that was designed to force you to bond with others? Thomas Jefferson understood that people come together by getting to know one another in natural, enjoyable circumstances. He knew that informal, social contact—between members of his own team, and with all stakeholders, especially opponents—was the key to getting things accomplished.

Thomas Jefferson combined traditional Southern hospitality, enhanced by a continental flair, with a genius for bringing people together to discover and achieve common purposes. He was masterful at reaching out to key stakeholders one-on-one while also orchestrating harmonious social events. He emphasized that these informal interactions served an important purpose: "that we may know one another and have opportunity of little explanations of circumstances, which, not understood, might produce jealousies and suspicions injurious to the public interest."

Ignoring formal rank, Jefferson treated everyone at his team-building dinners as an honored guest. He graciously drew all his guests into conversation and applied wit and charm to deflect or redirect controversy as it arose. Jefferson knew the value of wine and food in bringing people together. He served his guests French, Italian, and American cuisine accompanied by the finest wines of the world. And he did it all in a style that one of his guests described as "elegant simplicity."

Dennis Ratner, Founder and CEO of the Haircuttery, Comments on the Influence of Jefferson's Leadership Style

"Jefferson's leadership style is an inspiring expression of the approach that I have been attempting to execute for all of my business career. Long ago I discovered that bringing on the right people is truly the best investment I can make. And a culture of collegiality, built on shared values and strong relationships, is the way to get the most from those great people. We run meetings that are characterized by respectful, passionate, open communication with a strong, creative, problem-solving, results-oriented flavor. We are informal and at the same time totally commited to success.

"A few years ago I spent some time at the University of Virginia, Darden Business School, and came away with an even greater respect for Jefferson's legacy in supporting education. Continuous learning, on an individual and organizational basis, is another key to our success, along with our commitment to teamwork, integrity, and a high quality of life. And, if we were a public company, I'd have to be driven by finance as the overriding priority, but because we are privately held I can focus on my dream, which is to build an organization that is free to pursue the happiness of its people as its top priority."

Beethoven's Ninth Symphony, composed in the wake of the French and American Revolutions, is a supreme musical expression of the spirit of freedom championed by Thomas Jefferson. The amazing choral climax usually begins with the German word *Freude,* meaning "joy," and this masterpiece is widely known as the *Ode to Joy.* But the original first word by the German poet Schiller was *Freiheit,* meaning "freedom." German court censors of the time were uncomfortable with the notion of freedom and changed the first word to "joy." The unfortunate change stuck, until Leonard Bernstein conducted the Ninth at the ceremonies celebrating the fall of the Berlin Wall. Bernstein went back to the original word—"freedom!" This incredible music is the sound of the Enlightenment ideals that still drive the quest for liberty, brotherhood, and equality. Listen, and feel the joy that results from liberating the spirit of freedom.

ONWARD TO DARWIN

Thomas Jefferson was a naturalist; one writer calls him a "Romantic ecologist," who saw in nature convincing proof of the existence of a benign Creator.

Our next revolutionary genius loved nature as much as Jefferson, but his uncannily astute observations of nature led him to propose a theory that has proven to be a most vexing challenge to traditional Judeo-Christian beliefs about the nature of Creation.

Introverted, soft-spoken, and gentle, Charles Darwin promulgated ideas that provided, and continue to provide, a great test of the freedoms of speech and belief that Jefferson championed. Whether you accept his theories or not, Darwin, as man and scientist, offers a supreme role model for developing your power of observation and opening your mind.

Charles Darwin

(1809–1882)

Developing Your Power of
Observation and Opening Your Mind

Now comes the pain of truth, to whom 'tis pain;

o folly! for to bear all naked truths,

and to envisage circumstance, all calm,

that is the top of sovereignty.

—JOHN KEATS

O ur next revolutionary genius had this to say for his success: "With such moderate abilities as I possess, it is truly surprising that I should have influenced to a considerable extent the belief of scientific men on some important points . . . I think I am superior to the common

Darwin's power of observation for me is a very deep one, one that combines looking with thought. I'm struck by his unusual marriage of patience and passion, tinged somehow with a sadness that may have come from his illness or perhaps the deaths of his children.—Norma Miller

run of men in noticing things which easily escape attention, and in observing them carefully. My industry has been nearly as great as it could have been in the observation and collection of facts. What is far more important, my love of natural science has been steady and ardent."

Such plainspoken modesty is so rare these days that it almost sounds disingenuous. Many twenty-first-century skeptics might wonder why a man of great accomplishment would describe himself with such reserve. Could he truly be so naïve? Does he really regard the methodical procedures behind his accomplishments as the secret of his success? Could a man of historical influence actually approach his work with this much humility, letting his ideas speak louder than his personality?

In the case of Charles Darwin, the answer to all three questions is yes—and therein lies the essence of his genius. Darwin was not naïve in the ways of the world—far from it—but he maintained both an innocent, childlike fascination with the natural world and a wonderfully open and inquisitive mind. He repeatedly cited his powers of observation, "long pondering, patience and industry" as his strengths as a scientist. And he was a decidedly humble revolutionary of the mind, eschewing fame and controversy to keep the focus on his ideas and their dissemination.

But what powerful ideas they were! Darwin earns his place as one of our top ten revolutionary minds for one of the most free-thinking acts in the history of thought: his discovery of the theory of evolution by natural selection. Although tentative ideas about evolution had begun to emerge in the eighteenth century through the work of his own grandfather, Erasmus Darwin (1731–1802), and the French naturalist Jean Lamarck (1744–1829), Charles Darwin expanded these sketchy theories with meticulous and comprehensive observations. By popularizing the phrases "struggle for existence" and, most notably, "survival of the fittest," Darwin brought these ideas to a tremendous mainstream audience. Although, like Copernicus, he was hesitant to offend the religious community of the day, his theories provoked outrage in his lifetime from closed minds and continue to do so in the present day. But his proponents have won the argument, fully integrating his theories into the contemporary disciplines of anthropology, sociology, economics, and psychology. His influence is also apparent on a more personal level: it's hard for any of us not to think of him when we visit the monkey house at the zoo!

SETTING THE STAGE FOR DARWIN: THE AMAZING MARY ANNING

Early ninteenth-century enthusiasm for evolutionary theories was fueled by the discovery of perfect dinosaur skeletons by an amazing child prodigy, Mary Anning (1799–1847). At a time when even the leading paleontologists could not reconstruct dinosaur remains accurately, Mary Anning's achievements in unearthing specimens were revolutionary. She grew up playing on the cliffs of Lyme Regis in southern England, the daughter of a carpenter, but was orphaned at age eleven. As a child Mary was fascinated by the many fossils she found on the cliffs, and she swiftly learned how to extract the fossils in good condition. Her first coup came in 1811 when she excavated the skeleton of a complete ichthyosaurus! She also discovered the first complete plesiosaurus and, in 1825, the very first pterodactyl, the great flying reptiles of the Jurassic/Cretaceous periods.

Mary Anning's exceptional abilities were dismissed by some people as a freak of nature. Her brilliance was "explained" by those who still resisted the notion of women's intellectual powers as follows: it was said that she had been struck by lightning as a child and that the spark of electrical genius had embedded itself into her nervous system! Of course, this was utter nonsense—her success was due to local knowledge, tenacity, and, like Darwin, her remarkable skills of observation.

THE EVOLUTION OF A GENIUS

The childlike wonder we feel watching the monkeys at the zoo is an apt starting place for an examination of Darwin's genius, for his fascination with the natural world, and his openness to the full range of its beauty, took root at a young age. In the autobiography he wrote privately for his family, Darwin observed that his schoolmasters and his father considered him "a very ordinary boy, rather below the common standard in intellect." Surprisingly, one of the earliest signs of his potential emerged in his youthful passion and skill for hunting—which became so pronounced that his father warned him, "you care for nothing but shooting, dogs and rat catching and you will be a disgrace to yourself and all your family." The younger Darwin took the warning to heart, deciding that the pleasures of "observing and reasoning" were preferable to those of "skill and sport."

The cultivation of his observation skills was already under way. By the age of eight, the year that his mother died, his taste for natural history and for collecting specimens was already "well developed" as he put it. Perhaps as a solace to the unique heartbreak a boy experiences at the loss of his mother, he delighted in long solitary walks, collecting shells and minerals to add to his collections of seals, stamps and coins. By the age of ten he was carefully observing insects, and the boundless enthusiasm that a child can bring to such pursuits stayed with him through his schooling. In high school he was, by his own description, "possessed of much zeal for whatever interested me and a keen pleasure in understanding any complex subject or thing," already exhibiting the enthusiasm, attention to detail, and capacity for total absorption in his subject that would be the hallmarks of his later intellectual successes.

Darwin's grandfather and father were both doctors, and the plan was for Charles to follow in their footsteps at Edinburgh University. But Darwin was not attracted to the way medicine was taught. He found lectures "intolerably dull" and was so upset by watching operations performed without benefit of anaesthetic that he "rushed away" and could not be induced to return. Like several of our revolutionary thinkers, Darwin demonstrates that formal academic study is not necessarily the route to success or self-fulfillment.

He abandoned his medical degree after two years, in 1827, but it was at Edinburgh that he developed a serious interest in the natural sciences. Here he discussed the work of Jean Lamarck on evolution, which challenged the old ideas of immutable species, as had his own grandfather's *Zoonomia, or The Laws of Organic Life* (1794–1796), which Charles greatly admired. Despite his scientific interests, however, when he went to Cambridge University in 1828 it was with the intention of entering the Church. But the Bible was no match for the bugs he'd been watching since he was a boy; he later observed "no pursuit at Cambridge was followed with nearly as much eagerness or gave me so much pleasure as collecting beetles."

A PROFOUND INFLUENCE ON DARWIN: THOMAS MALTHUS

Thomas Malthus (1766–1834) was a brilliant academic at Cambridge University who went on to become a curate in the Church of England. His 1798 essay "On Population," revised 1803, influenced the conclusions Darwin drew from his own observations and contributed to his belief in natural selection. Malthus wrote, "there is a natural tendency for population to increase faster than its means of subsistence." And, Darwin concluded, "natural selection was the inevitable result of the rapid increase of all organic beings, for such rapid increase inevitably leads to the struggle for existence."

We can still sense the boy in him in the delight he took at the variation of nature as an adult. We can hear it in his words, through which he transforms what most people would view simply as a revolting bug into "a larval cirripede with six pairs of beautifully constructed natatory legs, a pair of magnificent compound eyes and extremely complex antennae." Or we can see it in his adventures in the field, such as the occasion when he had both hands full with a pair of rare beetles he had found under some bark, only to spot a third and new kind, which he could not bear to lose—at which point he popped the beetle in his right hand into his mouth. When that beetle burned his tongue with an immediate ejection of acrid fluid, Darwin was forced to spit it out at once, losing both it and the third beetle.

To understand truth one must have a very sharp, precise, clear mind; not a cunning mind, but a mind that is capable of looking without any distortion, a mind innocent and vulnerable.

—J. KRISHNAMURTI

His openness to the eccentric beauties of nature was matched by his lifelong openness to new ideas. Both served him well, helping him to accept fresh evidence and refute old certainties. He also noted, "I have steadily endeavoured to keep my mind free so as to give up any hypothesis, however much beloved (and I cannot resist forming one on every subject) as soon as facts are shown to be opposed to it." But it was evidence, and not opinion, that he sought, maintaining a mind as independent as it was open. "I am not apt to follow blindly the lead of other men."

THE POWER OF OBSERVATION

Darwin's unaffected passion for the natural world, of course, was no guarantee for greatness unless it was put to effective use. Summing up the essence of his thought processes in his autobiography, he wrote that his most important characteristics were "the love of science, unbounded patience in long reflecting over my subject, industry in observing and collecting facts, and a fair share of invention as well as of common sense." These were developed further at Cambridge by John Henslow, professor of botany, who in 1831 recommended the newly graduated Darwin for the voyage on which he would refine his skills even further, changing the course of natural history forever.

It almost didn't happen: Darwin was very nearly rejected for the naturalist post by Robert Fitzroy, captain of the HMS *Beagle*. A classic representative of the closed mind, the kind of mind that would resist the very changes that his own ship's voyage would ultimately set in motion, Fitzroy was convinced he could judge a man's character by the shape of his face. Astonishingly, he doubted whether anyone with Darwin's nose could have enough "energy and determination" for the five-year voyage that lay ahead! Darwin got the job, but it wasn't the last time that he and Fitzroy would view the world differently.

The *Beagle* sailed to Tahiti, New Zealand, Brazil, Uruguay, Argentina, Chile, and, most notably, the Galapagos Islands off the coast of Ecuador. Throughout this voyage Darwin painstakingly wrote up his detailed observations on flora, fauna, and geology. In his autobiography Darwin later wrote that "the voyage of the *Beagle* has been by far the most important event in my life and has determined my whole career . . . I have always felt that I owed to the voyage the first real training or education of my mind. I was led to attend closely to several branches of natural history, and thus my powers of observation were improved . . . I worked to the utmost during the voyage from the mere pleasure of investigation and from my strong desire to add a few facts to the great mass of facts in natural science."

As the voyage of the *Beagle* progressed Fitzroy and Darwin witnessed the variations in finches, and other species, from island to island, along with other observable evidence, for the evolving theory of natural selection. Darwin observed these phenomena with an open, curious mind and pointed them out to Fitzroy. But Fitzroy wouldn't accept what he saw with his own eyes because he believed that the implications might lead to a contradiction of the literal interpretation of the first chapter of the book of Genesis.

Although he speculated about evolution before his journey on the *Beagle*, Darwin shared the orthodox view of creation at least until 1834. As he noted in his journal in that year: "It seems not a very improbable conjecture that the want of animals may be owing to none having been created since this country was raised from the sea."

His publications after returning from the voyage of the *Beagle* made Darwin's scientific reputation, and in 1839 he was elected a fellow of the Royal Society. Darwin also started to suffer from a mysterious illness that dogged him for the rest of his life and that he may have picked up on the voyage. The symptoms included violent shivering and vomiting attacks, and he lost much time when he was afflicted. Darwin observed that the illness had "annihilated several years of my life." Nevertheless, he was determined to accentuate the positive, noting that his illness saved him from the distractions of "society and amusement."

Early in 1839 he married his cousin Emma Wedgewood, and the birth of their first child at the end of the year gave Darwin a new subject for observation. At once he set about noting down all the new expressions the baby made, as he was convinced that human expression had a "gradual and natural origin." In 1841 Darwin left London for the peace of a country retreat, Down House in Kent, and devoted himself to growing plants and rearing pigeons. By these means he gained more valuable knowledge of variation and interbreeding for his later work.

As with most of our revolutionary thinkers, Darwin kept copious notes and journals about his work. He was also a prodigious correspondent, and 13,000 of his letters have survived, along with many of the specimens that he collected. He was able to use these records to prove that he had been working on his theories of evolution for over twenty years when the Welsh naturalist Alfred Wallace (1823–1913) outlined his version of the theory of natural selection in an essay that he submitted to Darwin in 1858.

Wallace and Darwin jointly published their ideas later that year in an academic journal, and Darwin was astonished that at this stage their work attracted very little attention. He concluded that it is necessary to explain new views at length to arouse the attention of the scientific world. Accordingly the following year Darwin published *The Origin of Species by Means of Natural Selection or the Preservation of Favored Races in the Struggle for Life*, once again making use of his copious notes to write swiftly.

Although the idea of evolution had been around for a while, Darwin was the first to frame it as a comprehensive and well-supported scientific theory. One of the keys to his success was a remarkable attention to detail, a fundamental component of his self-described "methodical" working style. He always made his own index for any book he read to keep track of subjects relative to his own work. He also kept thirty to forty large portfolios for the storage of references and memos, and before investigating any topic he looked through his indices and portfolios. He thus had instant access to all the information he had collected on the subject in his lifetime.

It was his mastery of an abundance of information that made all the difference, for it was in the tiny details that he proved his grand points. As Professor John Burrow comments in the introduction to the 1968 edition of *The Origin of Species*, "The reader who knows that the *Origin* is the most important book of the last century . . . may initially be disconcerted to discover that it has so much to do with such matters as the relative size and hairiness of gooseberries."

He found it difficult to express his ideas clearly at the first attempt, but again he saw this as a plus as it forced him to think for a long time about each sentence he wrote. His methodical approach led him to spot and correct errors in his own reasoning or in the logic of others that he might otherwise have missed. And he remained determinedly optimistic throughout the arduous process; whenever he was criticized by his opponents, he took comfort in repeating the following mantra to himself: "I have worked as hard and as well as I could, and no man can do more than this."

He had originally planned to write a book four or five times the length, but shifted gears once speed became essential to prove that he had developed these theories independently. Darwin again saw the positive side and told himself that very few people would have read such a long book. But they clearly did want to read it in the form in which it was published; the first print run of 1,250 copies sold out on the first day, and by 1876 some 16,000 copies had been sold in England alone. It was translated into nearly every European language and received widespread reviews.

Darwin's meticulous and methodical pursuit of clarity quite obviously paid off. Among all the works of the scientific luminaries, his writing is arguably the most accessible to educated lay readers. One does not need special training, mathematical or otherwise, to read *The Origin of Species*, whose universal appeal is virtually unmatched by any other scientific masterpiece. At the same time, Darwin did not compromise his scientific integrity or effectiveness in producing such a popular work. It is rich in logic and fact—features that render the work all the more thought provoking and convincing.

Although Wallace and others were on the same track, Darwin's contribution is unique and far more comprehensive. To the argument that his was an inevitable conclusion based on the intellectual context of his time, Darwin replied, "It has sometimes been said that the success of *The Origin* proved 'that the subject was in the air,' or 'that men's minds were prepared for it.' I do not think that this is strictly true, for I occasionally sounded out not a few naturalists, and never happened to come across a single one who seemed to doubt about the permanence of species. Even Lyell and Hooker, though they would listen with interest to me, never seemed to agree. I tried once or twice to explain to able men what I meant by Natural selection, but signally failed. What I believe was strictly true is that innumerable well-observed facts that were stored in the minds of naturalists were ready to take their proper places as soon as any theory which would receive them was sufficiently explained."

A DARWIN GLOSSARY

On the way from Heathrow Airport to central London you can visit the Darwin Café whose slogan is: "Your Natural Selection!" Darwin's ideas are pervasive; they have become part of the fabric of intellectual life and popular culture. Below are a few key definitions that may guide your understanding.

Survival of the Fittest

This doesn't mean that regular attendance at the health club will enhance your chances for survival; rather, Darwin was referring to fitness vis-à-vis the environment. This basic premise of Darwin's theories is a strong echo of Malthusian thinking: that there are never sufficient resources available to feed populations of animals or competing populations; in the struggle against nature and the environment that inevitably results, the fittest or most successful animals will compete more effectively for the available resources. Any small, chance variation in an animal that aids it in this struggle not only contributes to the redefinition of its overall quality of "fitness" but will also tend to be perpetuated (and most likely enhanced) by its offspring. As he noted: "Favorable variations have a tendency to be preserved, unfavorable to be destroyed."

Natural Selection

The process by which natural forces determine which living beings are most successfully suited to their particular environment—and thereby reap the most benefits from it—is the dynamic that fuels evolution. Consider a population of thin-shelled tortoises that are regularly picked up and carried to great heights by members of a local population of eagles, who drop them so that their shells crack open and they can be eaten. If a random variation results in a slightly thicker shell that resists being picked up and broken, that strain of tortoise will flourish and become dominant. According to the theory of natural selection, the tortoise population's shells will become even thicker and heavier through the generations. As for the eagles, those who develop a taste for something other than the increasingly heavy tortoises will do better than those who attempt to maintain an all-tortoise diet.

Social Darwinism

Some political philosophers have applied the theory of natural selection to the arena of human relations, wherein the fittest who survive are a nation or a people. "Rule Britannia," "Deutschland uber Alles" and "Manifest Destiny" are reminders of the doctrines by which the British Empire, Germany, and the United States, respectively, sought to lay claim to evolutionary dominance. The idea that human history was a Darwinian struggle and that the Western powers had won by the dawn of the twentieth century was a very seductive one, but it is not true Darwinism, which operates over vast time scales and with microscopic forces.

The Darwin Awards

These morbid but popular awards are given for inadvertent self-destruction through the lack of common sense. The awards website announces that they "celebrate Charles Darwin's Theory of Evolution by commemorating the remains of those who improved our gene pool by removing themselves from it."

Creation Science

Regarded by many as the biological equivalent of flat-earth geology, creation science posits that all life forms were created at once by a supreme being, as per the book of Genesis. Creatures that no longer exist, but the remains of which are found, are said simply to have failed to make it to the ark on time. (It is noteworthy that both Leonardo da Vinci and Darwin came to challenge the prevailing creationist viewpoint by observing the shells of extinct marine animals in elevated places in which they should not have been present at all.) Nevertheless, recent polls indicate that almost 25 percent of Americans accept creationism over evolution, and another 30 percent are undecided.

The Missing Link

After science and society began to accept the idea that man is descended from primates, the question arose regarding the exact link between man and ape. The search for this so-called missing link began to dominate the minds of anthropologists and biologists in the early twentieth century in such a way that every country wanted to prove that it had the missing link. Darwin himself was not at all in favor of the idea of a missing link in any evolutionary chain, claiming that "the struggle acts . . . far more subtly, persistently, and over immense periods of time." In other words, the search for a single "missing link" is a wild-goose chase.

Sexual Selection

A variation of natural selection suggests that evolution is driven primarily by the competition to produce offspring to continue the parents' specific genetic lineage. If you've ever attended a high school dance or spent an evening at a singles bar, then you've probably already mused on this controversial theory.

A GENTLE NATURE, A GIANT IMPACT

The Origin of Species and Darwin's later work *The Descent of Man* (1871) provoked fierce opposition from those who continued to hold a literal belief in the biblical account of creation. Darwin's ideas are so mainstream today that we can scarcely imagine the reaction when they were first introduced into the comfortable Victorian ethos of established values and cozy faith in God, queen, and empire. By declaring that the top-hatted, brilliantly uniformed imperial grandees were actually descended from hairy tree-dwelling apes, Darwin lobbed a grenade at Western civilization's self-concept. The controversy surrounding Darwin's ideas traveled to American shores, as reflected in the play and film *Inherit the Wind,* which dramatizes the infamous Scopes Monkey Trial; more recently the Kansas State Board of Education made global news reports by attempting to limit the teaching of evolution in schools.

But the classic debate over evolution took place at a meeting of the British Society for the Advancement of Science at Oxford in 1860. Darwin did not enjoy such disputes, but his supporters, such as zoologist Thomas Huxley and botanist J. Hooker, relished the opportunity of refuting his opponents. Ranged against these men of science were the Bishop of Oxford, William Wilberforce, and Darwin's old captain, now

Admiral Fitzroy. Fitzroy waved the Bible and asserted its unquestionable authority. Wilberforce ended his arguments by turning to Huxley and asking, with a sarcastic smile, "Do you claim descent from monkeys through your grandmother, grandfather, or both!"

The normally staid British audience exploded with furious chants for and against the two sides, and a certain Lady Brewster fainted and had to be carried from the room. Huxley waited for silence and then proceeded: "I am here only in the interests of science," he began. "You say that development drives out the Creator. But you assert that God made you; and yet you know that you yourself were originally a little piece of matter no bigger than the end of this gold pencil case." After making an incisive and powerful defense of Darwin, Huxley finished by responding to the bishop's remarks about his ancestry: "I would rather have an ape for an ancestor . . . I should feel no shame to have arisen from such an origin. But I should feel it a shame to have sprung from one who prostituted the gifts of culture and of eloquence to the service of prejudice and of falsehood."

Darwin deliberately avoided such debates himself because he feared it would not do any good and would lead to a "miserable loss of time and temper," preferring to let his ideas speak for themselves. Perhaps to avoid such conflict, he had refrained from explicit claims of man's descent from apes in *The Origin of Species*, although the implications were there. Later, in *The Descent of Man*, he cautiously referred to man's immediate biological ancestor as "a hairy quadruped, furnished with a tail and pointed ears, probably arboreal in its habits." Nevertheless, when he heard of his champions' performance at Oxford, he commented, "It is of enormous importance, showing the world that a few first-rate men are not afraid of expressing their opinions."

INSPIRED BY DARWIN: GREGOR MENDEL

Darwin's breakthrough raised many questions that inspired other geniuses. One of the most fruitful was the question of how evolutionary information was transmitted from generation to generation. This question led to the birth of the modern science of genetics and was the specific inspiration for a Moravian monk named Gregor Mendel (1822–1884). After entering a monastery as a young man, Mendel devoted his life to understanding the laws of heredity. Mendel owned the German translation of *On the Origin of Species* published in 1863. He made copious notes in the margins of this and other books by Darwin. In 1865 Mendel produced his laws of heredity, by which he proved that the characteristics of parents did not merge in their offspring, but were transmitted as distinct traits. Mendel experimented with peas to develop and prove his theories. He demonstrated that the characteristics of different varieties of peas, such as the shape of the pod, were transmitted by a biological inheritance code now known as genes. Moreover, Mendel discovered and explained the distinction between dominant and recessive genes, laying the groundwork for the discoveries of Watson and Crick, the Human Genome Project, and the birth of bio-engineering.

A modest and gentle man, Darwin sought to prove the veracity of his work through scientific method rather than showmanship or bombast. "I have never turned one inch out of my course to gain fame," he wrote in his autobiography. Moreover, he was leery of the notoriety that some of his fellow scientists had achieved. "When I think of the many cases of men who have studied one subject for years, and have persuaded themselves of the truth of the foolishest doctrines," he noted early in his career, "I sometimes feel a little frightened, whether I may not be one of these monomaniacs."

Any doubts about the sincerity of his modesty disappear in the face of his famously gentle demeanor and consistent self-effacement. Rather than lay claim to an extraordinary mind, he gave credit to what he did with the mind he had. His dedicated effort to make the most of his mental abilities—and revolutionize the way we think about ourselves in the process—remains a shining example to us all.

Despite his scientific interest in his own family, Darwin's correspondence and autobiography reveal a warm, humble, and loving soul. These qualities are apparent in his moving description of his wife: "She has been my greatest blessing, and I can declare in my whole life I have never heard her utter one word which I had rather have been unsaid. She has never failed in the kindest sympathy towards me, and has borne with the utmost patience my frequent complaints . . . I do not believe she has ever missed an opportunity of doing a kind action to anyone near her. I marvel at my good fortune that she, so infinitely my superior in every single moral quality, consented to be my wife. She has been my wise adviser and cheerful comforter throughout my life, which without her would have been . . . a miserable one . . . She has earned the love and admiration of every soul near her."

Darwin eventually lost his religious faith, but it was not simply because he could not fit his scientific theories into a religious worldview. He was also devastated by the deaths of three of his nine children. There was no sudden break with his religious beliefs; "disbelief crept over me at a very slow rate, but was at last complete. The rate was so slow that I felt no distress and have never since doubted even for a single second that my conclusion was correct." Although he lost his religious belief, he nevertheless was a practitioner of kindness, an exemplar of gentleness, and an advocate of love for all of creation. As he noted:

"As man advances in civilization, and small tribes are united into larger communities, the simplest reason would tell each individual that he ought to extend his social instincts and sympathies to all members of the same nation, though personally unknown to him. This point being once reached, there is only an artificial barrier to prevent his sympathies extending to men of all nations and races."

Darwin died in 1882, and after great controversy, was buried in Westminster Abbey as a symbol of reconciliation between science and faith.

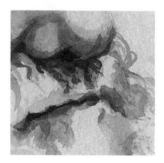

Summary of Achievements

▲ Darwin became the world's leading biologist through his observations made on the voyage of the survey ship *Beagle* while still in his twenties.

▲ He gave the first convincing explanation of the mechanism by which different species evolve in *The Origin of Species* (1859).

▲ He forced other thinkers to confront the problem of human evolution, especially after the publication of *The Descent of Man* (1871).

▲ To the end of his life he showed how even the greatest scientists have to be open to detailed studies of new evidence.

▲ He authored *The Expression of Emotion in Man and Animals,* published February 1872. It was written to demonstrate graphically—it was one of the first books ever with photographs—that animals and humans share certain facial expressions that indicate emotional states. It was a seminal work in the introduction of the concept of body language.

DARWIN AND YOU

It is ironic that the Genius Dream Team member most closely associated with the idea that genius has a genetic component so inspiringly reminds us that we have a choice in the extent to which we mobilize our inherited potential. Darwin's celebration of the power of patience, passion, observation, and methodology offers inspiration and encouragement as you strive to make the most of your inborn gifts. Imagine what you could do if you were as passionate in your pursuits as he was. Now imagine it again, remembering that you can be!

Darwin also provides an opportunity to reflect on how the brain you rely on evolved to its present state. Remember, you're part of an evolutionary continuum too—and there's a reason you are the way you are.

Our brains have evolved to manifest two distinctive attitudes toward the kind of change that Darwin's theories set in motion, one dominated by atavistic, repto-mammalian tendencies, the other by our evolving consciousness. Visionary philosopher and mathematician J. G. Bennett called these the psycho-static and psycho-kinetic, respectively. The psycho-static mind—the mind of a Captain Fitzroy—sees change as a threat, rejecting the unknown and avoiding ambiguity. This mind believes that the past determines the future, and seeks to justify its own status quo. It is motivated by fear and resists innovation, creative tension, and new ways of thinking. Alternatively, the psycho-kinetic mind—a mind like Darwin's—recognizes the ever-changing nature of existence and reconciles that awareness with a sense of a changeless, fundamental core of values.

This mind sees change as a promise, embraces chaos creatively, recognizes that the present creates the future, and welcomes the unknown. It is self-reflective and seeks the truth, however uncomfortable it may be.

As we become more aware of our own tendencies toward Fitzrovian attitudes it becomes possible to face down the fears that stand in the way of a more open, creative way of living—something to consider as you reflect on the self-assessment and exercises that follow.

DARWIN:
DEVELOPING YOUR POWER OF OBSERVATION AND OPENING YOUR MIND SELF-ASSESSMENT

☐ I have an open mind.

☐ My friends, family, and colleagues would agree that I am openminded.

☐ I am a patient, careful observer.

☐ I accentuate the positive in my life.

☐ I do not cling to old familiar ideas when they are proved wrong.

☐ I am methodical in my working habits.

☐ I am patient and persistent.

☐ I have empathy for other species.

☐ I do not let illness, childhood issues, or other people's criticism intimidate me, dampen my spirits, or affect my self-confidence.

☐ I am organized and thorough in documenting the process, progress, and effectiveness of my work.

☐ I can think inductively, studying specifics and details until patterns emerge.

☐ My love for truth is greater than my need to be right.

EXERCISES

THINKING LIKE DARWIN/
DEVELOPING YOUR POWER OF OBSERVATION
AND OPENING YOUR MIND

PRACTICE SELF-OBSERVATION

The chart below shows the relationship between the "triune" structure of your brain and Abraham Maslow's "hierarchy of needs." As an exercise in cultivating conscious evolution take Maslow's hierarchy as a theme for a day. Note the percentage of your time and energy invested in each evolutionary level.

How much of your attention and energy is focused on the survival level? What types of territorial behavior do you engage in on the average day? (For example, how does it make you feel when you discover that someone has taken two parking spaces by parking diagonally? Do you ever do anything like that?) What percentage of your life force is invested each day in mammalian concerns? What role does seeking approval and bonding with other Homo sapiens play in your daily life? And how much time and focus do you devote to big-picture thinking, self-awareness, altruism, and other neo-cortical activities?

Avoid placing value judgments on the levels, just observe yourself as objectively as you can . . . as Darwin might watch a beetle!

TRIUNE BRAIN MODEL:	MASLOW'S HIERARCHY:
Reptilian/brain stem	Lower level: survival focus, food, sex, power, etc.
Mammalian/limbic system	Mid level: bonding, affiliation, affection, and self-esteem
Human/neo-cortex	Higher level: consciousness, altruism, big picture, long-term good of society, self-actualization

David, a counselor at a community college, decided to view behavior at his weekly departmental meeting through this Maslovian/triune-brain lens. Here are some excerpts from his genius journal:

"I headed toward my usual seat, but quickly noticed that it was occupied by a new coworker-reptile; this particular reptile was obviously unaware he had invaded 'my' space/territory and was potentially in danger. Initially, I considered asking him to move or even giving him a shove but having judged better (higher functioning) I chose to ignore the matter, and suppressing a reptilian glare, I found a new seat.

"I was slightly preoccupied with the adjustment to the new and in my opinion, inferior seating arrangements, so I began making jokes with the person seated next to me (mammalian bonding) until we received disapproving glares from the other mammals. As the meeting started and we began to discuss issues, I noticed that my reactions were tinged with a reptilian desire to exert my standing in the hierarchy, and a mammalian concern that everyone would like and approve of me. This awareness helped me edit out those elements and speak in a way that was perhaps more truly about the issues themselves. I guess this is what 'higher cortical functioning' is all about.

"The final item on the meeting agenda was the announcement of the papers that had been accepted for an upcoming conference. Though I had not submitted a paper, I felt elated when I learned that my best friend had been chosen to receive a large grant and would be presenting her paper at a major conference (a warm, fuzzy mammalian reaction).

"Then I became aware of a rumbling in my stomach and a strong reptilian craving for a Big Mac with cheese . . . so much for higher-level thinking!"

FIND YOUR OWN "BEETLEMANIA"

At Cambridge Darwin met so many intelligent people who shared his interest in beetles that he joked that beetle collecting was obviously a sign of an eminent mind. Although Darwin meant this humorously, there is an element of truth in it. The human brain understands and remembers information by codifying and categorizing it into patterns. Plato's great student Aristotle understood this when he introduced classifications for human knowledge.

Did you ever have a passion for collecting things when you were younger? Perhaps seashells or stones, maybe baseball cards or butterflies? Experiment with renewing that old passion or discovering a new one. A particularly wonderful way to cultivate your Darwinian openness and observational powers is to share a collection with a child. What you collect isn't as important as the way you do it—Pokemon cards, stamps, coins, books, Beatles records, or beetles—anything that captures your imagination. Keep a "collection journal" together and set weekly goals for things you'd like to find. In addition to developing observational, organizational, and memory skills you'll learn how to better perceive the world with the childlike openness and passion that was the secret of Darwin's genius.

Charles Darwin once grew eighty different species of plants from seeds he found in the mud he scraped off a bird's foot.

LEARN FROM PETS

Darwin kept many pets, including dogs, tortoises, and of course a variety of beetles and other insects, and he learned from them all. He had a particular passion for pigeons and spent many years breeding them to learn how they inherited varying characteristics. He subscribed to the *Poultry Chronicle* and joined workingmen's pigeon clubs, where he was always known as "the squire." If you don't have a member of another species resident in your household, then invite one: cats, dogs, fish, parrots, rabbits, or snakes can all teach you new ways of understanding the world. And if you already have a pet, aim to see your animal friend in a new way. Experiment with keeping a family journal of your animal companion's behavior. Let your animals inspire creative family conversations on questions like these:

▲ How would your world change if smell was as important to you as it is to a dog?

- ▲ Why do dogs often seem to look like their owners?
- ▲ Why do cats seem to be more independent than dogs?
- ▲ How do different animals experience emotion?
- ▲ Does an insect have feelings?
- ▲ What are the greatest similarities and differences in the ways that animals and humans interact with other members of their own species?
- ▲ If you were another animal besides Homo sapiens, what would you be and why?

A NOVEL APPROACH TO THE POWER OF OBSERVATION

Darwin was very much a family man, and one of his favorite pleasures in later years was reading novels with his family, so long as they did not end unhappily, against which he said, "a law ought to be passed." Of course, great novels offer the pure pleasure of getting lost in the story. But reading novels is also a wonderful way to sharpen your appreciation of the power of observation. Great writers observe the world with Darwin-like perspicacity and patience, and as you savor their works, you can strengthen your own depth of appreciation for the amazing details of creation. Make a list of your favorite novels and read them again with a view toward deeper appreciation of observation. Share your list with a friend or your family and organize a novel-reading group—just as Darwin did with his family.

e.e. cummings referred to himself as a "wily observer of everything under the sun."

Here are a few brilliant masterworks of the power of observation to help you get started:

Thomas Hardy's *Tess of the d'Urbervilles*, one of the most visual, descriptive, and observant books ever written.
Anne Tyler's *Accidental Tourist,* nonjudgmental, pure observation of humans in psychologically challenging circumstances.
Annie Dillard's spectacular nonfiction book *Pilgrim at Tinker Creek,* widely acknowledged as a masterpiece of observation.

Tom Wolfe's *Bonfire of the Vanities*, fiction that reads like fact despite its exaggerations and stereotypes.

Kazuo Ishiguro's *Remains of the Day*, a novel of disillusionment told with sly attention to minute details.

EXPERIENCE THE EVOLUTION OF THE UPRIGHT POSTURE

Although it is particularly fun to do this exercise in a group you can still get the value by doing it on your own. All you need is some clean, carpeted floor space and a towel.

Begin by lying facedown on the floor, the towel under your face, with your feet together and your hands resting at your sides. Notice that it is now impossible to fall. Rest facedown for a minute or two and contemplate the consciousness of a creature with this kind of relationship to gravity. Experiment with slithering along the floor toward an imaginary morsel of food.

Now get ready for an evolutionary leap. You are about to mutate. Slide the backs of your hands along the floor beside you until they flip over so that your palms are now on the floor in front of you. Press down with your newly evolved paws to raise your head and upper torso off the ground. Look around and consider the leap in consciousness allowed by your expanded horizon. Experiment with using your paws to help you explore your environment and move toward food.

Next, evolve to become a mammalian quadruped. Choose your favorite: horse, dog, cougar, gazelle, water buffalo . . . Move up onto all fours and, just for fun, imitate the gait, sounds and other behaviors of your chosen animal. How does your range of behavior and potential awareness change in this disposition?

Your next huge evolutionary leap is to rise off your front paws and become a primate. Choose your favorite—chimpanzee, orangutan, gorilla— and enjoy moving around in monkey mode. How do the possibilities for awareness change? Does the changing relationship with gravity affect your options for communication and socialization?

Now rise up to your full stature as Homo sapiens. What's it like to be fully human?

After completing this journey through the process of evolution consider the following questions and record your observations in your notebook.

What vulnerabilities are inherent in a fully upright posture?

What are the advantages of a fully upright posture?

What are the implications of your upright posture for the development of intelligence and consciousness?

On a day-to-day basis do you observe a relationship between people's posture and poise and their level of awareness and alertness?

Is it possible to feel depressed when you are fully upright?

Is it possible to feel exultation when you are slumped and hunched over?

ORIGIN-ALL THINKING

Did God create the world and all its species simultaneously? What's the origin of our species? Do you believe that we are descended from apes? How did life on earth begin? Could life as we know it have evolved from a primal soup of random molecular particles? If Darwin's theory is accurate, what is the implication for belief in God?

IS CREATION SCIENCE AN OXYMORON?

Here's the view of Harvard biologist Edward O. Wilson: "Because I was raised in a predominantly antievolutionist culture in the Protestant southern United States, I am inclined to be empathetic to these feelings, and conciliatory. Anything is possible, it can be said, if you believe in miracles. Perhaps God did create all organisms, including human beings, in finished form, in one stroke, and maybe it all happened several thousand years ago. But if that is true, He also salted the earth with false evidence in such endless and exquisite detail, and so thoroughly from pole to pole, as to make us conclude first that life evolved, and second that the process took billions of years. Surely Scripture tells us He would not do that. The Prime Mover of the Old and New Testaments is variously loving, magisterial, denying, thunderously angry, and mysterious, but never tricky."

Can you read and think about these questions with an open mind?

One of Darwin's secrets for cultivating an open mind was what Sigmund Freud called "Darwin's golden rule." Freud noted, "It is an undoubted fact that disagreeable impressions are easily forgotten . . . The great Darwin was so much impressed by it that he made it a 'golden rule' to note down with especial care any observations which seemed unfavorable to his theory, since he had convinced himself that precisely they would not remain in his memory."

In other words, Darwin focused especially on remembering and thinking about the observations and information that his emotions might have led him to avoid. This disciplined approach to overcoming prejudices and preconceptions is one of the hallmarks of genius and independent thinking.

Experiment with applying Darwin's golden rule to your own observations and experiences. Challenge yourself to become more aware of your prejudices and preconceptions. Take "my prejudices and preconceptions" as a theme for a week and record your observations in your noteboook. Be sure to record the most discomforting observations before you forget them!

DARWIN AT WORK

Overcoming Fitzrovian closed-mindedness and cultivating a Darwinian openness to new ideas is a great challenge in the rapidly evolving, highly competitive corporate jungle.

Despite the intense information age imperative to innovate, many organizations are rife with Fitzrovian attitudes to new processes, procedures, and technologies A new idea, no matter how positive its implications, always suggests abandonment of the old. And there seems to be a direct correlation between the extent to which an idea is truly innovative and the amount of resistance it generates. Resistance to organizational innovation often manifests in "Fitzroyisms"—phrases designed to stifle new ideas. The top ten Fitzroyisms I've heard over the years are:

10. "We've always done it this way."
9. "That's not how we do things around here."
8. "It's not in the budget."
7. "You have to prove that it will work before we try anything."
6. "If it ain't broke don't fix it."
5. "Yes, but . . . "
4. "We're not ready for that kind of change."
3. "Don't rock the boat."
2. "The lawyers won't like it."
1. "If that were such a good idea, someone would already have done it."

Business services giant KPMG recently launched a major program to rethink every aspect of the way it runs its business. Their name for this radical program is Darwin! KPMG's effort is unusual in that the firm is, by any measure, extremely successful, but as Mike Rake, KPMG's senior partner in the UK and chairman of KPMG Europe, told me, "the pace of change is now so fast that being good at what the world needs today is no guarantee of success tomorrow. Businesses need to look at the world through Darwinian eyes—i.e., without preconception—to understand and respond to what's really going on out there."

DARWIN: THE EVOLUTIONARY ANTHEM

Le sacre du printemps (*The Rite of Spring*) by Igor Stravinsky is a perfect pairing with the great genius of Darwin. The elemental nature and fiery asymmetrical rhythms of Stravinsky's *Rite* introduced a whole new concept of music to the world. Stravinsky noted that he wanted listeners to "hear the whole earth cracking." The premiere of this work in 1913 caused a great uproar, akin to the initial furor that greeted Darwin's ideas. Of course, both Darwin's theories and this extraordinary piece of music have withstood the test of time. The most popular recording of *The Rite of Spring* is the Leopold Stokowski rendition in Disney's *Fantasia*. In this classic, you witness the evolution of life from a ball of gas swirling in space, through the dance of primitive life forms, to the extinction of the dinosaurs, and beyond.

ONWARD TO GANDHI

The desk at which Darwin wrote *Origin of Species* can still be seen at the Athenaeum Club, in the heart of London's clubland near Trafalgar Square. In the nineteenth century the Athenaeum was the focal point for the governing classes of the British Empire, and it was there, over cigars and port, that far-reaching decisions concerning global conquest and annexation of territory were often made.

Although the masters of the British Empire may have been initially disconcerted by Darwin's revelations that they, like the rest of humanity, were descended from tree-dwelling hairy apes, they quickly recovered their poise. The rulers of the empire, however, swiftly assimilated Darwin's insights and proceeded to reinterpret them in their favor. Soon after Darwin had published *The Origin of Species* the prevailing view had become that the British Empire now represented the evolutionary pinnacle of social, political, intellectual, scientific, and military development. The "fittest" had not merely survived, they were now well and truly in charge. (There is an interesting contrast here with the reaction of the Inquisition to the discoveries of Copernicus and Galileo. The Inquisition fought a desperate rearguard action, trying to suppress the new knowledge that the Earth goes around the sun.)

Darwin's writings were simply enlisted as irrefutable "scientific" proof of this self-declared assertion of global superiority. "Survival of the fittest" now became a virtual mandate, indeed a jingoistic slogan, to encourage yet more imperial conquest and aggrandizement.

Nevertheless, at almost exactly the same time that Darwin published his great book, a child was born in India, the jewel in the crown of Britain's imperial possessions. That child would grow into the most effective adversary the empire had experienced since George Washington accepted the surrender of General Cornwallis at Yorktown. This new adversary was also to develop a revolutionary approach to the problem of dismantling the empire's grip on his home country. The new element was to be nonviolent resistance, and this great innovator's name was Mahatma Gandhi.

Mohandas Karamchand

(Mahatma) Gandhi

(1869–1948)

Applying the Principles of Spiritual Genius to Harmonize Spirit, Mind, and Body

We must be the change we wish to see in the world.

—GANDHI

By now you couldn't have helped but notice the varied roles that God and religion have played in the lives of our dream team geniuses. Some (Copernicus, Darwin) made discoveries that put them in conflict with established religion; others (Brunelleschi, Columbus) were

In this portrait I remained more faithful to the source material than in any other portrait. I wanted to convey a dynamic mind-body relationship as if this is a freeze frame of a man in action in both thought and deed.—Norma Miller

driven by a desire to give glory to the God they knew; still others (Elizabeth, Jefferson) labored to liberate God from monopolistic power structures of church or state. Whatever the particular dynamic we've seen, God and genius have been historically linked.

Such is still the case today, although our modern world has made room for so many different notions of church, religion, and godliness that we often refer to any and all of them by the all-encompassing term of spirituality. Never in history has the individual had access to so many ways of finding and expressing his or her own spiritual life. Consequently, many of us are compelled to define our relationship with God in unique terms. And with so many potentially rewarding spiritual paths before us, how shall we—as seekers of an authentic, vibrant spirituality—proceed?

Our penultimate breakthrough thinker is a revolutionary genius of the spirit who can guide us to make the most of our abundant options. The first person to achieve a political revolution without the use of violence, Mohandas K. Gandhi changed the world through the power of what he called "soul force," an inspiring combination of integrity, service, forgiveness, prayer, self-reliance, self-purification, and love from which we all can learn. As a result of Gandhi's methods, his beloved homeland India won its independence from British rule in 1947. His unprecedented strategy of satyagraha, or nonviolent resistance, celebrated the ideals of truth (*satya*) and firmness (*agraha*), even while embracing the possibility of love for one's enemy. Gandhi's practical philosophy and its tactical manifestations have also influenced other great leaders including Martin Luther King, Nelson Mandela, the Dalai Lama, and others.

As the great civil rights leader Martin Luther King emphasized, "Gandhi was probably the first person in history to lift the love ethic of Jesus above mere interaction between individuals to a powerful and effective social force on a large scale." On a more personal scale, he is a profoundly useful role model for all seekers of expanded inner freedom and spiritual vitality in everyday life.

EXPERIMENTS WITH TRUTH

Gandhi was born in 1869 in Porbandar, India, into a high-caste family who had been merchants, but had more recently taken a leading role in local politics. Gandhi was brought up in a strict Hindu family, within which he began to express an unusually strong conscience and highly developed moral compass at a very early age.

The concept of the musical or mathematical prodigy is familiar, but Gandhi was a moral prodigy. His early, extreme sensitivity to questions of goodness and truth was the seed of his greatness, and it blossomed as he grew to manhood. As he writes in his autobiography, *Experiments with Truth*, "But one thing took deep root in me—the conviction that morality is the basis of things, and that truth is the substance of all morality. Truth became my sole objective. It began to grow in magnitude every day, and my definition of it also has been ever widening." Once, as an act of rebellion against his vegetarian parents, the young Mohandas secretly ate goat meat with a young Muslim friend. That night he had nightmares and dreamed that he had a live goat bleating inside him. Though he persisted, and tried meat half a dozen times during the next year, Gandhi eventually decided that deceiving his parents was worse than not eating meat. As he comments in his autobiography, "Lying to anyone was out of the question," he learned. "It was this . . . that saved me from many a pitfall."

In 1883, when they were both thirteen, Gandhi wed his wife, Kasturbai. It was an arranged marriage, but Gandhi was deeply fond of her. She bore his four sons and supported him throughout his struggles for independence and his quest for self-realization. Nevertheless, he later made public his opposition to the institution of arranged marriage, writing, "I can see no moral argument in support of such a preposterously early marriage."

In 1887 Gandhi's family reluctantly allowed him to leave India to study law in London, where his mother made him vow not to touch meat, wine, or women. In London he discovered that vegetarianism was becoming newly fashionable, and he joined the London Vegetarian Society,

where he was introduced to the writings of some of the great moralists of the age—Leo Tolstoy, Annie Besant, and John Ruskin. On his return home Gandhi practiced as a lawyer, but in 1893 he gave up his lucrative Bombay legal practice to live on just one pound sterling per week in South Africa. Traveling by train to Pretoria shortly after his arrival, Gandhi was told to leave the first class car, for which he had a ticket, because he was not white. When he refused to go to another compartment, he was thrown off the train—and remained in South Africa for the next twenty-one years, opposing that country's discriminatory legislation against people of color.

TRANSFORMING FEAR

In *Gandhi the Man* Eknath Eswaren describes the future "Mahatma" as a fearful child. "Even in high school," Eswaren comments, "he had been terrified of boys much less his size." Gandhi's nanny, Rambha, offered him this wise and ultimately life-changing advice:

"There is nothing wrong in admitting you are afraid," she assured him. "But when something threatens you, instead of running away, hold your ground and repeat the mantra Rama, Rama over and over again in your mind. It can turn your fear into fearlessness."

Gandhi's pursuit of the law did not inhibit his spiritual development. He studied all the world's leading religions and their guiding principles, looking for connections and shared themes. His ability to harmonize such disparate traditions as Buddhism, Christianity, Judaism, Islam, and of course Hinduism was a major facet of his spiritual genius. He would ultimately apply their combined wisdom, and their respective most compelling ideals, toward the political and social achievements that would become his life-long spiritual quest. "What I want to achieve . . . is self-realization, to see God face to face," he noted in his autobiography. "All that I do by way of speaking and writing, and all my ventures in the political field, are directed to this same end."

Gandhi realized that the love, forgiveness, and compassion could be found at the heart of any spiritual path, regardless of the tradition. Beginning with his own, he identified their signal expression in a passage from a Hindu sacred text:

> For a bowl of water give a goodly meal;
> For a kindly greeting bow thou down with zeal;
> For a simple penny pay thou back with gold;
> If thy life be rescued, life do not withhold.
> Thus the words and actions of the wise regard;
> Every little service tenfold they reward.
> But the truly noble know all men as one,
> And return with gladness good for evil done.

The passage "gripped my mind and heart" when Gandhi first read it. "Its precept—return good for evil—became my guiding principle. It became such a passion with me that I began numerous experiments in it." One experiment was to find the same message in the other traditions, which proved to be a landmark success. By removing his guiding principle from the restrictions of any one denomination, his quest became a truly spiritual mission that transcended the borders of religion.

Gandhi's approach to spirituality still resonates today: "There are innumerable definitions of God, because His manifestations are innumerable," he wrote. "They overwhelm me with wonder and awe and for a moment stun me. But I worship God as Truth only. I have not yet found Him, but I am seeking after Him. I am prepared to sacrifice the things dearest to me in pursuit of this quest. Even if the sacrifice demanded be my very life, I hope I may be prepared to give it."

By every indication, Gandhi lived up to his quest, honoring his words with his actions and displaying a level of integrity which can inspire us all. As Mahadev Desai, one of his closest associates, explained: "Most of us think in one way and speak in another way and act in yet another way. Not so with [Gandhi] . . . He said what he believed and put into practice what he said, so his mind, spirit, and body were in harmony."

Gandhi's beliefs were well reasoned and subjected to what biographer B. R. Nanda calls a rigorous form of "moral algebra," and his strong conscience was matched with an indomitable will. Once the ethical equations were calculated, he committed to a path of action and could not be swayed, ready to give his life to its fulfillment if necessary. His legendary integrity is illustrated by the story of a mother who came to Gandhi and pleaded with him to tell her young diabetic son not to eat sugar as it was bad for him, hoping that the boy would listen to a man with such moral force as Gandhi. To her surprise Gandhi instead asked the woman to bring her son back in three weeks' time. When she returned, Gandhi finally told the boy not to eat sugar. When she asked why he hadn't said this to the child three weeks ago, he replied, "Three weeks ago, I myself was still eating sugar."

GREAT SOUL

Gandhi was dubbed "Mahatma," meaning "Great Soul," by the Bengali poet and Nobel Prize winner Rabindranath Tagore (1861–1941). The name was a reflection of Gandhi's shining integrity and his ability to integrate universal spiritual truths. In old age Gandhi was also nicknamed "Bapu" or "grandfather."

SERVICE, FORGIVENESS, PRAYER

Gandhi's commitment to service, forgiveness, and prayer was forged in the family environment in which he was raised. The Hindu tradition views service to others as the key to happiness and enlightenment, as captured by the great sage and poet Rabindranath Tagore: "I awoke and saw that life was service. I acted and behold, service was joy."

For Gandhi, service began in his parents' home. Describing in his autobiography how he cared for his injured father, for example, he declared, "I loved to do this service. I do not remember ever having neglected it." Service rendered in a spirit of joy was, in Gandhi's emerging philosophy, the supreme pleasure and the secret of self-realization. He argued that service performed out of guilt, for external recognition, or as a result of pressure from others diminishes the spirit. His devotion to the principle of service expanded to include his community, country and ultimately, all of creation. "If I found myself entirely absorbed in the service of the community," he wrote, "the reason behind it was my desire for self-realization. I had made the religion of service my own, as I felt that God could be realized only through service. And service for me was the service of India."

Forgiveness was likewise learned in his boyhood home, most notably on the occasion, recalled in his autobiography, when he took something from his father, only to be tortured by the pain of his transgression. "I decided to at last write out the confession, to submit it to my father, and ask his forgiveness. I wrote it on a slip of paper and handed it to him myself. In this note not only did I confess my guilt, but I asked adequate punishment for it, and closed with a request to him not to punish himself for my offence. I also pledged myself never to steal in the future." His father's response to the confession created one of the inner turning points of Gandhi's evolution; instead of responding with anger, Gandhi's father offered "sublime forgiveness," Gandhi wrote. "He read it through, and pearl-drops trickled down his cheeks, wetting the paper. For a moment he closed his eyes in thought and then tore up the note. He had sat up to read it. He again lay down. I also cried. I could see my father's agony. If I were a painter I could draw a picture of the whole scene today. It is still so vivid in my mind . . . Those pearl-drops of love cleansed my heart, and washed my sin away. Only he who has experienced such love can know what it is."

The weak can never forgive.

Forgiveness is an attribute of the strong.

—GANDHI

Along with the appreciation of service and forgiveness came a profound respect for the power of prayer. While sailing from India to London in 1931 to appeal for Indian independence, Gandhi attended a prayer meeting and said that prayer had "saved my life . . . I had my share of the bitterest public and private experiences. They threw me into temporary despair. If I was able to get rid of that despair it was because of prayer . . . It came out of sheer necessity as I found myself in a plight where I could not possibly be happy without it." For Gandhi, prayer was the catalyst of "soul force" and the most important instrument of action. "Supplication, worship, prayer are no superstition; they are acts more real than the acts of eating, drinking, sitting or walking. It is no exaggeration to say that they alone are real, all else is unreal," he wrote, adding that heartfelt prayer "can achieve what nothing else can in the world."

SATYAGRAHA

The tradition of service, forgiveness, and prayer would find political expression in Gandhi's philosophy of satyagraha, or peaceful resistance, a result of his fateful encounter with prejudice on the Pretoria-bound train, after which he remained in South Africa over twenty years. "I began to think of my duty," he later wrote of that day. "It would be cowardice to run back to India without fulfilling my obligation. The hardship to which I was subjected was superficial—only a symptom of the deep disease of color prejudice. I should try, if possible, to root out the disease and suffer hardships in the process."

At the heart of the philosophy is the concept of ahimsa, or nonviolence, which derives from the idea that all life is interwoven in a divine fabric of love. "Complete non-violence is complete absence of ill will against all that lives," he wrote. "Non-violence is therefore, in its active form good will towards all life. It is pure Love. I read it in the Hindu scriptures, in the Bible, in the Koran." The practitioner of ahimsa, even when under attack, "is expected not to be angry with one who has injured him. He will not wish him harm; he will wish him well; he will not swear at him; he will not cause him any physical hurt. He will put up with all the injury to which he is subjected by the wrong doer."

SELF-MASTERY

Gandhi's pursuit of enlightenment led him to embrace a challenging spiritual training regimen designed to master the body and transmute the energy of desire through the practice of self-purification and the development of self-reliance. For him, this included a vow of celibacy, because he "could not live both after the flesh and the spirit," and a simple, ascetic diet than included periods of fasting, which he also used as part of the armamentarium of satyagraha. In the 1920s he started a series of fasts "to death" to apply moral pressure and to achieve political concessions from the British. He thought of fasting as "the greatest and most effective weapon . . . under given circumstances," but warned that it should not be undertaken without proper training.

In South Africa Gandhi set up the first of his many ashrams, or spiritual retreats, which were centers for his philosophy. This ideal sprang from Gandhi's pursuit of what he called the simple life or self-help. In this he was heavily influenced by the Russian writer Leo Tolstoy, author of *War and Peace* and *Anna Karenina*, an aristocrat of vast personal wealth who was alienated by the trappings of his fortune and the feudal powers of the tsarist regime in his homeland. Horrified by the widening gulf between rich and poor and the poverty of the Moscow slums, he set up soup kitchens in Moscow and gave away his wealth to the poor, electing to live as an ascetic on his own estate. Tolstoy also preached nonviolent solutions in his own writings and corresponded on the subject with Gandhi, to whom he wrote in 1910, "your activity in [South Africa] . . . is the most important work of all the work now being done in the world."

Self-help would later become an important part of Gandhi's battle with the British colonial powers in India, when he campaigned against giving charity to the poor. Instead he advocated that everyone should be given a spinning wheel, or *charkha*, to make their own cloth and become self-sufficient. The argument had serious political overtones, since Gandhi used it to object to the British elimination of the native cloth industry, and led demonstrations at which British-made clothes were burned. The *charkha* quickly became a tremendously successful icon, symbolizing a traditional Indian way of life at the same time that it honored Gandhi and his independence movement. Adopted by the Indian National Congress as the image on its flag, it united the Indian population against the British, who could do nothing to eradicate an everyday object despite its potency as a rallying symbol.

But more than a simple political image, the *charkha* gave expression to the practical spirituality that Gandhi practiced. He often used the *charkha* to spin as a form of meditation and was frequently photographed at the wheel. Also implicit in the image—and, by extension, in the idea of spinning the cloth for one's own clothes—was an endorsement both of simplicity and of the empowerment that derives from self-reliance. In a 1945 letter to Nehru, Gandhi outlined the scope of his chosen symbol: "I hold that without truth and non-violence there can be nothing but destruction for humanity. We can realize truth and non-violence only in the simplicity of village life and this simplicity can best be found in the *charkha* and all that the *charkha* connotes . . . Man should rest content with what are his real needs and become self-sufficient."

THE MARCH TO FREEDOM

Having published his manifesto for a free India in 1908, Gandhi returned to India for good in 1914, and soon took the leading role in the Home Rule Movement, eventually becoming leader of the Indian National Congress. From 1920 onward he organized campaigns of civil disobedience, always based on nonviolent methods. In 1922 he was arrested, but brilliantly turned his trial into an indictment of colonial rule. He did not hire a lawyer, nor did he defend himself—he pleaded guilty and used the occasion to explain why he had been forced into civil disobedience. The judge acknowledged that Gandhi's was an unusual case, but nevertheless sentenced him to six years' imprisonment, from which he was released two years later after an operation for appendicitis. Although he was to be imprisoned in the future, the British authorities never again put Gandhi on trial.

Gandhi at once renewed his efforts, and in 1930 he led a mass, 200-mile march to the sea to collect salt in a symbolic gesture against the government monopoly. To gain maximum publicity the march was conducted over eighty days, so that each day, after a few miles' walk, he and his followers could stop at villages to spread their beliefs. After starting with just a handful of fellow marchers, he was joined by thousands more en route.

In 1932, while in prison again, Gandhi embarked on his "epic fast unto death" in protest against British domination and official discrimination against "untouchables." He sparked support across India, and untouchables were allowed to enter temples where they had previously been barred, while higher-caste women publicly took food from the hands of untouchables to break down a centuries-old taboo. Gandhi achieved significant concessions and ended his fast with sips of orange juice.

WISDOM OF A GREAT SOUL

During the vicious battles over partition in 1947 between Muslim Pakistan and Hindu India, Gandhi was approached by a distraught Hindu whose son had been killed by Muslims. In revenge he had killed a Muslim child. The man came to Gandhi in great despair and asked him what he should do. Gandhi thought for a while and then said: "Go forth and find a Muslim child who has been orphaned by the riots. Take that Muslim child into your Hindu home and raise him as your own son, but as a Muslim."

After spending much of the Second World War in British jails in India, Gandhi negotiated the new constitutional structure with the British in 1946. He had achieved his goal, but his creed of nonviolence could not prevent the violent unrest between the Hindus and the Muslims (who eventually broke away to form Pakistan). Blamed by some militant Hindus for being too generous toward the Muslim minority, Gandhi remained a firm champion of tolerance, though his final months were darkened by the continuing strife. For the archetypal man of peace the ironic final tragedy was played out when he was assassinated in Delhi on January 30, 1948—not, as one might have expected, by a demented supporter of the recently defunct British Empire in India, but by a Hindu fanatic. As he died, Gandhi called out the name of God.

Critics have leveled charges of naïveté, stubbornness, and unrealistic optimism at Gandhi, often with just cause. Yet despite his failings and the strife that continues today in India, Pakistan, and elsewhere, Gandhi's message offers humanity's greatest hope. In an age of multiple nuclear warheads, biological death agents, and smart bombs, the Mahatma's path beckons all who care deeply about the future of life. After Gandhi's death, India's leader Jawaharlal Nehru came to Princeton to visit Albert Einstein. Einstein and Nehru discussed the paradoxical parallel between the development of the nuclear bomb and the evolution of Gandhi's principles. Einstein commented: "Gandhi had demonstrated that a powerful human following can be assembled not only through the cunning game of the usual political maneuvers and trickeries but through the cogent example of a morally superior conduct of life. In our time of utter moral decadence, he was the only true statesman to stand for a higher human relationship in the political sphere . . . Generations to come . . . will scarcely believe that such a one as this ever in flesh and blood walked upon this earth."

GANDHI'S SPIRITUAL HEIRS

Martin Luther King (1929–1968)

Gandhi's philosophy has had a remarkable influence on other modern political movements, most notably in the American campaign for civil rights led by Dr. Martin Luther King. A brilliant champion of freedom, King introduced the Mahatma's creed of nonviolent action to America, with historic results. He paid homage to Gandhi in his autobiography:

"Gandhi was probably the first person in history to lift the love ethic of Jesus above mere interaction between individuals to a powerful and effective social force on a large scale. Love for Gandhi was a potent instrument for social and collective transformation. It was in this Gandhian emphasis on love and non-violence that I discovered the method for social reform that I had been seeking.

"The intellectual and moral satisfaction that I failed to gain from the utilitarianism of Bentham and Mill, the revolutionary methods of Marx and Lenin, the social contract theory of Hobbes, the 'back to nature' optimism of Rousseau, the superman philosophy of Nietzsche, I found in the non-violent resistance philosophy of Gandhi . . .

"Gandhi was able to mobilize and galvanize more people in his lifetime than any other person in the history of this world. And just with a little love and understanding, goodwill and a refusal to co-operate with an evil law, he was able to break the backbone of the British Empire. This, I think, was one of the most significant things that ever happened in the history of the world. More than 390 million people achieved their freedom, and they achieved it non-violently."

Nelson Mandela (1918–   )

In the early 1950s Nelson Mandela and his supporters discussed whether they should campaign using Gandhian methods of nonviolence. In his autobiography, *Long Walk to Freedom,* Mandela explains that Gandhi's son, local newspaper editor Manilal Gandhi, argued for nonviolence on ethical grounds, saying that it was morally superior. Others argued that they should approach the problem as one of tactics and that any violence would be crushed by the powerful South African state, making nonviolence a practical necessity. Mandela himself saw nonviolence on the Gandhian model "as a tactic to be used as the situation demanded . . . I called for non-violent protest as long as it was effective." Mandela believed that Gandhi's approach had been successful in India because the British had adhered "to the same rules" as the Indians, but in South Africa peaceful protest was met by violence from the state. Mandela was willing to emulate the Mahatma in going to prison for his beliefs and in fasting in protest against the South African authorities. In 1964 Mandela was sentenced to life imprisonment for political offenses, including orchestrating a three-day national strike. He was released in 1990 after a mounting international campaign for his release forced the South African government's hand. In 1994 Mandela was inaugurated as the president of a newly democratic South Africa.

The Dalai Lama (1936–   )

Tenzin Gyatso, the fourteenth Dalai Lama, was recognized in 1938 at the age of two as the spiritual leader of Tibet. He was educated according to a strict monastic regime and at the age of fifteen became head of state. He fled Tibet in 1959 after Communist China overran the country, and he has campaigned ever since for the freedom of his homeland. Outside Tibet he has become a spiritual leader of immense influence for many people who are not themselves Buddhists. When he was forced into exile in India he made a pilgrimage to Rajghat on the banks of the Jamuna River where Gandhi was cremated. He saw a parallel between Gandhi's struggle against the British and the Tibetan struggle against Chinese domination. In his autobiography *Freedom in Exile* the Dalai Lama wrote, "As I stood praying, I experienced simultaneously great sadness at not being able to meet Gandhi in person and great joy at the magnificent example of his life. To me, he was—and is—the consummate politician, a man who put his belief in altruism above any personal considerations. I was convinced too that his devotion to the cause of non-violence was the only way to conduct politics."

Summary of Achievements

- ▲ Gandhi was the first person to achieve political revolution through the creation of a nonviolent mass political movement.

- ▲ He was the prime mover and architect of Indian independence from Britain in 1947.

- ▲ A spiritual genius, he synthesized the teachings of all the world's great religions to forge his own distinctive philosophies.

- ▲ A staunch advocate of religious toleration, he also helped to break down caste distinctions and taboos in India—a previously unimagined social breakthrough.

- ▲ He led the way in social and other reforms through the foundation of the ashram movement.

GANDHI AND YOU

Are you satisfied with the way your spiritual values are reflected in your everyday behavior? Do you sometimes yearn for a deeper experience of divine connection in daily life? What are the habits of body and mind that interfere with your sense of connection? Can you imagine how much better you would feel if you let go of those habits?

Though we may lead lives that often fall short of our highest aspirations, and struggle with limiting habits that we know get in our way, most of us will recognize that many of Gandhi's positions are too extreme to make him an exact role model.

However, his pragmatic spirituality offers countless lessons for us all, as do his integrity, dedication, and fealty to his governing principles.

Not everyone can carry self-restraint to the lengths that Gandhi practiced, but if you feel that the spiritual dimension in your life is lacking, you can emulate some of his methods. Moreover, his way of looking at the world can serve as a catalyst for our examination of our own worldviews—and our exploration of the spiritual ramifications of those views.

A shining example of the peaceful warrior at his most effective, Gandhi asks us not to compare or compete but to contemplate his legacy as we move forward into the following self-assessment and exercises.

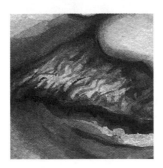

GANDHI:
APPLYING THE PRINCIPLES OF SPIRITUAL GENIUS TO HARMONIZE SPIRIT, MIND, AND BODY
SELF-ASSESSMENT

□ I have the willpower to change things in my life for the better.

□ I'm vigilant in monitoring my own integrity.

□ I believe in, and practice, nonviolence in my dealings with others.

□ I cherish all forms of life.

□ My life is too complex and I could benefit from simplification.

□ I take responsibility for my own actions.

□ I can forgive those who upset, offend, or oppose me.

□ I regularly experience service to others as a source of joy.

□ I appreciate and apply the power of prayer.

EXERCISES

THINKING LIKE GANDHI/
APPLYING THE PRINCIPLES OF SPIRITUAL
GENIUS TO HARMONIZE SPIRIT, MIND, AND BODY

In the beginning of *Experiments with Truth* Gandhi comments: "The experiments narrated should be regarded as illustrations, in the light of which every one may carry on his own experiments according to his own inclinations and capacity."

Gandhi knew that his own path was extremely rigorous and severe. He counseled seekers to look within and be guided to discover the right "experiments" for themselves. Guided by his light, let's explore some of the most important steps on the spiritual path:

PRACTICE FORGIVENESS

When Gandhi's father forgave him—washing his sin away in the flow of "pearl drops"—it changed his life. As he wrote, "This sort of sublime forgiveness was not natural to my father. I had thought that he would be angry . . . But he was so wonderfully peaceful, and I believe this was due to my clean confession. A clean confession, combined with a promise never to commit the sin again, when offered before one who has the right to receive it, is the purest type of repentance. I know that my confession made my father absolutely safe about me, and increased his affection for me beyond measure."

Asking for forgiveness is a wonderful exercise in humility but, as Gandhi counseled, be sure you're apologizing to the right person, at the right time, for the "wrong thing" you may have done.

Before attempting to ask for forgiveness from those you may have wounded, experiment with forgiving—in your heart—those who may have wounded you. Try the following.

In your notebook, make a list of some of the people who have hurt you and how you were hurt. Do this list stream-of-consciousness style, don't edit, and keep your pen moving on the paper continuously.

Keep writing even if you feel strong emotions arising. Stop after fifteen minutes and center yourself by taking seven deep, conscious breaths. Now look at your list and assign a number—from 1 (low) to 10 (high)—that reflects your subjective measurement of the level of the hurt in each recorded incident.

After you've ranked each incident, open yourself to the possibility of granting forgiveness to the people on your list. Begin with the people who are lowest on your "hurt index."

Of course, forgiving someone on a spiritual level doesn't necessarily mean that you'll give him or her the chance to hurt you again. And sometimes it seems as though only a truly gifted spiritual genius like Gandhi or Mother Teresa has the ability to forgive someone who has committed a "10." Yet forgiveness provides a possibility of healing not only for the offender but also for the forgiver.

But How Do I Do It?

Empathize. Understanding helps. It's easier to forgive when you understand why someone hurt you. Of course, that can be very challenging when you feel deeply wounded. But if you can put yourself in the other person's position and imagine looking at the world from his or her point of view, you may find it a bit easier.

Prayer. Just as you might pray to be forgiven you can also pray for the strength to forgive. True forgiveness seems to be an act of grace that cleanses the spirit of the giver as much as the receiver.

Access Spiritual Genius. Call on the example of one of your spiritual heroes, someone like Gandhi, Nelson Mandela, Mother Teresa, the Dalai Lama, or Pope John Paul II (who forgave Mehmet Ali Agca, the man who shot him).

Like most disciplines, learning to forgive takes time and practice, and it's best to start small. You can strengthen your ability to forgive through another simple but challenging Gandhi-inspired exercise.

"POCKET" AN INSULT

Gandhi suffered many insults and humiliations on his path to greatness. He learned to free himself from ego-centered responses as part of his personal spiritual development program. In *Experiments with Truth* he describes an incident in which he was kept waiting and then "scolded" by a bureaucrat without being given a chance to reply. As he describes it: "I smarted under the insult, but as I had pocketed many such in the past I had become inured to them. I therefore decided to forget this, and take what course a dispassionate view of the case might suggest."

In your notebook, record a few examples of recent insults that you feel that you have suffered. Examples might include:

- ▲ A caustic comment from a colleague.
- ▲ A snub by your boss.
- ▲ A hurtful remark from your spouse.
- ▲ A rude remark (or gesture!) from a passing car.

My religion is very simple.
My religion is kindness.
—THE DALAI LAMA

Note how you reacted. What were the bodily responses you experienced? What happened to your breathing? How long did the feelings associated with the insult persist? What would you do differently if you found yourself in the same circumstances again?

PRACTICE JOYFUL SERVICE

Gandhi believed that service to others, rendered in a spirit of joy, was life's supreme pleasure. He wrote, "The deeper the search in the mine of truth the richer the discovery of the gems buried there, in the shape of openings for an ever greater variety of service."

Seek out opportunities for discovering different facets of joyful service that you can perform in your life. Start by looking for small acts of kindness that you can perform in your everyday life. As Shakespeare commented: "How far that little candle throws his beams! So shines a good deed in a naughty world."

In your notebook, make a list of seven simple acts of selfless service that you could perform in the course of a week. Examples might include:

- Cooking a meal for a friend.
- Cleaning a room for a relative.
- Picking up some of the litter in your neighborhood.
- Baby-sitting for a young couple.
- Volunteering at a homeless shelter or hospital.
- Doing the dishes or other household chore when it isn't your turn to do so.
- Tutoring a child.
- Giving a massage to a loved one.
- Running some errands for a housebound neighbor.

After you've made your list plan to do at least one act of conscious service each day for a week. Don't talk about it, just record your reflections in your notebook. Aim to discover the type of service that gives you the most joy and then make it a regular part of your life.

GANDHI, MOTHER TERESA, AND THE WIMBLEDON EFFECT

Each summer the Wimbledon Tennis Tournament is held in London and shown every day on television. Tennis coaches from all over England report a marked improvement in the performance of their students and club members in the weeks following the tournament. This phenomenon has been dubbed the Wimbledon effect.

Could watching films of altruism in action have a similar effect on your well-being and inner life as watching Wimbledon has on your tennis game?

Yes, according to renowned expert on human motivation Professor David McClelland. Exposure to the loving attitude of someone like Gandhi, the Dalai Lama, or Mother Teresa may strengthen your immune system and stimulate altruistic feelings, even via film. McClelland showed his Harvard undergraduates movies of Mother Teresa caring for the sick in Calcutta. He measured students' immune system responses as they watched the Nobel Prize—winning nun in action. Almost 50 percent of the students reported that they felt inspired by the film, but the other half were unmoved or skeptical. Despite the variation in attitudes, most of the students showed a significantly higher immune response. And those for whom immunity improved reported a welling up of desire to serve others without asking for anything in return.

So take every opportunity to expose yourself and your family to images and examples of loving-kindness.

RENOUNCE AND REJOICE

Gandhi lived a life of increasingly severe asceticism. He fasted regularly, renouncing meat, fish, eggs, spices, and condiments. And at age thirty-seven he took a vow of celibacy for life. This path is far too extreme for most of us. Moreover, one can make a strong case that our sensory pleasures are divine gifts to be enjoyed with reverence and gratitude. As Rabindranath Tagore, the Nobel Prize–winning poet, rhapsodizes in the *Gitanjali*: "Deliverance is not for me in renunciation. I feel the embrace of freedom in a thousand bonds of delight. Thou ever pourest for me the fresh draught of thy wine of various colors and fragrance, filling this earthen vessel to the brim. My world will light its hundred different lamps with thy flame and place them before the altar of thy temple. No, I will never shut the doors of my senses. The delights of sight and hearing and touch will bear thy delight. Yes, all my illusions will burn into illumination of joy, and all my desires ripen into fruits of love."

Nevertheless, you may find that a little renunciation will support your sense of inner freedom and awareness while eliciting a surprising sense of joy.

> *We must radiate God's love.*
>
> —MOTHER TERESA'S "MISSION STATEMENT" TO HER NUNS

Practice a Talking Fast

Gandhi's study of the world's great spiritual traditions made him aware of the potentially transformative power of silence, expressed in its essence by the thirteenth-century Christian mystic Meister Eckhart, who noted, "There is nothing in all creation so like God as stillness."

Gandhi put these words into practice. He emphasized, "Experience has taught me that silence is part of the spiritual discipline of a votary of truth."

Experimenting with silence is a wonderful way to make yourself more susceptible to grace. Take a vow of silence, consciously, for a set period of time. Start by being silent for an hour, then try a morning or afternoon, and work your way up to a whole day without speaking. Conscious silence is a

Be still and know that I am God.

—THE TORAH

powerful practice for consolidating your energy and finding inner peace. Of course, this practice is much easier if you are alone or outside your normal environment. Avoid being silent in a way that inconveniences others. As a professional speaker, I find that a day of not speaking is a special blessing.

Give Up Something That Isn't Good for You

Experiment with eliminating something that you'd be better off without, perhaps, for example, junk food, margarine, or colas. You don't have to swear off these things forever. Start with giving up something for a day or maybe a week. Begin with something that is relatively easy to give up and then try giving up things that you really like.

Fast!

One thing I really like is food! But I've also found that fasting occasionally is good for my health and energy level and that it provides a sense of expanded "spiritual space," allowing me to view myself and others with deeper compassion. Gandhi conducted many experiments with diet and fasting. As he noted, "dietetic experiments came to take an important place in my life. Health was the principal consideration of these experiments to begin with. But later on religion became the supreme motive."

Experiment with consciously choosing to miss a meal. Instead of eating, take the time for prayer, contemplation, or an act of service.

When you're ready, try a fast for a day.

SOME GUIDELINES FOR FASTING

Set a time limit.

Do it consciously.

Dedicate the fast to a higher purpose.

Commit 100%.

Don't do it without deep consideration for those it may affect . . . if your fast inconveniences others against their will, wait for a better time and place.

Be very careful about breaking the fast—avoid gorging! Eat something light, chewing consciously and slowly.

TRAIN YOUR WILLPOWER

The idea of willpower has been out of fashion for a while. Many people, for example, consider drinking excess alcohol, overeating, and smoking to be "diseases" outside the realm of volitional control. Although genetic predispositions and other physiological phenomena certainly influence behavior, we are nonetheless possessors of a considerable degree of free will. But the exercise of will requires practice. Gandhi was a master of willpower. During his wife's illness Gandhi entreated her to give up salt and lentils. She would not agree and told him that even he could not give up these foods. Instantly he undertook to give them up for a year. His wife said at once that she would follow his advice, but urged him to take back his vow. Gandhi responded, "I cannot retract a vow seriously taken . . . it will be a test for me, and a moral support to you in carrying out your resolve." Gandhi once told an English admirer that if he could not give up smoking he would find it difficult to do anything— "if you cannot master yourself in this how can you hope to do anything else?" he asked.

The secret of developing will is to start small. Instead of tackling your worst habits right away, try instead to make a clear decision about something relatively easy. Each night before you go to sleep, write in your notebook an action-oriented commitment to yourself for the next day. Then visualize yourself completing the commitment you made. Treat this commitment as a sacred bond with yourself, and see yourself succeeding. You might, for example, make a commitment to polish your shoes, clean your compact discs, or walk a mile . . . *what* you do isn't as important as the idea of doing it *consciously*. Start with a simple conscious action each day and record your observations about the quality of conscious action in your notebook.

Also, take a few minutes and consider if you might be able to help someone close to you to keep his or her resolutions, as Gandhi did for his wife. Ask a loved one, "How can I support you in keeping your commitments to yourself?"

PRACTICE WALKING FOR GOOD

Gandhi wore spectacles and was quite thin; he looked somewhat like the nerdy stereotype that many people hold for those who are intellectually or spiritually advanced. But like so many of our other great minds, Gandhi was a physical powerhouse. He possessed amazing stamina, endurance, flexibility, and strength.

He was a lifelong devotee of "body-mind fitness," and noted that "no matter what amount of work one has, one should always find some time for exercise, just as one does for one's meals. It is my humble opinion that, far from taking away from one's capacity for work, it adds to it."

Gandhi's exercise of choice was the same as Jefferson's: walking.

He wrote, "I had read in books about the benefits of long walks in the open air, and having liked the advice, I had formed a habit of taking walks, which has still remained with me. These walks give me a fairly hardy constitution." Both Jefferson and Gandhi knew walking was an ideal way to strengthen the body and relax the mind. And, as he demonstrated in the famous salt march, Gandhi also saw walking as a form of political action.

A marvelous way to invoke the spirit of these two giants—while also improving your fitness—is to participate in a march for a good cause. Fund-raising walks supporting research or treatment for AIDS or breast cancer, for example, are commonly held in locales around the world.

TURNING THE OTHER CHEEK

Aikido, the way of harmonious energy, is a spiritual and martial art developed by Gandhi's Japanese contemporary Morihei Ueshiba (1883–1969). Ueshiba achieved an enlightenment in which he realized his oneness with all creation, and as paradoxical as it may seem, he created an effective method of self-defense (used by "enlightened" police and security forces around the world) based on nonviolence and compassion for one's opponent. Just as Gandhi applied the spiritual ideals of compassion, forgiveness, and love in his approach to large-scale political conflict, Ueshiba applied them to small-scale, interpersonal conflict. Ueshiba's particular genius was to develop a series of practical movements and partner exercises that, with regular and sincere practice, allow individuals to embody the ideal of ahimsa.

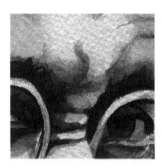

PRAY

Prayer from the heart can achieve what nothing else can in
the world . . . Properly understood and applied, it is the
most potent instrument of action . . .

—Mahatma Gandhi

~ゥ

As a student of many paths to truth, Gandhi knew the value of prayer, but believed that we should each find our own best way to walk the path. As he expressed it: "peace comes from prayer . . . I am indifferent as to the form. Everyone is a law unto himself in that respect . . . Let everyone try and find that as a result of daily prayer he adds something new to his life."

Dr. Larry Dossey is a pioneer in scientific research on the benefits of prayer. His research supports Gandhi's intuition that the essence of prayer is more important than the form. Dossey writes, "Science shows . . . that prayer does not belong exclusively to any particular religion but to a unity of all religions, classes, and creeds. Science universalizes and democratizes prayer."

In addition to documenting the many wonderful benefits of prayer, Dossey has attempted to discover the most effective ways to pray. Is there an essential ingredient that makes prayer effective? His research indicates that the inner act of surrender to a Higher Power, subsuming one's ego in a spirit of love—expressed as empathy, caring, and compassion—is the key to gaining maximum benefit from prayer.

Dossey offers a wonderful prayer to help us cultivate our receptivity to prayer, entitled "May We Let Prayer Be."

May we let prayer be.
May we allow it to follow
The infinite patterns of the human heart.
May we learn to practice the most difficult art,
The art of noninterference.
May we be guided by prayer
Instead of attempting to guide prayer.
May we allow prayer to be what it needs to be,
To be what it is.
May we let prayer be.

Using your notebook, make a practice of recording prayers from different traditions that resonate in your soul, and then share them with your friends and loved ones.

Prayers of Dedication

All spiritual traditions teach the importance of prayer at the beginning and end of each major activity of the day. Waking up and going to sleep, eating, working, meditating, or cleaning—each starts and ends with a prayer, or in Tibetan Buddhist terms, a dedication.

"Dedication practice" takes only about thirty seconds but can profoundly enrich your experience of the spirit in any activity. Before meditating, for example, you might say, "I dedicate this practice to my awakening in order that I may serve and awaken all beings." Before eating, you might ask: "May these substances which I now receive with gratitude be transformed in me for the growth of my spirit and my service to life." Of course, a similar effect can come from a few moments of silent gratitude, or saying grace. The important element, whatever the form, is the sincerity of your heart. Consult your own tradition, seek out the wisdom of other traditions, or find your own way to the dedications that work best for you.

FROM DARKNESS TO LIGHT

Wendy Palmer is a fifth-degree black belt in aikido and author of *The Practice of Freedom* (Rodmell Press). She leads workshops around the world on conflict resolution and personal development. I asked Wendy to comment on Gandhi's influence in her life and work.

"I was totally inspired by the information that he had started from a place of fear and found a way to transform that energy into an incredibly powerful force, merging faith, love, and respect which could, ultimately, transform an entire nation.

"That ability to effect such a change in himself is far more inspiring than the idea that he was always strong, capable, and spiritual. Gandhi was actually able to take himself from a place of darkness to a place of light. For me it is extremely important to remember that real strength is born in response to our weaknesses and vulnerabilities."

Mantra Practice

Repeating a brief prayer or a name of God (Rama, Allah, Jehovah) is known in the Hindu tradition as a mantra. Gandhi's nanny taught him to repeat the name of God as a way of dealing with his fear of being bullied at school. Gandhi said, "The mantra becomes one's staff of life and carries one through every ordeal . . . Each repetition . . . has new meaning, each repetition carries you nearer and nearer to God."

A few simple mantras to repeat and remember throughout the day:

Thy will be done.
Om Mane Padme OM.
Thou art with me.
Om Namah Shivayah.

Shalom.
Wisdom and Love.
La Ilaha Ilallah.

Wendy Palmer comments on mantra practice:

"My understanding is that Gandhi constantly repeated his mantra. I
think that people should realize that once a day is not enough. Sometimes I
joke with my students. I say we need to take a commercial break—have a
word from our sponsor before we resume our involvement with the soap
opera of our lives. If we stopped and prayed and centered as often as there
are commercials, we would be growing our connection to universal wisdom
at a wonderful rate."

Breathing as Prayer

Thomas Merton, a Catholic monk and author, noted, "I pray by breathing."
Every spiritual tradition links breath with God. Buddhist monk Thich Nhat
Hanh offers a wonderfully simple prayer of gratitude linked to the breath.
Experiment with repeating these words a few times a day as you enjoy
breathing consciously:

Breathing in I smile,
breathing out I relax.
This is a wonderful moment.

EXPLORE NONVIOLENT COMMUNICATION (NVC)

One of Gandhi's few possessions was a set of three monkey dolls representing the notion "See no evil, hear no evil, speak no evil." A Gandhian approach to learning how to look, speak, and listen beyond evil, to the truth of the heart, has been developed by Marshall B. Rosenberg, author of *Nonviolent Communication: A Language of Compassion* (PuddleDancer Press, 1999). NVC is a simple set of tools that leads to thinking and communicating with respect and compassion. NVC teaches the how-to of nonviolence in everyday thought, speech, and action. It offers simple, elegant strategies for individuals and organizations to embody the values for which Gandhi lived, and died.

NVC begins with an awareness of the myriad ways we tend to judge others and ourselves. As we become mindful of our reactive, dismissive, and invasive patterns of thinking and communicating, we can learn to let them go and cultivate a new language of the heart. As NVC trainer Bridget Belgrave comments, "It's amazing to discover that compassion, when fully alive, is far more fun than insulting people!"

Experiment with NVC by making nonviolent communication a theme for a day. Observe and record the ways you judge, blame, and label others, and yourself, and then specifically look for ways that these uncompassionate elements manifest in your language.

For more information contact the International Center for Nonviolent Communication (www.cnvc.org).

GANDHI AT WORK

In the industrial machine age hierarchical structures and an emphasis on the production of material things often sucked the spirit and soul from the workplace. In the industrial age personal life was clearly distinct from the job, and the pace of change was relatively steady and slow.

In the information age the movement to more flexible, organic structures (mirrored in the World-Wide Web) and an emphasis on intellectual capital creates more potential for the liberation of spirit and soul. But the pace of change is greater, and so, therefore, is the level of uncertainty. And for many the old distinction between job and personal life has faded. More of us are seeking a sense of greater meaning and purpose in what we do "for a living."

Now we have more options, more freedom to pursue Gandhi's ideal of self-realization in the context of work. However, if we don't discipline ourselves to take advantage of that freedom, we will get caught in an agenda not of our own making.

Gandhi emphasized, "The purpose of life is not to increase its speed." But it's all too easy to be trapped in the ever-accelerating, complex web of corporate life and to forget what *is* the purpose of life. And we are all subject to the seductive notion that a bigger job, higher status, and more money will bring us happiness.

Whatever you do, whether you are a CEO or a clerk in the mailroom, Gandhi's relevance to your work is expressed in these lines from his beloved *Bhagavad Gita*:

> *work is holy*
> *When the heart of the worker*
> *Is fixed on the Highest . . .*
> *Action rightly performed brings freedom.*

In other words, it's not what you do but the spirit in which you do it. For Gandhi, the spinning wheel was a symbol of the dignity of work, no matter how simple.

As Gandhi legatee Dr. Martin Luther King expressed it:

"No work is insignificant. All labor that uplifts humanity has dignity and importance and should be undertaken with painstaking excellence. If a man is called to be a street-sweeper, he should sweep the streets even as Michelangelo painted, or Beethoven composed music, or Shakespeare wrote poetry. He should sweep the streets so well that all the hosts of heaven and earth will pause to say: 'Here lived a great street-sweeper who did his job well.'

Marcia Wieder is the best-selling author of *Making Your Dreams Come True*. She teaches visionary thinking and team building to clients such as American Express, Wells Fargo Bank, and the Young Presidents' Organization. Marcia comments on Gandhi as an inspiration in her own work:

"As a professional speaker and motivator I'm often asked where I get my motivation. Well, there is a statue of Gandhi near my home in San Francisco. For years I have visited this place. It's become a sacred spot for me. I approach this master with reverence. I make eye contact with him as I stand in his line of sight. I open my heart, and a question always bubbles up from the depths of my soul. The answers that I receive from him are priceless.

"He tells me, 'Feel my peace, feel my soul, feel yourself as me, know us as one. Begin here. Our beating heart is the pulse of the universe. It is the one vibration. Slow down and be quiet to know this pulse. Beyond thinking, beyond feeling, come to know. Then may you speak it, then may you share it. Go deeper, deeper, deeper.'

"Gandhi provides me with the much needed messages I long to hear. Always delivered with piercing clarity and sweet simplicity. Sometimes, when I feel tired, afraid, or confused, invoking his presence reminds me that I have a calling, a unique purpose, a reason why I am here. My destiny is to lead so I may follow, to teach so I may learn, to communicate so I may hear. Gandhi is more than a role model, he is a living presence who reminds us that gentleness can move mountains and that a still place of oneness lives in all of our hearts."

GANDHI: THE MUSIC OF COMPASSION

The sitar is the great instrument of India, evocative of the incredible richness and complexity of the Hindu pantheon. Indian music is a marvelous complement to meditation and is designed to free the mind and spirit. Ravi Shankar is the most well-known exponent of this great musical tradition, and his recordings offer a wonderful auditory journey through Gandhi's world.

Shankar created the film score for the movie *Gandhi* and introduced the rock world to the Indian spiritual tradition through his tutelage of George Harrison. Shankar also greatly influenced the minimalist modern composer Phillip Glass. Glass composed an opera written in honor of Gandhi, entitled *Satyagraha*. Glass also collaborated with Shankar to create a marvelous original work entitled *Passages*, which is available on the Private Music label.

In addition to the works of Shankar and Glass you can also hear the Mahatma's spirit in Michael Fitzpatrick's compelling album *Compassion*. This compilation of chant and cello features the voices of the monk Thomas Merton and His Holiness the Dalai Lama.

ONWARD TO EINSTEIN

The ancients knew something which we seem to have for-
gotten. All means prove but a blunt instrument, if they
have not behind them a living spirit.

—ALBERT EINSTEIN

~♪

The "living spirit" was the driving force in the poltical revolution led by
Mahatma Gandhi. But, as we've seen, Gandhi's work is relevant to personal
as well as national liberation. Albert Einstein, our final breakthrough thinker,
dramatically changed our understanding of time, space, and the whole physical universe. Yet his work also speaks profoundly to our inner lives. As he
noted in comments that echo the great concerns of Plato and Gandhi:

"A human being is a part of the whole called by us universe, a part limited in time and space. He experiences himself, his thoughts and feelings
as something separated from the rest, a kind of optical delusion of consciousness. This delusion is a kind of prison for us, restricting us to our
personal desires and to affection for a few persons nearest to us. Our task
must be to free ourselves from this prison by widening our circle of compassion to embrace all living creatures and the whole of nature in its
beauty."

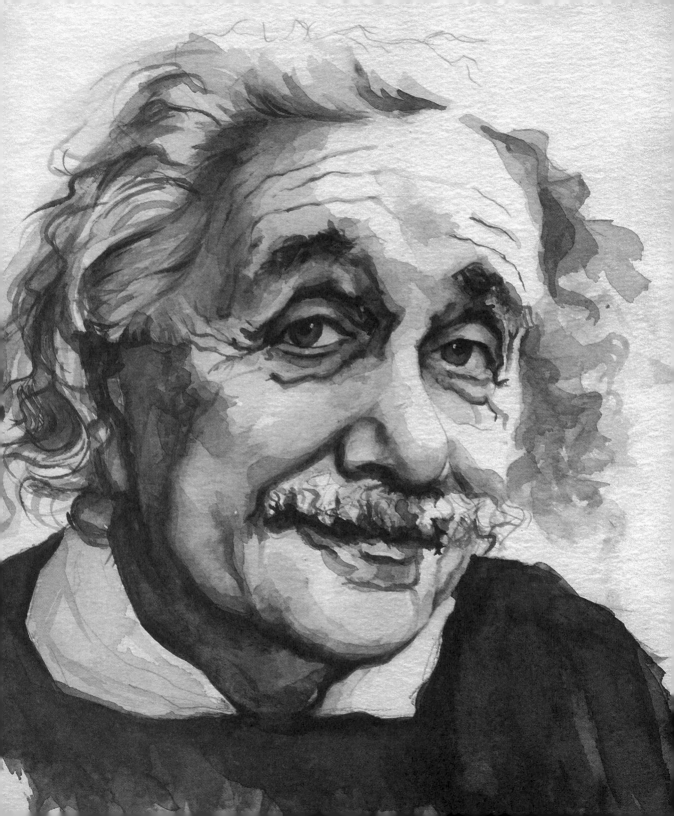

Albert Einstein

(1879–1955)

Unleashing Your
Imagination and Combinatory Play

Study and in general the pursuit of truth and beauty

is a sphere of activity in which we are permitted

to remain children all our lives.

—ALBERT EINSTEIN

S igmund Freud wrote of Leonardo da Vinci, "The great Leonardo continued to play as a child throughout his adult life thus baffling his contemporaries." The quality of play and childlike imagination was also embodied by Freud's contemporary, Albert Einstein.

One of my favorite subjects for many portraits I have done of him, but this one proved quite challenging. There could be a fine visual line between play and nonseriousness of purpose; by definition play needs to convey a certain childlike wonder. In this portrait he emerged as showing the fun of imagination, but with the intelligence to know how to use it.—Norma Miller

Freud indulged in playfulness himself in describing one of his meetings with Einstein: "He understands as much about psychology as I do about physics, so we had a very pleasant talk."

Freud may not have been very sophisticated in his knowledge of physics, but Einstein's understanding of psychology was actually quite profound. And his comment on the relationship between these disciplines is worth noting: "Body and soul are not two different things but only two different ways of perceiving the same thing. Similarly, physics and psychology are only different attempts to link our experience together by way of systematic thought."

We tend to think of Einstein as the archetypal genius of the twentieth century—a scientist, of course, a professor with the world as his student. Despite his image as the supreme absentminded professor—the tousled hair, the disheveled clothing—Einstein has a great deal to offer anyone who seeks to awaken body and soul and link experience together. Einstein was inspired by the quest for pure truth and beauty that so inspired Plato two and a half millennia ago. He viewed the sense of wonder as the wellspring of science and art as he proclaimed, "The most beautiful thing we can experience is the mysterious. It is the source of all true art and science. He to whom this emotion is a stranger, who can no longer wonder and stand rapt in awe, is as good as dead."

And although he's most famous for his science, we approach him for what he offers us about the art of living. Indeed, Einstein has far more to say to us than his deservedly famous—and famously difficult—theories and equations might lead us to believe. For our purposes, the physics could be considered beside the point; you don't have to understand Einstein's theories to learn from him.

Even Einstein at times found his discoveries daunting. Recalling the period when the special theory of relativity was just beginning to unfold in his mind, he confessed that he would "go away for weeks in a state of confusion, as one who at that time had yet to overcome the state of stupefaction in his first encounter with such questions." A complete appreciation of Einstein's revolution requires an understanding of the work of Galileo, Newton, Faraday, Maxwell, Hertz, Michelson and Morley, Mach, Lorentz, and Helmholtz, as well as a mastery of advanced mathematics. You're not going to get that here; I don't have that background, and I doubt that you do, either.

But we do share with Einstein—and Plato, and the rest of our dream team—an interest in how we learn and what we can do with that knowledge. And for all the sophistication of his intellectual constructs, a look into the workings of his mind reveals that Einstein is the perfect guide to some of the least sophisticated powers we all have, the childlike sense of play, possibility, and humor that is the essence of his genius.

There are only two ways to live your life:

one is as if everything is a miracle,

the other is as though nothing is a miracle.

—ALBERT EINSTEIN

BOY WONDER

Born in Ulm, Germany on March 14, 1879, the young Albert Einstein was a dreamy, curious individualist. According to Howard Gardener, author of *Creating Minds*, young Einstein "loved to make constructions of all sorts. He built giant houses out of cards . . . pored over jigsaw puzzles; and he was fascinated by wheels and all other objects with moving parts." Most fascinating of all was the compass his father, Hermann Einstein, showed him when he was five years old. The compass arrow pointing true north, as it floated in space, became a compelling symbol for Einstein's fascination with electromagnetism and his lifelong quest for the true and the beautiful. Albert's mother nurtured her son's interest in beauty through exposure to literature, music (especially the violin), and art, leading to his enduring fascination with the work of Michelangelo. His Uncle Jacob encouraged his search for truth by supporting his love of mathematics, giving him books on geometry and algebra. In his formal schooling, however, Einstein was a rebellious and difficult student. Like Leonardo, he was dyslexic, and his language development proceeded very slowly, leading one of his teachers to tell him that he would "never amount to anything." The popular notion that Einstein failed mathematics, however, is a myth. Einstein actually failed French, English, zoology, and botany because he preferred to explore mathematics, read about physics, and play imagination games about the nature of light, space, and time.

Young Albert was a voracious reader outside the classroom, partial to works of Darwin and Kant as well as the popular science books of the period. This reading affected him profoundly and fueled his other noncurricular pursuits. "Through reading of popular scientific books I soon reached the conviction that much of the stories in the Bible could not be true," he later wrote. "The consequence was a positive orgy of free thinking . . ."

Einstein's first positive academic experience was his attendance at a Swiss school with a progressive, humanistic philosophy. Located in Aarau, near Zurich, the school encouraged a balance of theoretical work with practical application, and emphasized the role of visual imagination in the learning process. Finally in a sympathetic academic environment, the teenaged Einstein flourished, combining "the curiosity and sensibility of the young child with the methods and program of the mature adult," according to Gardener, who refers to Einstein as "the Perennial Child." Einstein's physics teacher guided him to focus on the problem of reconciling Newton's mechanical view of the world with the emerging understanding of electromagnetism, the fundamental challenge that would lead to his revolutionary discoveries.

Einstein graduated from Aarau in 1896. His success there led to acceptance by the elite Zurich Polytechnic Institute, where Einstein soon decided that the mathematics was too abstract and the physics unimaginative. He began to cut class, using the excellent physics lab on his own, once again reading and researching independently. But his most important mode of research didn't take place in the library or the lab. Rather it was through what he called *Gedanken*: imagination games and thought experiments. Einstein took time every day for creative daydreaming. "A normal adult never stops to think about problems of space and time," he later said of these daydreams. "These are things which most people think about when they are children. But my intellectual development was retarded, as a result . . . I began to wonder about space and time only when I had already grown up."

And from those daydreams history was made. One day while still in his early teens, Einstein went for a walk on a grassy hillside. He closed his eyes, enjoying the warmth of the sun, and imagined that he was riding on a sunbeam out into the universe. In his mind's eye, he traveled into eternity and was shocked to discover himself returning to the place from which he began. If you travel forever in one direction and return to the place where you began, what does that tell you about the universe? Obviously, it must be "curved."

As a result of this and other imagination games, Einstein intuited his theory of relativity.

Remarkably, though their popular public personae are dramatically different, the scientist whose work was most dramatically upended by Einstein's was another dreamer: Sir Isaac Newton. The definer of an orderly "clockwork universe," Newton is often portrayed as a dour, pinched-faced scientist, though he reveals his childlike and playful side in his notebooks. His theory of gravitation was inspired by watching, with a sense of openness and wonder, as an apple fell from a tree. His great work *Optiks* was inspired when a glass broke in his cabin, creating a prism effect when sunlight passed through the glass and cast a tiny rainbow on the wall. Quickly Newton collected all the glass he could find, smashed it, and wrote in his journal, "I filled my cabin with rainbows." In describing his own process of thinking, Newton wrote: "I do not know what I may appear to the world, but to myself I seem . . . like a boy playing on the seashore . . . diverting himself, and then finding a smoother pebble or prettier shell than ordinary, while the greater ocean of truth lay all undiscovered before me." Newton's imaginative play led to his revolutionary idea that intervals of time and space are absolute and the speed of light is relative; Einstein's led to his revolutionary idea that the speed of light is absolute and that intervals of time and space are relative.

Unable to secure an academic position after the Polytechnic, Einstein got a job at the Swiss Government Patent Office in 1901. Four years later he published his revolutionary idea in a simple, three-page paper that changed the world forever.

COMBINATORY PLAY

In a landmark survey of the working methods of great scientists and mathematicians, Dr. Jacques Hadmard found that their thinking process was characterized not by language or standard mathematical symbols, but rather by visual imagery. Such was clearly the case with Einstein, who participated in the survey. "The words of the language, as they are written or spoken, do not seem to play any role in my mechanisms of thought," he wrote, adding that his own processes instead "rely, more or less, on clear images of a visual and some of a muscular type."

The study offers us a rare and uniquely explicit look at the great genius's thought process, which clearly shows how he harnessed the insights he would develop during his periods of creative daydreaming and put them to work. After the associations are made visually, he continued, "conventional words . . . have to be sought laboriously . . . in a secondary stage, when the mentioned associative play is sufficiently established . . ." He called this two-stage visual-to-verbal process "combinatory play," which he considered "from a psychological viewpoint . . . the essential feature in productive thought."

By a strange and infamous quirk of science—rooted in the notorious actions of a doctor on duty the night Einstein died—we know something about how physiologically equipped Einstein's mind was for just this sort of associative work. Princeton Hospital pathologist Thomas Harvey's unsanctioned removal and preservation of Einstein's brain for future study has been well documented, but less familiar are the results of the research that was eventually done on the pilfered organ. Three decades after Einstein's death, Dr. Marian Diamond and her colleagues at the University of California at Berkeley published a paper entitled "On the Brain of a Scientist: Albert Einstein." One area of focus was the brain's "glial" cells, which bind neurons (nerve cells) together and provide a medium for the transfer of electrochemical messages between them; Diamond's analysis of a slice of Einstein's brain demonstrated that it contained 400 percent more "glial" cells per neuron than the average. Diamond also reported that Einstein's enhanced glial endowment was especially significant in the left parietal lobe, an area of the brain she refers to as "the association area for other association areas in the brain."

In other words, Einstein's "neurological switching station" was super-developed. Did Einstein's brain develop these connections as a result of his combinatory play, or was his skill at such play a result of an extraordinary neuro-anatomical gift? Much as we'd like to know the answer, which could suggest how much the rest of us really can think like Einstein, we'll never know for sure. But other research by Dr. Diamond does shed fascinating light on this question. In a famous experiment, Diamond placed rats in two distinct environments: "stimulus rich" and "stimulus deprived." The stimulus-deprived rats spent their days in an empty cage while the stimulus-rich rodents spent their hours racing on treadmills, climbing ladders, and scurrying through mazes. The results were unequivocal: the stimulus-deprived rats showed stunted brain development and poor social adjustment before dying young; the stimulus-rich group lived longer, formed successful social networks, and developed bigger brains with dramatically enhanced glial connections between neurons.

Since the pioneering work of neuro-anatomist Ramon y Cajal over ninety years ago scientists have suspected that brainpower is a function of interconnection between brain cells. We now also know that the conduits of interconnection—glial cells, dendrites, axons, and synapses—can continue increasing in number throughout the course of an individual's lifetime. Diamond's research suggests that combinatory play and a stimulus-rich environment—like the one that Einstein maintained throughout his life— are keys to increasing the mind's ability to make the connections from which genius is born.

Einstein's desire for combinatory play led him to exchange and test ideas with friends in an informal environment. He found great stimulation and inspiration through his participation in a group called the Olympiad. Einstein and his Olympiad friends, including his future wife, Mileva Maric, met for intensive discussions on topics ranging from mathematics and physics to philosophy and literature. These forums provided Einstein and his friends a safe haven for the expression of personal dreams and doubts, and were usually combined with camping trips involving hiking, swimming, and much good humor.

HUMOR AND HUMILITY

In fact, humor—which is another expression of the brain's ability to make connections—was always an important component of Einstein's outlook. Even the special theory of relativity was fair game for his famous wit, as on this occasion when he tried to make his theory intelligible to the press: "If you will not take the answer too seriously and consider it only as a kind of joke, then I can explain . . . as follows. It was formerly believed that if all material things disappeared out of the universe, time and space would be left. According to the Relativity Theory however, time and space would disappear together with the things."

His sense of humor and his humility were evident before his theory was confirmed as well. "If Relativity is proved right," he quipped prior to its proof and acceptance, "the Germans will call me a German, the Swiss will call me a Swiss citizen, and the French will call me a great scientist. If relativity is proved wrong, the French will call me a Swiss, the Swiss will call me a German, and the Germans will call me a Jew."

After receiving the Nobel Prize in 1921 Einstein became an international icon of genius for the rest of his life, besieged by autograph seekers, fans of all kinds, and the world's press. Nevertheless, as revealed in a poem he included in a note to an old friend, he became more humble, playful, irreverent, and humorous as his fame magnified:

> *Wherever I go and wherever I stay,*
> *There's always a picture of me on display.*
> *On top of the desk or out in the hall,*
> *Tied round a neck, or hung on the wall.*
>
> *Women and men, they play a strange game,*
> *Asking, beseeching; "Please sign your name."*
> *From the erudite fellow they brook not a quibble,*
> *But firmly insist on a piece of his scribble.*
>
> *Sometimes, surrounded by all this good cheer,*
> *I'm puzzled by some of the things that I hear,*
> *And wonder, my mind for a moment not hazy,*
> *If I and not they could really be crazy.*

A letter to another friend made clear his resistance to the seductive magnetism of fame: "Schopenhauer once said that people in their misery are unable to achieve tragedy but are condemned to remain stuck in tragicomedy. How true it is . . . Yesterday idolized, today hated and spat upon, tomorrow forgotten, and the day after tomorrow promoted to Sainthood. The only salvation is a sense of humor . . ."

Humor and humility went hand-in-hand, at least in his public persona. Like Socrates, Einstein knew how much he did not know. "As a human being, one has been endowed with just enough intelligence to be able to see clearly how utterly inadequate that intelligence is when confronted with what exists," he wrote to the queen of Belgium. "If such humility could be conveyed to everybody, the world of human activities would be more appealing."

His vast array of writings makes clear his fealty to the ideals of Socrates and Plato on many occasions. "What a man can wrest from Truth by passionate striving is utterly infinitesimal," reads another letter. "But the striving frees us from the bonds of the self and makes us comrades of those who are the best and the greatest." And in a clear echo of Platonic wisdom, he asserts that "the most important human endeavor is the striving for morality in our actions. Our inner balance and even our very existence depend on it. Only morality in our actions can give beauty and dignity to life."

A gentle soul offended by the rising tide of Nazi madness, Einstein left Europe in the early 1930s for a position at the Princeton University Institute of Advanced Studies. In 1933 Einstein collaborated with Freud to produce an antiwar pamphlet entitled "Why War." A strong advocate of world peace throughout his life, Einstein was moved, nevertheless, to write to President Roosevelt in 1939 to warn him of German progress in developing a nuclear bomb. He urged the United States government to beat the Germans to the punch. Einstein's warning was instrumental in the launching of the Manhattan Project.

After World War II Einstein campaigned for nuclear nonproliferation and raised his voice, in concert with Charlie Chaplin, against the evils of

McCarthyism. In 1952 he was offered the presidency of the newly formed state of Israel, an offer he graciously refused. As he commented at the time, "Equations are more important to me, because politics are for the present, but an equation is something for eternity."

In the second half of his life Einstein aimed to find the equations that would reconcile his discoveries about the macrocosm with the microcosmic insights of quantum physics. His ambition as he described it was truly Olympian: "I want to know how God created the world. I am not interested in this or that phenomenon, in the spectrum of this or that element. I want to know His thoughts, the rest are details."

Einstein's lofty goals and principled stances on world issues contrasted with some personal qualities that weren't always as admirable. Although never abusive, he could be curt, if not devastating, in his critiques of colleagues. He preached the importance of "harmony and beauty in human relationships," but was an inattentive, distant father and a philandering husband. He was not, however, unaware of the irony. "My passionate interest in social justice and social responsibility has always stood in curious contrast to a marked lack of desire for direct association with men and women," he noted, adding that "such isolation is sometimes bitter . . ."

Neither his marriage nor his quest for a unified field theory was successful. If his later work in physics never matched his early leaps of genius, however, he generously applied his mind to questions of psychology, philosophy, education, ethics, and world peace, and in the process became more than just the most famous scientist in history. Albert Einstein reigns, along with Leonardo, as a supreme archetype of the creativity of the eternal child within, dreaming of a world alive with goodness, beauty, and truth.

Summary of Achievements

▲ The special theory of relativity was introduced in a paper entitled "On the Electrodynamics of Moving Bodies" (1905).

▲ The "General Theory of Relativity" was introduced in a paper of the same name (1916).

▲ He was awarded the Nobel Prize for Physics in 1922.

▲ He revolutionized humanity's understanding of the nature of the universe.

▲ His equation $E=mc^2$ (energy equals mass times the speed of light squared) gave birth to the nuclear age.

▲ He inspired President Roosevelt to accelerate the U.S. nuclear program to compete and win against the Axis Powers in World War II.

▲ He serves as an international icon of wisdom, imagination, and peace.

EINSTEIN AND YOU

Do you like to doodle or daydream? Have you ever solved a problem by sleeping on it? Are you more likely to get your breakthrough ideas when daydreaming—resting in bed, driving in your car, or taking a shower—rather than when you are at work? If you answered yes to any of these questions, you may be surprised to discover that you are already thinking like Einstein.

Like Leonardo, Einstein cultivated his creative daydreaming and powers of visualization. But chances are that "Introduction to Creative Daydreaming" and "Visualization 101" weren't in the curriculum when you were in school. Perhaps you were even admonished to stop daydreaming. As a result, you may feel that you haven't fully developed your creative imagination. But what if you could learn new ways to use your imagination to solve complex problems? What if you could bring Einstein's strategy of combinatory play to managing the serious issues of daily life?

"Sure," most folks would say, "but that's not possible . . . Einstein's brain must have been different."

But do we know how different Einstein's brain was from yours? Can you cultivate a brain like his? The possibilities are worth keeping in mind as you consider the self-assessment and Einstein exercises that follow.

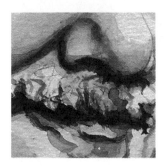

EINSTEIN:
UNLEASHING YOUR IMAGINATION
AND COMBINATORY PLAY
SELF-ASSESSMENT

- ☐ I like to daydream.

- ☐ I can take serious challenges and play with them in my mind.

- ☐ I balance logic with my gut feelings in making decisions.

- ☐ I have my own equivalent of Einstein's Olympiad Group.

- ☐ I seek solace and inspiration in nature.

- ☐ I maintain my sense of humor in the face of serious problems.

- ☐ I maintain my sense of humility in the face of great successes.

- ☐ I nurture the rational and imaginative sides of myself.

- ☐ I create a brain-nourishing environment at work and at home.

- ☐ I can take an open, childlike approach to problems.

- ☐ I notice things that others wouldn't think were important, and wonder about them.

EXERCISES

THINKING LIKE EINSTEIN/ UNLEASHING YOUR IMAGINATION AND COMBINATORY PLAY

THE SECRET OF EINSTEIN'S HAIRDO!

Einstein was famous for his wild hair that seemed to go freely in many different directions. (Einstein said that the secret of his hairstyle was "negligence"!) The freedom of his follicular expression is a marvelous metaphor for the freedom of his mind. Try this simple creativity test to make yourself an heir of Al's genius.

Alternate Use Exercise 1

In your notebook or on a piece of scrap paper, take two minutes and write down as many uses as you possibly can for a paperclip.

How many uses did you write down? Take the total number of answers and divide by two to calculate your score in terms of uses-per-minute.

The international average score is four uses per minute. A score of eight is excellent and a score of twelve or more correlates significantly with other genius-level measures of idea generation ability.

Does the alternate use test really test creativity? Probably not. Rather it tests one's comfort with free association, and free association is an important aspect of the creative process.

Remember that Einstein called the ability to move from associational play to more conventional analysis "the essential feature in productive thought." He let his imagination play freely with an idea and only then began the analysis, "in a secondary stage, when the mentioned associative play is sufficiently established . . ."

One of the most distinguishing characteristics of geniuses from all walks of life is the ability to shift back and forth from combinatory play— imaginative free association—to logic and careful analysis. Geniuses intuitively understand the importance of letting the mind go outside traditional constraints. Once you understand, as Einstein did, the secret of free association, you'll know how to get your mind "out of the box."

Alternate Use Exercise 2

Try the alternate use exercise again. This time, in two minutes, write down as many uses as you possibly can for a brick. To think like Einstein, you'll focus on pure free association. In other words, treat this as a test of writing speed. Write down answers as fast as you can without analysis or criticism. Then after you have generated a genius-level score, go back and use your imagination to explain your off-the-wall answers.

THINKING IS LINKING

The ability to see unexpected relationships and make unfamiliar connections was a delightful secret of Einstein's creativity. Linking things that seem to be unrelated is a wonderful way to strengthen your abilities in "combinatory play." Practice looking at things that, at first glance, seem unrelated, and find different ways to link them. Or consider things that are obviously related and find connections between them that are not so obvious.

In your notebook, write down at least three links between the following things. There are no "right" answers in this exercise, only creative ones, so have fun!

Isaac Newton and fruit.
Einstein's hairstyle and your job.
The speed of light and your favorite cousin.
$E=mc^2$ and Catholicism.

Synapses and interpersonal intelligence.

Gandhi's idea of ahimsa and Einstein's quest for a unified field theory.

Einstein and Marilyn Monroe.

Sheri Philabaum holds a Ph.D. in English and is a successful playwright. She comments on the "thinking is linking" exercise, "This kind of associational play wakes up creativity and frees the mind. Making apparently random links opens up infinite avenues for thematic exploration, and serves as a way to get out of the box of conditioned thinking. It's also a particularly useful tool to help overcome writer's block, and it's just plain fun."

These are my first reflections on the relationship between Einstein's hairstyle and my job:

- ▲ They both often seem out-of-control.
- ▲ A little conditioning might have helped Einstein's hair, and I have to stay in good mental and physical condition to do my job well.
- ▲ Einstein's hair reminds me that substance is usually more important than appearances: I can do a great job even on a bad hair day!

OPTIMIZE SIMPLICITY

"What can be done with fewer assumptions is done in vain with more."

Occam's Razor, quoted above, is an expression of the wisdom of a fourteenth-century philosopher. It became one of the guiding principles of modern science and an inspiration to Einstein.

Einstein's world-changing paper on relativity was only three pages long. He once said, "Things should be made as simple as possible, not simpler." This is a wonderful guide for scientists and for anyone who seeks a balanced, happy life. Sharpen your focus on "optimal simplicity" by making it a theme for a day. In your journal, record examples of things that are unnecessarily complex (perhaps a colleague's presentation at work, or the instruction manual for your latest electronic purchase). Seek examples of things that are oversimplified or dumbed-down (perhaps a political speech or an advertisement). As you record observations on this theme and attune yourself to the powerful idea of optimal simplicity, experiment with applying it to your life. Contemplate the questions: In what areas is my life, or my attitude toward it, overly complex, or too simple? What adjustments can I make to discover my state of optimal simplicity?

TURN ASIDE FROM THE INESSENTIAL

Einstein often forgot to put on his socks and sometimes used uncashed checks as bookmarks. He once stopped a group of students on the Princeton University campus and asked them, "Which direction did I just come from?' The students pointed out that he had emerged from the direction of the faculty club. "Good," Einstein replied, "that means I must have already had lunch."

Einstein's famous absentmindedness was a symptom of his all-consuming love affair with the "essentials" of truth, goodness, and beauty. He said that one of the keys to his creativity was "Turning aside from the inessential." Of course, most of us need to wear socks and put our checks in the bank on a timely basis; but we can nevertheless benefit from an element of Einstein's example. In your notebook, make a list of potentially inessential activities from your daily life. Are there a few things you could turn aside or eliminate that might open more time and space for your creativity and full self-expression?

Paul is an architect in New York. He reflects on a simple way that he practices turning aside from the inessential— "I've decided that I refuse to let the cell phone control my life! I have two rules:

"I always keep the phone turned off, unless I'm making a call. (This prevents people from interrupting me, and imposing their schedules on my life.) I never walk in the city and talk on the telephone at the same time. (If

I feel a desperate need to make a call while hurrying from a job site to a client meeting, I will stop, step into a doorway, and make the call.)"

Paul finds that his cell phone–free walks through the city help him relax while stimulating his imagination. He notes, "I like to do one thing at a time, and do it as well as I can. I work hard, and need breaks! Since I came to Manhattan in 1996, walking in the city has felt to me like a stroll through an amusement park. After six years, I find it as thrilling as I did the first day. To me, even dashing down Thirty-eighth Street is a tiny vacation, and I refuse to ruin that with an electronic business meeting."

> *I believe that a simple and unassuming manner of life is best for everyone, best for both the body and mind.*
>
> —ALBERT EINSTEIN

Turning aside from the inessential in your everyday movements is a simple secret for balancing body and mind. What are your inessential habits of sitting, walking, and talking? Do you stiffen your neck, hold your breath, raise your shoulders, or brace your knees to type on your keyboard, pick up your toothbrush, talk on the telephone, or turn your steering wheel? Freeing yourself fromthese little inessentials liberates a surprising amount of energy for creativity. A wonderful means for cultivating this freedom is the technique developed by F. Matthias Alexander. Leo Stein, brother of Gertrude, described the Alexander Technique as "the means for keeping your eye on the ball applied to life!" To learn more about the Alexander Technique contact: Michael Frederick of Alexander Associates at 800-260-5133.

CREATE YOUR OWN OLYMPIAD SOCIETY

When Gandhi was a young man living in London he formed what he called "a seeker's club," just as Einstein and his friends convened regular meetings of their Olympiad Society. Indeed, all our geniuses benefited from exchanging ideas with others in an informal context. They all seemed to have an intuitive understanding of the importance of balancing solitary, individual contemplation with free-flowing exchange of ideas with others. Take a few minutes to reflect on the optimum balance in your life between sharing ideas with others and spending time in solitary contemplation. Consider forming your own Olympiad group or seeker's club to explore creative ideas and enhance personal and professional development.

REFLECT ON LIGHT

When he was still a young man Einstein noted: "For the rest of my life I want to reflect on what light is." Plato, our first genius, was also fascinated by light and saw it as the beacon of truth, beauty, and goodness; and in the Plato chapter you were introduced to a delightful meditation on light that I hope you've had the chance to enjoy. Now, in the spirit of both Plato and Einstein, make light a theme for a day. Observe the effects of different kinds of light on your perception and emotions. How do you respond to overhead light versus lamplight? What would it be like to travel on a beam of light? How do you feel in halogen light versus fluorescent and incandescent? Do you prefer morning light to the reflected rays of the late afternoon? How about moonlight? Does awareness of light make you more attuned to shadows? What's your favorite experience of light? (Mine is watching it dance on water or in the eyes of someone I love!) A day reflecting on light may just prove to be enlightening.

CREATIVE VISUALIZATION 101

Creative visualization is a secret of genius and of high performance in any discipline. Just as Brunelleschi envisaged the completed Duomo, Einstein visualized the fundamental nature of the universe. His vivid imagination was developed through practicing *gedanken,* or thought experiments. You can develop your own genius talents by experimenting with the following imagination games:

Fruits of the Imagination

Find a red apple, an orange, a lemon, a green fig, some purple grapes, and a handful of blueberries. Place them on a table in front of you and sit quietly for a few moments, following the flow of your breathing to help you relax. Then look at the apple carefully, studying its shape and color for about thirty seconds. Now close your eyes and recreate the image in your mind. Do the same with each of the fruits in turn. Then repeat the exercise, only this time hold the apple in your hands as you study it. Inhale its aroma and take a bite. Bring your full attention to the taste, smell, and texture of your juicy apple. When you have swallowed your bite, close your eyes and see the apple, enjoying all the luscious multisensory associations. After you have sampled each fruit (don't take a big bite of your lemon, a little nibble will do the trick), picture each one in your mind's eye. Then, in your imagination, create an internal image of each fruit magnified 100 times. Shrink the fruits back to regular size and imagine viewing them from different angles. This playful exercise will strengthen the vividness and flexibility of your creative visualizations.

Visualize and Describe "the Beautiful"

In the Plato chapter you were invited to make a list of the ten most beautiful things you've ever seen. Go back to that list and choose one item from it for visualization practice each day for ten days. Devote one minute in the morning when you wake up and one minute in the evening as you go off to sleep, to evoking the image in your mind's eye as vividly as you can. Then take another minute and describe the details of your beautiful thing aloud or in writing. By describing it in detail you'll sharpen and vivify the image of beauty, further enriching your appreciation. As you savor the beauty, your powers of creative visualization will multiply.

Create Your Own Internal Masterpiece Theater

When he was a child Einstein's parents exposed him to the great masterpieces of the world, stimulating his gifts for visual thinking and the appreciation of beauty. Einstein developed a particular fascination and love for the works of Michelangelo. Choose one of the masterpieces of a great artist, for example, Michelangelo's *Pietà* or a panel from the Sistine Chapel. Hang a reproduction on your wall and study it for five minutes each day for a week. Then, as you drift off to sleep each night, aim to recreate the masterpiece in your mind's eye. Visualize the details. Bring all your senses to this exercise. Imagine, for example, the feeling of the weight of Christ's body in his mother's arms in the *Pietà* or the sound of God giving life to Adam in the central panel of the Sistine Chapel. Experiment with describing the masterpiece in detail, either aloud or in writing.

Do not picture Einstein surfing on a beam of light! If you failed to carry out this instruction, it is because your power of visualization is so strong that it takes any suggestion, positive or negative, and turns it into an image. Many people, however, are burdened by the mistaken assumption that they can't visualize. What they usually mean is that they do not see vivid, Technicolor, internal visual images. It is important to realize that you can get the full benefits of creative visualization practice without seeing clear Technicolor images. If you think you cannot visualize try answering the following questions: What is the model and color of your car? Can you describe Einstein's face? What's the difference between a square, triangle, and circle? Chances are you answered these questions easily by drawing on the internal image databank in your cerebral cortex. This databank has the potential to store and create more images, both real and imaginary, than all of the world's film and television production companies combined.

EXPERIMENT WITH IMAGE STREAMING

Dr. Win Wenger, author of *The Einstein Factor,* has been researching genius for more than thirty years. He emphasizes that "geniuses are little more than ordinary people who have stumbled upon some knack or technique for widening their channel of attention, thus making conscious their subtle, unconscious perceptions."

Through his Project Renaissance, Dr. Wenger explores the most effective means for ordinary people to develop the knack of genius. His remarkable insights into methods of problem solving and innovation are predicated on his exploration of the marvelous question he poses to himself on a regular basis:

"If you have a good method for solving problems, isn't one of the best problems to work it on the problem of how to create better methods for solving problems?"

One of his most delightful discoveries is the power of what he calls "image streaming." Image streaming is a deceptively simple way to energize your right hemisphere and access your inner Einstein.

To begin, find a comfortable place to sit, and enjoy a few full, easy "sighing" exhalations to help you relax. Gently close your eyes, and then, simply describe aloud the stream of images that flows through your mind. To get the most from this simple but powerful practice you'll want to follow these important guidelines.

Describe the images aloud, ideally to another person or to a tape recorder. Silent description doesn't produce the desired Einstein effect.

Make your descriptions multisensory. Use all five senses. If you see an image of a sandy beach, for example, be sure to describe its texture, aroma, taste, and sound as well as its appearance. Of course, it may seem strange to describe the taste of a beach, but remember, this is an exercise in thinking like one of the most imaginative people who has ever lived.

Descriptions in the present tense are much more effective in eliciting vivid imagination, so express your flow of images as though they are happening in the "now."

You can use image streaming without a theme as a free-form, spontaneous adventure in imagination and combinatory play. Image streams usually gather their own momentum and express themes without your conscious instruction. And you can also use the technique to ask a specific question or explore a particular theme. Dr. Wenger has used the method to develop numerous practical inventions and educational innovations.

MAKE YOUR LIFE A WORK OF ART

Is there not a certain satisfaction in the fact

that natural limits are set to the life of the individual, so

that at its conclusion it may appear as a work of art?

—ALBERT EINSTEIN

To help make your life a more wonderful work of art, play with making a work of art about your life. Using some scrap paper, play with creating colorful images—these can start as image streams or daydreams that become doodles—that represent major goals in your life. Start by musing on each of the following questions, and then play with generating some creative doodles in response to any or all:

Love and relationships: What kind of communication and caring do I want in my life every day?

Work and Career: What's my ideal job?

Finances: What would true prosperity feel like for me?

Learning: What skills or hobbies would I like to learn?

Spirituality: What kind of relationship do I seek with the divine?

Creativity and self-expression: What's my most authentic, joyful form of self-expression?

Travel: Where would I like to go?

Health: What would optimal wellness look and feel like?

Service and altruism: What is my most joyful form of service to others? (In an article on the meaning of success, Einstein noted, "Only a life lived for others is a life worthwhile.")

As you create colorful images reflecting these different life themes, allow them to become the topic of more image streams and creative Einstein-inspired daydreams about living your life with more beauty, truth, goodness, and happiness.

EINSTEIN AT WORK

Where are you when you get your best ideas? Over the past twenty years I've asked thousands of people this question. Most people answer that they get their best ideas while resting in bed, driving in their cars, or relaxing in the shower or bath. It is very rare for people to say that they get their best ideas at work.

What happens in the car, in bed, or in the shower that isn't happening in the workplace? Relaxation. And the freedom from the fear of criticism that allows our natural process of combinatory play to flourish. How can we create an atmosphere in the workplace that encourages the generation and application of our best ideas? Experiment with the following.

Take Brain Breaks

Punctuate meetings and problem-solving sessions with ten minutes of play every hour or two. Juggling, stretching exercises, or a whistling contest will not only lighten up the proceedings and stimulate creativity but will also improve recall.

Take a Child to Work

Many companies sponsor "Take your daughter/son to work" days. The idea is to help children understand their parents' jobs and to educate them about the world of work. All in all, an admirable activity. If Einstein were in charge, however, he might suggest a different emphasis: invite your children to the workplace and ask them to offer ideas on how to make work more like play.

Create an Einstein Room

Einstein's parents encouraged his natural talent for imagination by creating a stimulus-rich, brain-nourishing environment. Psychologists have known for many years that the quality of stimulation provided by the external environment is crucial to brain development in the early years of life. Brain researcher Dr. Richard Restak emphasizes that this holds true for adults as well:

"Throughout life, not just during the first few months, the brain's synaptic organization can be altered by the external environment." Alter your external environment to liberate yourself from "cubicle-consciousness" and promote creativity in the workplace. Take over a conference room and transform it into an Einstein Room. Replace the standard office furniture with comfortable chairs and a couch, bring in fresh flowers and live plants, and hang inspiring art on the walls. Install a stereo and assemble a collection of favorite music (Einstein particularly loved Bach and Mozart). Fill the room with large whiteboards and flip charts and stock it with colored pens. Use this room for combinatory play sessions on important work issues.

David Chu, president and co-founder of Nautica, comments on thinking like Einstein in his work: "The concept of Nautica arose from creative daydreaming sessions. The idea was to create an expression of a vibrant and fulfilling lifestyle that would be universally appealing. In playing with this blueprint for a design philosophy the image of the ocean kept surging to the front of my mind. Suddenly it became clear—water is everywhere—the ocean represents adventure, life, and unlimited possibility. After Einstein intuited his theory he had to do the math to prove it, just as we had to do the business, strategic, and financial planning to make the dream of Nautica real. The balance of imagination and play with hard, disciplined business thinking is what we've tried to create as the basis of our culture, and Einstein provides the perfect inspiration for balancing these two sides."

EINSTEIN'S MUSIC: "GIRD YOURSELF WITH PERCEPTIVENESS!"

Einstein's passion for the violin was born when he began lessons at the age of six. As a teenager he carried his violin everywhere and enjoyed playing pieces by Bach, Beethoven, and Mozart. He also loved improvising on the piano. For Einstein, music and physics were complementary pursuits, as he noted: "Both are born of the same source and complement each other." Moreover, music served as a catalyst for his creative process. As Einstein's eldest son observed, "Whenever he felt that he had come to the end of the road or into a difficult situation in his work he would take refuge in music, and that would usually resolve all his difficulties."

"Music," as Einstein's sister recalled, "put him in a peaceful state of mind, which facilitated his reflection."

Listening to the great works for violin by Bach (Double Violin Concerto in D Minor), Mozart (Sinfonia Concertante for Violin and Viola) and Beethoven (Die Grosse Fugue) is a wonderful way to evoke and celebrate the spirit of Albert Einstein. But to capture his special genius quality of "Imagination and Combinatory Play," you may also want to listen to the music of composer Erik Satie. Satie's music has a timeless, directionless quality playfully combined with a poignant, quirky incisiveness. His subtle, dreamy, minimalist pieces will nurture your imagination and free your mind.

Satie's creative spirit is also evident in the instructions he offers to pianists who attempt to play his works. Rather than traditional suggestions such as "allegro" or "andante," Satie includes admonitions such as "open your mind," "go further," and "gird yourself with perceptiveness." Satie and Einstein clearly share Keats's belief in "the truth of imagination."

ATTENTION, PARENTS

If you have a child with adjustment problems in school, a little boy who seems lost in his own daydreams, or a little girl who marches only to the sound of her own idiosyncratic drumbeat, take heart! You may be raising another Einstein or Darwin. Over the course of his formal education, Einstein failed a number of subjects, was told by one of his teachers that he would "never amount to anything," and was expelled from one of his schools for being "a disruptive influence."

Nevertheless, Einstein's parents were consistently supportive and nurtured their son's highly individual approach to learning. Einstein's parents understood, intuitively, that their son had what we now call an alternative learning style.

If you have a child with a different style of learning, you'll want to guide that child's education accordingly, as Einstein's parents did when they found the alternative school in Aarau that was based on the educational philosophy of Johann Pestalozzi. Three modern geniuses of education—Maria Montessori (who was inspired in part by Pestalozzi), Rudolph Steiner, and J. Krishnamurti—created developmental curricula that are particularly valuable for children with learning differences.

You may also find that the ten geniuses form the core of a powerful curriculum for nurturing the genius potential in your children. You can easily modify most of the exercises in this book for use with them. Children's natural orientation to question everything makes them highly receptive to your using the Socratic method to guide them through the pantheon of genius. And you'll find that, in many cases, your children are already applying the exercises from the book, such as "practice wonder" from the Plato chapter—on their own. You may be surprised and delighted to discover how much more you can get out of the exercises by doing them with your kids.

In the Plato chapter you were also introduced to an exercise in "appreciating and nurturing potential," and of course there's no more powerful way to practice that exercise than by raising children. As you learn to view the world from your child's perspective you can experience your own renaissance of the pure and creative mind. From Brunelleschi, the seminal figure of the Renaissance, we learned about the importance of expanded perspective. As a parent, one of your greatest challenges is to keep an expanded perspective in the midst of the daily trials of your child's life. This is something you teach by your own actions and attitudes, more than words.

Columbus's great relevance to kids is through the emphasis on optimism and positive explanatory style. Encouraging a resilient, winning attitude is one of the great gifts you can give your children. Dr. Martin Seligman has written a marvelous guide to help you, entitled *How to Raise an Optimistic Child.*

Enjoy introducing your children to the wonder of the heavens through exploring the genius of Copernicus. Visiting the planetarium and looking through a telescope studying the phases of the moon are marvelous activities to develop your children's love of science and beauty. As you encourage their natural curiosity and ability to think independently, you'll prepare them to be better able to deal with the world of unprecedented change that they are inheriting.

Consider Elizabeth's words to her Parliament: "We princes [parents] are set on a stage in sight of all the world; a spot is soon spied on our garments, a blemish quickly noted in our doings." And her advice to another queen: "if your subjects [children] see your words so honeyed while your acts are envenomed, what can they think." These statements serve as powerful reminders of the impact of parental role models. And Elizabethan skill in mastering the art of listening is most important with children.

The emotional intelligence you cultivate through your own study of Shakespeare can guide you to be a more sensitive and effective parent. The works of the Bard are an incredible gift to share directly with your children. Just be sure to protect them from the unnecessarily dry, stuffy academic approach to these treasures. (Please extend that protection to all their studies!)

Jefferson offers a powerful metaphor for guiding your children to appreciate and celebrate the gift of freedom. If possible, organize a family trip to the Cradle of Liberty in Philadelphia, and then to the Jefferson Memorial and Library of Congress in Washington, D.C., followed ideally by a visit to Monticello.

In the Darwin chapter you were introduced to an exercise in finding your own "beetlemania," or passion for collecting. Encouraging your children to collect and categorize is a wonderful way to develop their powers of observation and natural love of wisdom. Kids also thrive by developing relationships with other species, so please be generous in exposing them to the opportunity.

Mahatma Gandhi reminds us that, whatever our religious or spiritual orientation, we must be disciplined to embody our ideals in order to model them for our children.

Of course, these genius personalities are also very useful in teaching the facts of history, the skills of philosophy, the appreciation of art, and the orientation of science. As your children learn about the strengths and weaknesses of these extraordinary individuals, you can use them to impart lessons in character development as well. Make the most of these great characters for yourself and for your kids.

A final word from Einstein, who counseled his students at Princeton to regard their studies "as the enviable opportunity to learn to know the liberating influence of beauty in the realm of the spirit for your own personal joy and to the profit of the community to which your later work belongs."

I Link, Therefore I Am

The lunatic, the lover and the poet

Are of imagination all compact:

One sees more devils than vast hell can hold,

That is, the madman: the lover, all as frantic

Sees Helen's beauty in a brow of Egypt:

The poet's eye, in a fine frenzy rolling,

Doth glance from heaven to earth, from earth to heaven;

And as imagination bodies forth

The forms of things unknown, the poet's pen

Turns them to shapes and gives to

airy nothing

A local habitation and a name.

—WILLIAM SHAKESPEARE, *A MIDSUMMER NIGHT'S DREAM*

The educator Neil Postman lamented, "Children start school as question marks and leave as periods." Our journey through the minds of history's great breakthrough thinkers is designed to help you rediscover yourself as a question mark by contemplating these extraordinary exclamation points.

Creativity is the ability to make links that make a difference. All the members of our Genius Dream Team made connections of thought and action that changed the world forever. If you've experimented with the genius exercises, you've begun to link yourself with these great minds in a practical way. In this final section we'll aim to deepen these links by reviewing each genius quality and by introducing one last delightful exercise. I'll also share some personal reflections on the role of each genius in my life and offer some thoughts on contemporary geniuses who reflect these same qualities. Let's start with the most recent and then work our way backward in time.

In ninth grade my teacher told me, "You'll never amount to anything." You can imagine how happy I was when I discovered that Einstein was told the same thing by one of his teachers. The vision of Einstein intuiting the theory of relativity by riding out into eternity on a beam of light is a commanding image that fires my creative imagination. Einstein's quality of combinatory play is a wonderful recipe for living; it's the way I cook and write. His humanity, humility, and humor remind me to keep a soft, light touch when dealing with hard, heavy subjects.

Muhammed Ali is a playful example of a living genius who embodies the Einstein qualities of imagination and play. In addition to being one of the greatest athletes of all time, Ali has become a beloved world symbol of compassion, love, and resilience in the face of adversity. Ali's imagination and combinations in the ring are legendary, and his poetry and playful interactions with reporters and crowds around the world have made him one of the most well-known figures in human history.

Lucille Ball is another delightful modern exemplar of imagination and combinatory play. Her amazing talents as a comedian and actor were matched by her pioneering work as an innovator in the world of television. In addition to being the first female studio head, she and her husband,

Desi Arnaz, invented the concept of the live television audience, and the three-camera approach that revolutionized viewers' perspective. An embodiment of the very best this powerful medium has to offer, I must confess that I Love Lucy.

Although Gandhi's emphasis on renunciation and austerity isn't my path, he represents, in a unique and compelling way, my most important interest—how to integrate the great teachings of the world's spiritual traditions while facing the conflicts and challenges of daily life. The exercises in the Gandhi chapter are natural expressions of the perennial philosophy that he embodied. They are treasures that have enriched my life immeasurably. Through the study of aikido—humbling as it is—I strive to embrace the principles of nonviolence and love for all creation that he championed.

The Dalai Lama is an inspiring contemporary exemplar of the Gandhi quality. Although he is the highest ranking figure in the hierarchy of Tibetan Buddhism, he touches people of all creeds by transcending the boundaries of formal religion. Like Gandhi, he also serves as an inspiration for peaceful but firm opposition to tyranny. Nobel Peace Prize recipient Aung San Suu Kyi is another living exemplar of Gandhi's tradition. Her courageous nonviolent campaign for freedom and democracy in Burma is an expression of the intelligent "soul force" that Gandhi believed could change the world.

Darwin's example of what Leonardo da Vinci called "knowing how to see" has sharpened my view of the world. Even as he inspires me to hone my powers of pure observation—viewing the world in a more objective and scientific way—Darwin also evokes a sense of wonder at the miracle of creation. Despite my study of spiritual paths that teach reverence for all sentient beings, it's Darwin who inspired me to see the divine in beetles and other insects. Darwin reminds me that an open mind is a point of departure for understanding the world and for the process of personal evolution, a process that requires me to question my assumptions, preconceptions, and prejudices on a daily basis.

Dr. Oliver Sacks, author of *The Man Who Mistook His Wife for a Hat*, and primate behavior expert Dr. Jane Goodall are two wonderful modern representatives of Darwin's quality. Sacks and Goodall each demonstrate Darwinian patience and care in their detailed observations, made over many years. In the process, Sacks gives us a new understanding of ourselves through an original and compassionate approach to mental illness, while Goodall offers profound insights into our evolution through her empathic approach to our closest ancestors. Both of these modern geniuses are gifted with minds that are remarkably open and, like Darwin's, almost innocent in their clarity.

Thomas Jefferson changed the world forever by giving perfect voice to the human yearning for freedom. I can't read the Declaration of Independence without being moved to tears. Jefferson reminds me to treasure the gift of freedom, especially when so many people still live under tyranny. Jefferson's ability to savor the beauty and joy of life, even in the midst of stressful circumstances, makes him a delightfully inspiring hero.

Nelson Mandela is a powerful modern representative of the Jeffersonian quality of celebrating freedom. After enduring thirty years of imprisonment, Mandela understands and celebrates freedom. He assumed leadership of a previously racist and now multiracial state with minimal bloodshed and with inestimable grace. This is a modern miracle that would have delighted Thomas Jefferson.

When I went to school Shakespeare was a form of torture, and now it's one of the great joys of life. I just can't get enough! The most delightful aspect of my research for this book was immersing myself in the works of the Bard. Since launching this project, I've been rereading the plays and sonnets, attending every available performance, watching the movies, and—most fun of all—experimenting with playing different roles (*Richard III* is my favorite). My pilgrimages to the Globe Theatre in Stratford and the Folger Shakespeare Library are also highlights. In addition to my love affair with the pure magic of his words, Shakespeare reminds me that egotism leads to tragedy, or at best buffoonery.

Playwright Arthur Miller is a contemporary genius who manifests Shakespeare's genius quality. Miller has taken the lessons of the great Greek tragedies and the Bard and moved them from Thebes and Elsinore to the Bronx. Placing elegiac poetry in the mouths of common men and women, Miller keeps the universal themes of great drama alive. Julie Taymor, MacArthur Fellow, interpreter of Shakespeare, and creator of the theatrical version of *The Lion King* is another current figure who expresses Shakespeare's genius quality. Taymor's comments on crafting *The Lion King* reflect the profound emotional intelligence that informs her work:

"Quite often, with this kind of story, you know it already. It's nothing new. It's a reaffirmation of something you know. That's why it falls into the ritual mode. You look at an artist for *how* he interprets, not *what* he interprets. We've heard Beethoven's Ninth Symphony a million times, but that doesn't mean we don't want to hear it again. We want to hear a new artist's interpretation. So, it's the telling of the story, the communicating, the nuances. It's like, we know we die; therefore, how do we choose to live until then. We're not shocked by the ending of our tales—it's nothing new. It's how you live it that's important, how you experience life."

When corporations ask me how I might be able to help them, I don't usually say, "By guiding you to better apply the feminine principle in power and leadership in order to achieve greater balance and effectiveness." But that is the way I think of it. So I'm thrilled that the supreme role model for using power intelligently just happens to be a woman. Elizabeth's amazing inner strength as she moved from the Tower to assume and maintain power is tremendously inspiring to me. Her combination of masculine and feminine leadership styles makes her a supremely relevant role model today.

Former British Prime Minister Margaret Thatcher was inspired by one role model above all—Queen Elizabeth I. Like Elizabeth, she assumed power during a time of cultural malaise and economic stagnation. With Elizabethan toughness, "the Iron Lady" whipped the country into better shape. Although never renowned for her softer side, Thatcher set Britain on a path to vastly improved prosperity, renewed international influence, and revived confidence, fulfilling much the same role 400 years later that Elizabeth had in the sixteenth century.

Jack Welch, retiring CEO of General Electric, offers a powerful example of Elizabeth's quality in the realm of business. Despite his short stature and lifelong speech impediment, Welch exudes a radiant sense of self-confidence and inner power. In his two decades at the helm, he led the astonishing increase in GE's market value from $12 billion to over $500 billion.

Renowned for his compelling people skills and sensitivity to his coworkers and customers, Welch, like Elizabeth, has kept a constant watch on the bottom line while charting a longer-term vision for his empire.

When I was in college I read Thomas Kuhn's classic *The Structure of Scientific Revolutions,* in which he introduced the idea of the paradigm shift. Kuhn offers Copernicus's revolution as the supreme example of his thesis. The image of Copernicus reorganizing the cosmos has guided me since in attempts to manage change in my personal and professional life. Copernicus also inspires me to look at the sky with wonder and to seek beauty in the universe.

In addition to easy choices like Bill Gates and Stephen Hawking, *Star Trek* creator Gene Roddenberry offers a delightful contemporary exemplar of the Copernicus quality. In addition to introducing millions of people to a credible vision of space travel, Rodenberry championed—in a marvelously entertaining and unforgettable fashion—the emergence of a new paradigm of true equality between races, genders, nations and galaxies.

I agonized about including Columbus in the dream team because of the unconscionable acts he committed in the second half of his career. But his example of sailing perpendicular to the coastline to discover a new world is so vivid and inspiring, and his embodiment of the qualities of optimism, vision, and courage is so profoundly accessible, that I decided he had to be included, with appropriate disclaimers. In 1973 I left the comfort of a familiar coastline and optimistically moved to another country to pursue a new world of learning; I've made similarly bold changes in my life six or seven times since, and each one has been a turning point in the realization of my personal vision.

Although it's easy to take it for granted now, the American moon landing team, spearheaded by astronaut Neil Armstrong, provides a most vivid example of "going perpendicular." The optimism and courage of President Kennedy and the entire NASA organization made the new world of space travel a reality. More recently, Dr. Mae Jemison became the first African-American woman in space. As a physician, engineer, environmentalist, and astronaut, she is a magnificent and multidimensional example of "going perpendicular" to old paradigms and prejudices. Jemison's autobiography designed for young readers, *Find Where the Wind Goes: Moments from My Life*, is a delightful evocation of the Columbus metaphor.

Florence is my favorite place on earth and the Duomo is my favorite place in Florence. The Renaissance is my favorite period of history, and just after Leonardo, Brunelleschi is my favorite figure of the Renaissance. The *capomaestro's* down-to-earth toughness, savvy, and practical problem-solving ability made his magnificent dream a reality. When the hassles of everyday living draw me away from focusing on the big picture of my dreams, I find that if I can just picture the dome in my mind I instantly regain my sense of proportion and expand my perspective.

Buckminster Fuller is a contemporary genius who represents the Brunelleschi quality of expanding your perspective. A modern Renaissance man, Fuller coined the term "Spaceship Earth" and pioneered the emerging discipline of systems thinking. He combined an exceptional inventiveness with an expanded perspective on the interconnectedness of all creation. Just as Brunelleschi's dome is a symbol of the transformation from the Middle Ages to the Renaissance, Fuller's geodesic dome is a symbol of the shift from the industrial to the information age.

If humanity is to pass safely through its present crisis on

earth, it will be because a majority of individuals are now

doing their own thinking.

—BUCKMINSTER FULLER

⁓

As a freshman at Clark University in 1970 I started as a political science major. I hoped to make a difference in the world through political action, but it soon became evident that people on both sides of the liberal/conservative divide were rarely thinking or acting with consciousness. This was the time of the Vietnam War, and in the distant shadow of Plato, I "drew back from the wickedness of the times" and sought answers in the study of psychology and philosophy. Of course, that search continues, but the disciplines of the examined life and the quest for beauty, truth, and goodness have formed the through lines of this book and of my quest.

The most powerful representative of Plato's quality may not be any single individual. Rather, it may well be the emerging mega-mind we now call the Internet or Web. The exponential increase in speed, power, and sophistication of computers is creating a new dimension of intelligence that is already revolutionizing our world. This evolving global brain has the potential to store and integrate all human knowledge and ultimately to think and create independently.

ONE LAST EXERCISE
GENIUS DISCOVERY

Beauty is eternity gazing at itself in the mirror.

But you are eternity and you are the mirror.

KHALIL GIBRAN

~ꙅ

The student of enlightenment approached the hot dog stand. The vendor asked her, "What'll ya have?" She responded: "Make me one with everything!"

The experience of oneness with all creation is an essential feature of enlightenment, and oneness with the subject of investigation—whether a dome, a declaration, or a new cosmology—is an essential feature of genius.

Einstein's fascination with light led him to imagine riding on a beam out into eternity, and ultimately to imagine being one with the light.

In a similar spirit Einstein sought to identify with Newton by keeping the great man's picture above his bed. And it was Newton who emphasized the importance of "standing on the shoulders" of previous giants.

In the "How to Get the Most from this Book" section of the introduction, you learned of Machiavelli's practice of "resurrecting" and conversing with giants from history.

Chances are, if you've read and reflected on the lives and qualities of our Genius Dream Team, you've begun at least an informal conversation with some of these great minds. You may find yourself asking, "What would Elizabeth advise?" when confronted with a problem at work, or "What would Shakespeare say?" when facing a relationship challenge.

The approach you're about to learn for discovering your genius is even more powerful than Machiavelli's genius dialogue. This final exercise is adapted from the pioneering work of Dr. Win Wenger in *Borrowing Genius*. In this genius discovery exercise you'll experiment with becoming one with the genius of your choice and looking at the world from his or her extraordinary perspective.

Wenger points out that aboriginal shamans prepared their tribes for the hunt by dancing the dance of the intended prey. At the climax of the dance, the headman "became" the spirit of the prey by putting on the hollowed-out head of a moose, stag, or bear. In the genius discovery exercise that follows you'll use your imagination in a similar way by "putting on the head" of the genius whose consciousness and spirit you want to capture.

Choose one of the geniuses whose qualities you most wish to acquire— Shakespeare, for example.

Begin warming up your imagination by visualizing being in the center of an exquisitely beautiful garden. Close your eyes and describe the scene as richly as possible, to a listener or to a tape recorder. Make a slow, 360-degree turn, describing everything you see, to establish a strong sense of your position in space. Focus on the details of the uniquely beautiful qualities of your imaginary garden.

Describe the garden to your tape recorder or partner in great sensory detail, using present-tense language, as you did in the image streaming exercise in the Einstein chapter. Continue this for three to five minutes.

(Go with the flow of your image stream. If the garden morphs into something else, just enjoy it and let it be. You can continue the genius discovery exercise in whatever setting your unconscious mind chooses.)

Imagine that Shakespeare has come to join you in the garden.

Begin describing him in rich, multisensory language.

As you describe the Bard, imagine that he is projecting a warm, welcoming presence. Revel in his welcoming presence for one to two minutes.

Now that you have established strong neurological contact with Shakespeare, it's time to go for the inside view. You are about to find out what it's like to discover your genius from the inside out.

Move the image of Shakespeare's body around so you are facing his back and stand arm's length away from him. Now slowly move forward and merge into his presence. There are two ways to do this. You can "float" inside, or you can gently take hold the ears, lift off the head, and place it over your own head like a helmet and then pull the rest of the body around you like a rubber suit.

Align yourself with Shakespeare's body. Put your eyes where his eyes are so you can see through them. Put your ears where his ears are so you can hear through them. Continue the procedure with all the other parts of the body.

Now look around the garden through the eyes of the greatest writer and empath of all time. You will notice immediately that certain things look different. Describe those differences, from Shakespeare's perspective.

Continue for three to five minutes.

Next, maintaining your Shakespeare identity, use your notebook and describe in rich sensory detail everything you see, hear, taste, touch, and smell as Shakespeare. What are Shakespeare's characteristic gestures? What is his posture like? How does each part of his body feel as he writes at the height of his powers? What expressions does he have on his face? Focus intently on body-related feelings. Continue this for up to five minutes.

Now enter into the moment in Shakespeare's life when he experienced his greatest insight into human nature, a peak moment of epiphany, when everything came together and made perfect sense.

Describe that moment and the perceptions and understandings that were part of it. Write your description of this "aha" moment in present-centered terms.

Continue this step for up to five minutes.

When you are ready to end your genius discovery experience, walk, in your mind, in front of a big, full-length mirror. See your Shakespeare reflection standing there facing you in the mirror. Now vaporize the mirror. The mirror disappears, but Shakespeare is still standing there facing you. You and Will are no longer a single entity. You have returned to your own body.

Project a warm feeling of thanks to Shakespeare for allowing you the use of his mind and body. Imagine him projecting thanks back to you for the privilege of sharing such a remarkable experience with you. Before you leave, Shakespeare has something to say to you—he will share some especially important insight about this experience. Listen closely. Thank him, and report what he says to your partner, tape recorder, or journal.

As soon as possible after your genius discovery experience, debrief yourself. In your genius journal write a description of everything you experienced, especially the differences you noticed in the garden when you looked through your genius's eyes.

Of course, you can use this genius discovery exercise with all the members of our dream team (a most delightful and enriching way to get to know them better), and with anyone whose perspective you'd like to savor. You can also use it to help you answer a specific question, gain insight into a particular problem, or prepare for a presentation. Dr. Wenger has documented the use of this kind of process in dramatically accelerating improvements in musical performance and other disciplines. Over the years, I've found this process to be valuable not only for deepening my understanding of genius, but also as enhancer in practical performance. Just prior to my black-belt test, for example, I did a genius discovery session with aikido founder Morihei Ueshiba. The session filled me with a sense of radiant energy and utter confidence that helped make the test a pleasure—my attackers seemed to be coming at me in slow motion! And a few years ago, in the midst of an exceedingly stressful negotiation, a genius discovery session with the Mahatma helped me find a deeper empathy for the other side that allowed a successful, win/win solution to emerge. (You can learn more about how to use image streaming and "Borrowed Genius" exercises by consulting Dr. Wenger's website, www.winwenger.com.

This book began with the words: "You were born with the potential for genius. We all were; just ask any mother." Well, when you were a baby your parents were responsible for giving you unconditional love and creating an environment that would stimulate and inspire your potential for genius. They did the best they could. Now you are responsible for nurturing your own gifts in an unconditionally loving way. The ten geniuses we've met are ready to help you. As you embrace them you'll discover that they are projections of your own amazing mind, and that their genius is yours to discover.

Michael Gelb and his associates offer a variety of programs based on the ideas in "Discover Your Genius." Formats include keynote speeches, 1–5 day seminars, and executive coaching and organizational development programs. For more information please call 201-943-5303 or contact *www.michaelgelb.com* or send an e-mail to: DaVincian@aol.com.

(((LISTEN TO)))

DISCOVER YOUR GENIUS

WRITTEN AND READ BY
MICHAEL J. GELB

"Gelb is undoubtedly an engaging guide with an appealing approach to self-help."—*Publishers Weekly*

"A brilliant, practical guide to awakening and training our vast, unused resources of intelligence and ability."
—Ted Hughes, author of *Birthday Letters*

ISBN 0-06-001186-6 • $25.95 ($38.95 Can.)
6 Hours • 4 Cassettes • ABRIDGED

ISBN 0-06-001187-4 • $29.95 ($44.95 Can.)
6 Hours • 5 CDs • ABRIDGED

 HarperAudio
An Imprint of HarperCollins*Publishers*
www.harperaudio.com